NORTH AMERICAN AVIATION IN THE JET AGE

VOL. 2

The Columbus Years | **1941–1988**

MARK A. FRANKEL

SCHIFFER MILITARY

4880 Lower Valley Road   Atglen, PA 19310

Dedication

Mark Frankel visited Columbus, Ohio, several times when researching this book and dedicated it to the two retirees who most assisted him: Nolan Leatherman is a local historian who joined North American Aviation at Columbus as a mechanical engineer in 1957 and retired in 1991; Archie Lane is a pilot who flight-tested the Rockwell OV-10 Bronco, an innovative twin-turboprop developed for jungle warfare in Vietnam.

Other Schiffer books by the author

Training the Right Stuff: The Aircraft That Produced America's Jet Pilots, 978-0-7643-5030-6

Other Schiffer books on related subjects

North American Aviation in the Jet Age: The California Years, 1945–1997, John Fredrickson, 978-0-7643-5874-6

Boeing Metamorphosis: Launching the 737 and 747, 1965–1969, John Fredrickson, 978-0-7643-6162-3

Designed by Justin Watkinson
Type set in Impact/Times New Roman

ISBN: 978-0-7643-6647-5
Printed in India

Published by Schiffer Publishing, Ltd.
4880 Lower Valley Road
Atglen, PA 19310
Phone: (610) 593-1777; Fax: (610) 593-2002
Email: Info@schifferbooks.com
Web: www.schifferbooks.com

For our complete selection of fine books on this and related subjects, please visit our website at www.schifferbooks.com. You may also write for a free catalog.

Schiffer Publishing's titles are available at special discounts for bulk purchases for sales promotions or premiums. Special editions, including personalized covers, corporate imprints, and excerpts, can be created in large quantities for special needs. For more information, contact the publisher.

We are always looking for people to write books on new and related subjects. If you have an idea for a book, please contact us at proposals@schifferbooks.com.

Contents

Introduction

Mark Frankel was an attorney by education, a Philadelphia automobile dealer by occupation, and an aviation historian by avocation. As part of the postwar baby boom, he was reared in an era when every form of technology raced forward at a dizzying pace. Naval service as a JAG (military lawyer) during the Vietnam War found Mark shuttling aboard aircraft carriers. Military law is found in a 330-page manual titled the *Uniform Code of Military Justice* (or UCMJ). Brief visits aboard the aircraft carriers planted within him an abiding appreciation for naval airpower. He noted that aircraft designs came and went. Some were great, some were awful, but most were in between. In any case, naval aviation remained an enduring interest.

The nexus of this project is the US Navy–owned airplane factory at Columbus and its portfolio of products from 1941 until abandonment in 1988. The plant was built quickly in 1941 because President Franklin D. Roosevelt had the foresight to gird the nation for the coming global war. Curtiss-Wright Aeronautical Corporation was the original tenant. North American Aviation, Inc. (NAA), with headquarters in Los Angeles, replaced them in late 1950 as the primary occupant.

John Fredrickson and Mark Frankel were collaborating on creation of a trilogy of books documenting NAA from inception to demise. The first book, *Warbird Factory*, tells the story of NAA before and during World War II. The second book, *North American Aviation in the Jet Age, Vol. 1*, focuses on California operations, while this current book focuses on aerospace manufacturing at Columbus, a rich topic previously ignored.

Frankel's on-site research included face-to-face interviews with NAA retirees in Columbus and attending a retiree group meeting in Long Beach, while also visiting museums and aviation archives in distant cities. The diagnosis of a serious illness derailed progress when the project was about 80 percent complete. Sadly, Mark passed away shortly thereafter, in July 2020. We mourn his passing. The family believed that completing this book would be an excellent tribute to their late father's memory. John Fredrickson, an accomplished author of aviation history books, who was already participating in the research, volunteered to tidy up the draft, winnow images from those already collected, craft captions, and deliver a print-ready manuscript to the publisher.

Mark was a gregarious person who expanded his circle of friends, contacts, and sources by writing books. People, while living far apart, pulled together to bring the book to fruition. Nolan Leatherman, Archie Lang, and other veterans of the Columbus plant contributed as subject matter experts. Aircraft profiles were prepared by retired USAF colonel Jack Morris (1940–2021) of Santa Fe, New Mexico. Canadian Terry Panapolis provided technical assistance. Carl Fredrickson of Wichita, Kansas, an aircraft stress engineer by day, was the after-hours proofreader. The Frankel family appreciates the contribution of all.

The US military-industrial complex runs rampant with titles, acronyms, rank, and jargon; therefore, a glossary has been added to the back of this book to keep the text brief, clear, and concise. Boeing acquired the aerospace business units of Rockwell International (including North American Aviation) on December 6, 1996. Images were gathered from many sources both private and public. Unattributed photographs and graphics are primarily from the Boeing Historical Archives and are used with permission.

The Curtiss-Wright Era (1941–1950)

Ohio, the Buckeye state, became known as the "birthplace of aviation" because it was the Wright brothers (Orville and Wilbur) of Dayton who first achieved powered flight in 1903. Other aviation luminaries with roots in Ohio include Eddie Rickenbacker, World War II cigar-chomping bomber general Curtis LeMay, and astronaut John Glenn. Further, the Museum of the Air Force at Dayton is a massive repository of military aviation artifacts and history.

Columbus is in the geographic center of Ohio and has a metropolitan population of nearly two million people. It is the largest municipality in the state and the capital city. Some descendants of the pioneers abandoned agrarian life and moved there in search of challenging indoor work utilizing their minds and hands. The tradition of manufacturing excellence at Columbus began with fabrication of the finest horse-drawn buggies in the nineteenth century. Craftspeople take satisfaction in manufacturing durable items bigger than themselves. Building airplanes demands undivided attention to detail because the laws of physics governing flight are unforgiving. A mistake of design, manufacture, or maintenance can prove fatal.

Airfields of Columbus

A century ago, the civic leaders recognized that Columbus needed an airport both for military and civil purposes. Returning pilots from World War I wanted an airfield where they could maintain their aeronautical skills. Starting in 1920, the requisite flat and underutilized acreage was found in the suburb of Whitehall at the corner of South Yearling Road and East Broad Street and earmarked for that purpose. Like many airfields, it was named for a local aviator killed in action during World War I. The actual dedication plaque from 1923, bearing the name "Fred Norton," now resides within the Catholic Church at that intersection. Norton Field was in operation from 1923 until 1949.

Separately, but nearby, Transcontinental Air Transport Airline (or TAT) was another of the many business enterprises created by aviation mogul Clement Melville Keys. In 1928, it was engaged in an innovative joint venture

An airfield located on the Pennsylvania Railroad main line was an ideal site for an enduring airplane factory. Both people and freight traveled by rail during World War II. Parts and supplies arrived while outbound shipments included spare parts, scrap, and shipping fixtures.

with the Pennsylvania and Santa Fe (AT&SF) Railroads to operate premium passenger service (forty-eight hours) between Los Angeles and New York City. For a fare of $352, travelers would rest at night in luxury sleeping cars and by day aboard Ford trimotor airliners (sometimes derisively referred to as a "tin goose"). Columbus, Ohio; Waynoka, Oklahoma; and Clovis, New Mexico, were where passengers made the transition between rail and air. Starting in 1927 as Columbus Municipal Hangar (yielding the initials CMH), the airport's name subsequently became "Port Columbus." A bond was floated for improvements to the new Columbus airport, lying immediately adjacent to the Pennsylvania Railroad's main line. Luminaries who arrived for the dedication included Henry Ford and his son, Edsel; Harvey Firestone; and Amelia Earhart. Charles Lindbergh, a perpetual booster of better local airports, was a principal in TAT. The service was short lived because of the Great Depression, night-flying innovations, and the advent of progressively longer-ranging airliners.

Another local legend, Mr. Foster Lane, set up operations on the north side of the primary east–west runway. As a "fixed base operator" (FBO), the Foster Lane company remains a purveyor of aircraft parking, fueling, repair, and other general aviation services. Lane's business has outlasted the aircraft manufacturing and continues to thrive. Most recently (in 2016), the Columbus airport was renamed again—this time for a famous astronaut who also became an accomplished US senator—John Glenn (1921–2016). An ambitious project is underway to restore the original 1927 air terminal into a museum.

With global war looming, the Navy assumed total operation of Port Columbus in 1941. It became a naval air facility replete with an aircraft delivery unit in 1942. The naval unit's mission was onsite acceptance of the 5,780 airplanes from Curtiss and fly-ins from nearby plants, including 4,017 FG-1D (license-built F4U) Corsairs from Goodyear at Akron. Canadian-built airframes arrived from Canadian Car and Foundry in Fort Williams, Ontario; Fairchild of Canada in Montreal. Navy operations at Port Columbus were scaled back in 1946 and ceased in 1959. The aeronautical legacy of Columbus is significant and merits preservation, celebration, and sharing.

Construction of a sprawling new industrial plant located on that same airfield east of downtown started in 1941. It began as part of President Roosevelt's "arsenal of democracy" and was a place where military secrets were created behind wire fences secured by armed guards.

This major defense plant remained in operation for almost a half century. The airplanes fabricated there found their way into World War II, Korea, Vietnam, and beyond. Yes, it was an incubator where emerged an eclectic mix of the most-capable airplanes of their era. Propeller-driven airplanes gave way to jets—some of them supersonic.

Older citizens of Columbus still recall casting their eyes skyward and glimpsing for themselves the winged progeny of their hometown. Researchers probed the contents of various archives and confirmed that detailed photographs and other records were preserved. The emergence and history of each type of airplane can now be shared.

The Curtiss-Wright Era

The Curtiss-Wright Corporation was formed in 1929 by aggregating the business interests of three legendary aviation pioneers: Glenn Curtiss plus Orville and Wilbur Wright. The resulting airplanes most often bore the brand name "Curtiss," while engine division products were trademarked "Wright."

On May 16, 1940, with German troops boldly marching across Europe and war already raging in Asia, President Roosevelt went before Congress to request funds for a massive (but unwelcomed) arms program. Production of fifty thousand airplanes per year was the cornerstone of the proposal. Industrialists of that era were dumbstruck by that number. Why, fifty thousand was approximately equal to the entire output of the American aircraft industry since the first Wright Flyer of 1903! A presidential pronouncement moved the need for aircraft plant expansion and new factories from urgent to dire. Automobile-style assembly lines would be the key to boosting production.

The biggest producers faced the most acute need—and Curtiss-Wright Corporation was America's largest aviation manufacturer. Built on the tradition of the World War I biwing Jenny, their portfolio of products included the leading Army Air Corps fighter planes (P-36 and P-40), the Navy SB2C Helldiver, an advanced transport aircraft (C-46), aircraft engines, propellers, and other components. Already stretched thin by the onslaught of war-driven domestic and foreign orders, Curtiss-Wright was forced to undertake the addition of some 3 million square feet of plant space spread across three cities: Buffalo, New York; St. Louis, Missouri; and Columbus, Ohio.

Curtiss-Wright Columbus Plant, 1941–1950

Model	No. built	First flight	Length	Span	Empty lbs.	Gross	Max. mph
SB2C Helldiver	5,516	1940	36 ft., 8 in.	49 ft., 9 in.	10,547	16,616	295
SO3C Seagull	795	1939	36 ft., 10 in.	38 ft.	4,284	6,729	172
SC-1 Seahawk	576	1944	36 ft., 4 in.	41 ft.	6,320	9,000	313
XP-87 Blackhawk	2	1948	62 ft., 10 in.	60 ft.	25,930	49,900	360

Note: General characteristics (as above) help the reader grasp the size and other attributes of an airplane. Empty weight varies. It is determined by weighing each airframe on scales, and it changes with the passage of time. Metrics further vary by source and are subject to change by series, age, modification, or overhaul status.

Curtiss-Wright (C-W) Aeronautical Company headquarters were at Rockefeller Plaza in New York City. The primary products included airplanes, aircraft engines, and propellers. With a national workforce of 180,000

Surging demand for airplanes combined with the drafting of men for wartime military service provided the opportunity for women to fill the industrial void, provide leadership, and demonstrate their ability to perform demanding work—both mental and physical.

wartime workers, the Curtiss-Wright payroll was second only to General Motors. Columbus was a new "greenfield" venture (raw land freshly developed for industrial use). The $14 million project was funded by the government's Defense Plant Corporation and leased back to Curtiss-Wright. President Roosevelt nurtured a strategy of establishing (or expanding) several plants spread about various cities "between the mountains." Coastal plants were considered at greater risk of enemy attack; therefore, locations west of the Appalachians and east of the Rocky Mountains were preferred. Requisites for a new plant included a host city sufficient to provide employee housing and other amenities, an airfield, a railroad line, and electricity, plus potable water sufficient for drinking, cooking, toilets, and firefighting.

With additional factory space forthcoming at Columbus, the Curtiss-Wright Corporation set about to screen, hire, and prepare a workforce. Airplane factories always included women. When airplanes were fabricated of wood covered by doped cloth, it was primarily women who sewed the fabric—because only they had the dexterity. Nurses, bookkeepers, typists, telex, and switchboard operators were usually women. Now, for the first time, females were needed to perform engineering, manufacturing, and other technical tasks. Seventy women were graduated from several universities with an accelerated engineering program to go into plants and perform engineering, logistics, or whatever else was needed. The list of schools included Penn State, Cornell, Iowa State, Texas, Purdue, Minnesota, and Poly Tech Institute (State University of New York).

Separately, another four hundred women were sent to the Buffalo plant for training. The female engineers were known as "Curtiss-Wright Cadets." Assembly and manufacturing workers (now called "touch labor") of either gender were sent with full pay to the Ohio State Fairgrounds and into the pavilions for training during the period of plant construction. The curricula included industrial mathematics, blueprint reading, machining operations, workplace safety, and general aircraft familiarization.

Other Curtiss-Wright Factories

The proposed Columbus plant would occupy 85 acres at the southwest corner of the airfield. Ground for a new Curtiss aircraft factory was broken on November 28, 1940. Curtiss-Wright initially settled into fairgrounds structures for interviews, hiring, training, and even small-parts production. Early occupancy of the half-built airport factory came on July 1, 1941 (or 147 days into the project), because of stipulations the fairgrounds be cleared in time for the annual community celebration. Factory plans included two main aircraft doors (each with an opening of 200 feet), blackout equipment, a large basement with integrated bomb shelters, 45 acres of employee parking, a million square feet of roof tile, a kitchen to feed eight thousand daily, and cafeteria seating for 1,428. Amazingly, the rushed prewar construction was totally completed in only 319 days. The plant was officially opened on December 4, 1941, only three days before the attack on Pearl Harbor.

No doubt, Americans were the world's best-nourished wartime workers. Clean air-conditioned break rooms were set aside in the basement because many of them carried their own lunch bucket. The cafeteria's typical daily requisition included 1,200 pounds of meat, 350 loaves of bread, 1,200 rolls, 2,500 quarts of milk, 40 quarts of cream, 94 pounds of coffee, 400 pies, 16 bushels of potatoes, a whole 2-ton truckload of vegetables, 100 gallons of ice cream, and 140 pounds of butter. In addition, a carload of canned goods passed through the commissary every month. The price of a full-course dinner consisting of soup, an entrée—complete with potatoes and vegetable, bread and butter, a choice of beverage (tea, coffee, or milk) and desert—was thirty-five cents[1]—but remember, wartime pay for factory workers was government-established at seventy-five cents per hour.

A sister Curtiss plant located at Buffalo-Niagara International Airport suffered a lethal assault of its own making, when on September 11, 1942, a Curtiss P-40 Warhawk on a test flight crashed through the roof of Plant #2, killing 14 workers and injuring many others. By 1943, the P-40 was outclassed by newer aircraft. A new assembly line was established in Plant #2 to build a second type of pursuit aircraft. This time it was a fighter with a radial engine. They were P-47 Thunderbolts, a Republic Aviation Corporation design, built under license by Curtiss-Wright. After P-40 production stopped in 1944, Plant #2 (Buffalo, New York) built 2,674 Curtiss-Wright C-46 Commando cargo planes, which were best known for flying supplies into China from India over the "Hump" (the Himalaya Mountains) during World War II. The Buffalo plant was demolished in 1999 to make way for expanding the current airport terminal, tarmac, and second runway. Today, the only remnant of Plant #2 is a plaque dedicated to the workers lost in that P-40 crash on September 11, 1942.

Curtiss assigned its Navy contracts to Columbus, initially consisting of the SB2C Helldiver III and the SO3C Seagull III.[2] Columbus was a troubled venture from the outset. The products intended for the new plant seemed jinxed. Both the Helldiver and Seagull prototypes, built and test-flown in Buffalo before the Columbus plant was completed, displayed serious design deficiencies:

> The SO3C-1 was trouble from start to finish. The cause lay mostly with the immature engine and its cooling challenges, which led to numerous cowling changes that transformed the airplane's nose. An engine failure on July 21, 1941, left the prototype sunk in shallow water. Rebuilt

The "greatest generation" eagerly reports to work as the sun rises in the east. Airplane factories were vital to victory. The typical wartime shift was ten hours, and a world at war demanded twenty-two newly built SB2C Helldivers each day—weekends included.

Cafeteria workers prepare for a mealtime stampede they know is inevitable. Companies did their best to prepare appealing food at reasonable prices. A bad experience at mealtime erodes the good morale needed after lunch.

in Buffalo, the engine failed again in November, leading to a forced landing resulting in more damage. Navy-dictated design changes contributed to a weight increase of 463 pounds, which rendered the machine underpowered.

Stability deficiencies were evident in both landplane and seaplane configurations. The wing dihedral was too low for the desired lateral stability but altering this would require jig changes that were actively discouraged in the headlong rush to high-rate production.[3]

Likewise, the SB2C Helldiver also experienced difficulties from the start. The airplane was initially ordered by the Navy on May 15, 1939. Expected to carry a heavier load under more-restrictive conditions than any previous naval aircraft, it was required to sustain a 10,000-foot vertical dive and pull out with a maximum of 8 g (eight times the force of gravity). This forced the Curtiss-Wright designers into a new regime of aerodynamics by pushing the state of the art to its limits. The prototype Helldiver, designated XSB2C-1, was built at the Buffalo plant and first test-flown on December 18, 1940.

By August 5, 1941, construction on the new Columbus factory was well underway. Plenty of workers are on hand. The number of automobiles in the parking lot suggests some newly hired employees are already at work. Their tasks included training and setting up the assembly line. Museum of Flight

The maiden flight revealed serious stability and slow-speed-handling deficiencies. During further testing, the XSB2C-1 suffered minor mishaps (engine failure and landing-gear collapse), which delayed the test program significantly. But the need for space was so acute at Buffalo that the aircraft was ferried 320 miles to the unfinished Columbus plant on November 12, 1941. One month after the test program moved to Columbus, the XSB2C-1 suffered a structural failure during a dive test. By now the United States had entered the war, and the Navy ordered production of 3,865 Helldivers. Flight testing continued using the first production SB2C-1, which was also lost in a crash. Early production at Columbus was discouraging:

> Design problems continued to plague the program. The production aircraft also suffered from poor workmanship and substandard systems. It has been said that the fuel, electrical, and hydraulic systems on the aircraft were what one might expect to find on a farm tractor rather than a combat aircraft.[4]

Consistent with peer plants elsewhere, the C-W Columbus plant faced staggering challenges. Moving to a new facility, recruiting and training a workforce with the skills necessary for aircraft production, and assembling the Navy's most complicated carrier airplane were but a few of the problems. Despite the training previously mentioned, only 2 percent of the initial applicants had aircraft-related experience. In addition, a second production line for the SO3C observation plane forced a further expansion of the Columbus facility. By the summer of 1943, four years after the initial contract, no Helldivers were ready for combat. The first combat-ready example became part of the Navy air arm in November 1943 and ultimately performed well. A workforce of 24,000 people produced twenty-two Helldivers a day as production peaked.

With the improved models that emerged in late 1943 and 1944, Columbus-built Helldivers participated in numerous Pacific air battles, thus finally winning back a measure of respect. It was nicknamed the "Big-Tailed Beast," sometimes abbreviated to "Beast," because pilots found it a challenge to fly. The ultimate test of a weapon is performing its combat role. Starting in 1937, Japan built the two largest battleships that ever went to sea—the *Musashi* and *Yamoto*. It was on October 24, 1944, that scouts from the aircraft carrier *Intrepid* spotted *Musashi* underway. The first wave of attackers consisted of eight Curtiss Helldivers. The second wave was another eight

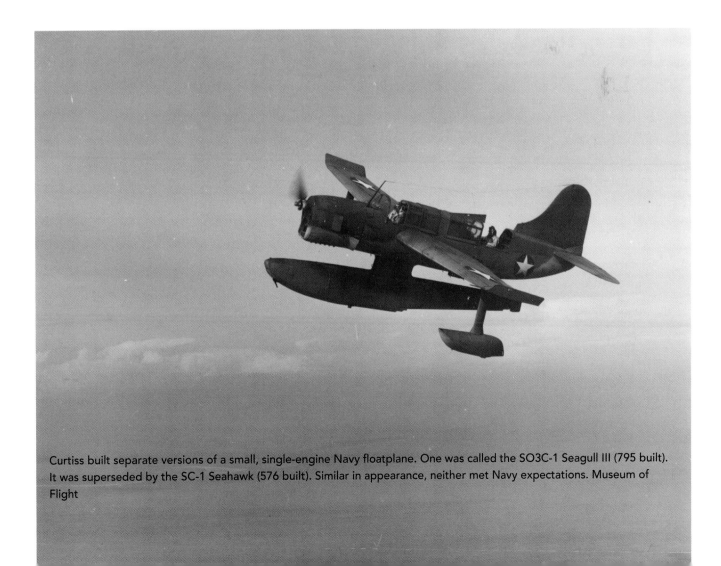

Curtiss built separate versions of a small, single-engine Navy floatplane. One was called the SO3C-1 Seagull III (795 built). It was superseded by the SC-1 Seahawk (576 built). Similar in appearance, neither met Navy expectations. Museum of Flight

The SB2C Helldiver had several nicknames, including "Big-Tailed Beast," which was sometimes shortened to "Beast" because pilots found it challenging to fly. Museum of Flight

Helldivers. In the end, *Musashi* was sunk. Six months later, Japan dispatched *Yamato* jointly with other vessels to help defend imperial forces holding the island of Okinawa. By April 7, 1945, the US Navy presence in Japanese waters south of Honshu was overwhelming. *Yamato* attracted swarms of US Navy aircraft and endured a massive aerial thrashing that lasted roughly two hours. Over three thousand Japanese sailors, almost the entire crew, perished either during the attack or when the dreadnought exploded, overturned, and quickly sank to the bottom. By this phase of the war, the US held a decisive quantitative advantage; however, when called upon, the Curtiss Helldivers delivered their share of devastation from above.

While grappling with the Helldiver and Seagull development difficulties, Curtiss-Wright submitted yet another proposal to the Navy in response to a request for a high-performance floatplane with fighter capability. The proposal, submitted on August 1, 1942, resulted in a

The only flyable Curtiss SB2C-5 Helldiver (BuNo 83589) performs at a Wichita, Kansas, air show in 2010. Ownership resides with the Commemorative Air Force, Cactus Squadron, in Graham, Texas. Carl Fredrickson

Helldivers were built by the thousand and saw extensive wartime action in the Pacific theater of operations. Dive-bombing is one of several strategies to sink a ship. Geysers of salt water erupt as bombs menace their target.

contract for two prototypes and five hundred production articles on March 31, 1943. The SC-1 Seahawk, as it was designated, was intended to be a simple single-seat, all-metal design that could be rapidly produced in large numbers. However, it grew into the largest and most advanced, powerful, and heavily armed floatplane to ever enter Navy service.

The Seahawk's maiden flight occurred on February 16, 1944. Powered by a nine-cylinder turbosupercharged Wright R-1820-62 Cyclone producing 1,350 horsepower and a four-bladed Curtiss Electric propeller, the Seahawk displayed remarkable performance. But it also displayed difficult spin recovery, and one test aircraft was lost during spin testing. A dorsal fin extension and a shallow strake were added to the Seahawk's tail, but spin recovery remained a problem. In service the turbosupercharger proved to be unreliable even though it gave the Seahawk exceptional performance at altitude. To cure persistent problems with the SC-1, Columbus undertook a substantial redesign that resulted in the SC-2. The tail area was increased and a new engine that produced an additional 75 horsepower was installed. Only ten examples of the SC-2 were produced.[5]

Workers can be seen interspersed with the Curtiss SB2C Helldivers on the Columbus assembly line. Folding wings save precious space on the crowded decks of an aircraft carrier. Newly invented mercury vapor (fluorescent) lights enabled day and night operation. Museum of Flight

In all, Curtiss-Wright Columbus produced 5,516 SB2C Helldiver IIIs, 795 SO3C Seagull IIIs, and 576 SC Seahawks by the end of the war.[6] But Curtiss-Wright's reputation was seriously tarnished. The company that Glenn Curtiss founded at the dawn of flight emerged as the industry's preeminent airplane manufacturer by the end of World War I. It amassed the largest plant capacity and most respected engineering force during the interwar years, yet it performed erratically during World War II and thereby suffered a dramatic loss of prestige. Curtiss-Wright fell behind its competitors in developing new designs or even producing reliable examples of existing designs. It was estimated that Curtiss was at least six months behind other manufacturers in producing new aircraft, a serious deficiency in an industry that requires rapid innovation.

The company was so troubled that it came to the attention of investigators from the respected Truman Committee. Senator Harry S. Truman, the straight-talking former haberdasher from Missouri, was the chairman of a Senate committee that probed for potential fraud in wartime defense contracting. In a scathing July 10, 1943, report, the committee denounced Curtiss-Wright's poor management policies and inferior products. Curtiss-Wright, the report noted, was the largest contractor in the aviation industry, yet it was unable to meet many of its obligations because of facility overload and an engineering staff spread too thin by its diverse product line. Worst of all, Curtiss-Wright managers had colluded with military officials to falsify inspection records. Truman was replaced by Senator James M. Mead (D-NY, 1885–1964) when Truman sought the vice presidency in 1944.

Curtiss-Wright's difficulty in developing new aircraft was illustrated by its performance in the Navy's BT torpedo bomber program. The BT was conceived as a new class of dimensionally large, single-seat, single-engine warplanes with enormous load-carrying capability, intended to replace the obsolescent SB scout bomber. Curtiss-Wright along with Kaiser-Fleetwings, Martin, and Douglas received

The Truman Committee visits NAA Inglewood in August 1941. From the left, Senator Harry S. Truman (D-MO), Kindelberger, unknown, Senator James M. Mead (D-NY), and Lt. Col. Charles E. Branshaw (chief of the Air Corps Santa Monica procurement office).

Three themes dominate wartime propaganda posters: Racial or ethnic slurs with an insulting or demeaning theme were often directed toward the foe. Second, the marketing of war bonds. Third, favorable depictions of allies included farmers, miners, and factory workers, but primarily those in military uniform.

YOU SUPPLY 'EM -WE'LL FLY 'EM

orders for BT prototypes. Curtiss-Wright was first to receive an order on December 31, 1943, yet their airplane, the XBTC-1, was the last to fly (in July 1946)—sixteen months behind the Douglas XBT2D and eight months behind the Martin XBTM. Douglas and Martin received production contracts, but Curtiss did not.

Curtiss-Wright, along with almost every other American builder, was hard hit when many military aircraft contracts were abruptly canceled in mid-August 1945. Desert airfields were already tightly packed with factory-fresh warplanes headed for scrap. Both Boeing and North American were also reeling. Fresh corporate strategies were needed to regain their own economic footing, and the government was not always helpful. War's end yielded an 84 percent reduction in aircraft contracts for Curtiss-Wright. Faced with the severe burden of excess plant capacity, the plants in St. Louis and Buffalo were closed and the entire Airplane Division was consolidated at Columbus. By 1947, Curtiss-Wright Columbus was surviving on overhaul work and subcontracts for other manufacturers. Nevertheless, Curtiss-Wright was still in excellent financial condition. Cash reserves of $178 million made it the financial giant of the aviation industry.

Lustron Homes

Military planners, most of them unaware of the top-secret Manhattan Project and its atomic bombs, expected a bloody invasion, urban street fighting, and the war with Japan to drag on until 1947. Industrial production remained at full throttle during the early summer of 1945. Therefore, it was a surprise when many American war plants received telex messages in mid-August 1945 to cease production immediately. Workers were told to gather their personal hand tools and go home. A handful remained to clear the assembly lines of work in process.

Consumer demand for automobiles, appliances, and new homes was held in abeyance for the duration of the

emergency, yielding a huge pent-up demand. Some of the still-new aviation plants reverted to government control and were put to novel uses. Part of the Boeing B-29 factory in Renton, Washington, was rented to a circus so the elephants and other large animals could work out and train indoors. General Motors leased the former Kansas City B-25 factory, and by mid-1946, new Pontiacs, Oldsmobile, and Buicks were rolling forth. The Dallas plant became a Naval Reserve drill facility.

Under auspices (and a $15.5 million loan) of a Depression-era government agency called the Reconstruction Finance Corporation, a private company named Lustron Corporation set up shop in part of the Columbus plant now surplus to the needs of Curtiss-Wright. The nationwide shortfall of automobiles, homes, and furnishings helped America avoid sliding back into economic depression.

Akin to service stations or large appliances, Lustron promised to build homes from porcelain-enameled steel panels measuring 2 feet square. Carl G. Strandlund, an executive with Chicago Vitreous Enamel Products, led the enterprise. Sample homes with two bedrooms measuring 1,025 square feet were fabricated. An aggressive nationwide marketing campaign was undertaken, and 2,500 homes were sold.

How could an innovative company fail? The final average price tag of $10,500, including lot, exceeded many budgets. Further, steel homes ran afoul of local building codes and banks were hesitant making loans for nontraditional factory-built residences. Political finger-pointing ensued regarding government support of an unproven private company during peacetime. Foreclosure and liquidation followed in 1951.[7]

XP-87 Blackhawk

The last Curtiss-Wright aircraft program at Columbus was the XP-87 Blackhawk (redesignated XF-87 on June 11, 1948).[8] Defined as a two-place, side-by-side, midwing, high-performance, all-weather fighter, the Blackhawk was powered by four Westinghouse J-34 turbojet engines, each capable of an anemic 3,000 pounds of thrust. The airframe was extra-large for a fighter, nearly 63 feet long with a 60-foot wingspan, standing 19 feet tall, and a maximum gross weight of 49,200 pounds—which is obese by airplane standards. A fully loaded B-25 medium bomber weighed in at about 31,000 pounds. Blackhawk designers argued that the size was dictated by the equipment and fuel capacity necessary to accomplish the all-weather night-fighter mission.

The Blackhawk project began in November 1945, three months after the end of World War II, when Curtiss-Wright submitted a proposal to the Army Air Forces in response to air technical service command's new military characteristics for all-weather fighters. Procurement of the first XP-87 was approved on December 26, 1945. The second was authorized on January 31, 1946. Delivery of the first article was expected in May 1947, with the second to follow in July. The first Blackhawk was not completed and inspected by the engineering acceptance board until October 6, 1947, four months behind schedule, and it was delivered with some tactical equipment missing.

On November 9, 1947, the XP-87 was disassembled, loaded on a convoy of trucks, and shipped to Muroc Army Airfield, California (now Edwards AFB), for Phase I flight testing to prove its airworthiness and explore its flight envelope. Misfortune seemed to follow the Blackhawk. The truck hauling the fuselage hit a roadside obstacle only a few miles west of Columbus and had to return to the plant for repair of the damaged tail. Six days later, a second accident inflicted more serious damage to an engine nacelle.

The XP-87 finally arrived at Muroc Field on December 1, 1947, where the nacelle damage was repaired; the aircraft was reassembled and readied for flight. The first flight was made on March 1, 1948, at a gross weight of 42,000 pounds. The best fighters are small, nimble, and fast. A fully loaded P-51 Mustang weighs only 12,100 pounds. There was nothing small, nimble, or fast about the bloated XP-87. Swept wings, a missing ingredient from the Blackhawk, were essential to achieve the 600 mph speed stipulated by Army Air Forces for the F-86 Sabre Jet.

The Blackhawk reached 360 mph true airspeed at an altitude of 15,000 feet, but a tail buffet was experienced at 190 mph. Further flight testing was marred by incidents of elevator, rudder, and fuselage vibrations. Violent tail buffeting was encountered on a descent from 20,000 feet. In an era when speed was king, the Blackhawk was unable to keep pace with the P-51 Mustang.

In all, Curtiss-Wright performed forty-five Phase I test flights totaling forty-seven hours of flight time—most of which was spent investigating the buffeting conditions.

The Curtiss XP-87 was a four-engine Air Force jet fighter aircraft with gross weight over 40,000 pounds and a top speed of 360 mph. Overweight, underpowered, and straight wings ended not only this model but also aircraft-building operations at Curtiss-Wright Aeronautical Corporation. Nolan Leatherman collection

A bullet-shaped fairing at the intersection of the vertical and horizontal stabilizers was installed, but the buffeting persisted. On September 21, 1948, Curtiss-Wright turned the XF-87 over to the Air Force for Phase II tests, which consisted of nineteen flights from September 24 to October 2, 1948. Phase II tests were flown by Air Force pilots to verify the manufacturer's Phase I data. The final Phase II flight was made to verify maximum-weight takeoff distance and climb performance to 25,000 feet. The results were satisfactory, but buffeting continued to plague the Blackhawk.

With Phase II testing concluded, the XF-87 was flown to Wright-Patterson AFB in Dayton, Ohio, to undergo a modification program. A nose gun turret and photographic equipment were to be installed. More-powerful engines were also needed. The four Westinghouse J34 engines were intended to be replaced by two more-powerful General Electric J47 jet engines in production.

Considerable debate surrounded the XF-87 modification program. Some Air Force officials argued that it would be more efficient to make these changes on the incomplete second airplane rather than retrofit them to number one. In addition, a new wing configuration increasing the area from 600 square feet to 740 square feet was investigated to lower the stalling speed and improve maneuverability. A serious disagreement arose between Curtiss-Wright and the Air Force over funding these changes. Finally, on October 14, 1948, the program was terminated after a team of qualified Air Force night-fighter pilots evaluated the XF-87 against the Northrop XF-89 and Douglas XF3D and unanimously reported that the XF-89 was superior.[9]

For Curtiss: The End

The files of every aircraft company are rife with ideas for airplanes never built. They are evidence that management was constantly probing for new opportunities. The success of the World War II C-46 Commando provided Curtiss valuable transport aircraft experience. The proposed Curtiss-Wright model 32 (CW-32) was named Sky Truck. It featured a tail that hydraulically folded upward for ease of cargo loading. Sized slightly smaller than a Douglas DC-6, it was to be powered by four Wright turbocharged R-1820 Cyclone engines. Design was started in November 1946 and progressed to mockup phase in 1948; however, the project died in an era of military budget cutbacks.

Curtiss operated in the national arena, where competition was cutthroat and stumbles were visible to all. Every new design was a gamble. Would it be a home run or a strikeout? Weak performers were benched. By the end of 1948, Curtiss-Wright's prospects looked very dim—even while holding the strongest balance sheet in the industry as measured by cash in the bank. The first-place company at the start of the war tumbled to last place by 1950. Managing cash was more important to the executives at Rockefeller Center than excellence of design or manufacture. The XP-87 Blackhawk was a strikeout with fatal corporate consequences.

With the green-eyeshade-wearing accountants dominating the company, it was time to exit the business of airplane building. Lacking any production contracts, Curtiss-Wright shut down the Aircraft Division and sold the assets to North American Aviation, Inc. The exit from aircraft engines came later. Today, the Curtiss-Wright Corporation survives as a respected and diversified company of nine thousand employees with a portfolio of advanced electronic products—many of them for the control of surface vehicles.

Who Was North American Aviation, Inc.?

The enduring two-seat trainer debuted in 1935 and was the launching pad for North American Aviation (NAA). Over 20,000 iterations of variants were built before, during, and after World War II. The initial design team included Dutch Kindelberger and Lee Atwood.

The name first appeared on December 6, 1928, when an aviation holding company was formed by a Canadian immigrant, Clement Melville Keys (1876–1952). Keys was the railroad reporter for the *Wall Street Journal* in the early 1900s. Having studied railroading during the formative years, his attention switched to aviation because railroads were already mature, stodgy, and fully regulated. Like now, the American dream in the 1920s was to become rich. Akin to sharks detecting blood in the water, savvy financiers and like-minded small investors sensed fortunes ahead for those on the ground floor of a technology with sky-high potential. Unfortunately, the allure of aviation-derived wealth was already a false promise for most small investors.

Keys was a major player. He would be better remembered had his name been attached to any of the many aviation companies he guided. No doubt, Keys's primary inspiration was emulating the economic juggernaut of William E. Boeing, a Seattle-based timber baron who was building a profitable nationwide aviation empire consisting of airframes, engines, and airlines. In 1929, Keys vied with Boeing by cobbling together his own consortium—which included the Curtiss-Wright Corporation.

Anthony Fokker departed Europe for America after the German defeat of 1918. Fokker's Atlantic Aircraft Company along with several airlines (predecessors to TWA, Eastern, and Western) came under the umbrella of

North American Aviation, Inc. (NAA). It was a powerful mix including airplane engine builders, airframe fabricators, and airline operations.

Meanwhile, automobile-building goliath General Motors Corporation (GM) was flush with cash. GM president Alfred P. Sloan (1875–1966) and his colleague, Charles Kettering, decided NAA would be a lucrative place for equity investment. Kettering was already on the board of directors of Bill Boeing's United Air Lines, with firsthand knowledge of the airline's surging income statement.

Unfortunately, three problems beset Anthony Fokker. First, a worldwide economic calamity was imminent. The arrival of the Great Depression starting in October 1929 caused Atlantic Aircraft to retrench operations into a single factory in Dundalk, Maryland (near Baltimore). Next, some of Fokker's business dealings were unethical, and his relationships with others were too often riddled with distrust. Finally, the worst disaster arrived in the wake of a fatal crash. A scheduled Transcontinental & Western Airlines (T&WA) flight destined for Los Angeles broke apart over Kansas on March 31, 1931. The aircraft was a trimotor Fokker model F-10. The name of legendary Notre Dame college football coach Knute Rockne was conspicuous on the list of the deceased. Was delamination of plywood wing spars triggered by exposure to rainwater the culprit? A litany of national newspaper headlines and breathless radio reports caused passengers to shun Fokker's airliners—which were wood framed and clad in thin veneer. In any case, new inspection requirements imposed on aircraft fabricated of wood were onerous. Bottom line: future airplanes, both military and civil, would be fabricated of metal.

General Motors Corporation acquired the remaining shares of Atlantic Aircraft in 1931. The final piece of the jigsaw came under the GM umbrella with the purchase of Berliner & Joyce, another airplane builder with a separate plant also located at the Dundalk airport. Meanwhile, with the Fokker brand name sullied and the namesake vanquished, the business was renamed General Aviation Division of General Motors Corporation. Anthony Fokker departed but did not survive the decade. After a three-week bout with meningitis, Fokker died in December 1939 at the age of forty-nine in New York. His ashes were returned to Holland for burial in the family cemetery plot.

Handpicked by Alfred P. Sloan, Ernest Breech (1897–1978) was a young, savvy, and fast-rising accountant and the executive responsible for General Motors' expansive

Ernest Breech was appointed by General Motors president Alfred P. Sloan to become the leader of the North American Aviation consortium. After solid footing was achieved, Mr. Breech departed for Bendix, another GM subsidiary. By 1948, he was president of the Ford Motor Company.

Considered by many to be the greatest industrialist of the twentieth century, Alfred P. Sloan first built General Motors before making a side trip into aviation with the incremental purchase (1929–1931) of North American Aviation, Inc.—then an aviation holding company.

aviation holdings. These included General Aviation (née Anthony Fokker's Atlantic Aircraft), parts plants, and multiple airlines. Hauling airmail was profitable. Eastern Airlines under Capt. Eddie Rickenbacker was in better shape than T&WA (the precursor to TWA). The promotion of Jack Frye from within launched TWA onto a successful trajectory. Meanwhile, the airframe business of General Aviation was floundering. All plants except the former Atlantic Aircraft plant at Dundalk, Maryland, were shuttered. A leadership vacuum ensued in the wake of the Anthony Fokker's exit. Lacking the guidance of a charismatic, decisive, and visionary leader, the General Aviation professional staff at Dundalk was adrift. Rampant bickering and backbiting existed among manufacturing, marketing, and engineering. Not a single worthwhile modern airplane was in the production pipeline.

Workers gather at the entrance to Building 3A, the Columbus headquarters complex, on June 15, 1951. Signaling new management and new products, the winged logo of North American Aviation was proudly lofted high overhead for all to see.

Ernest Breech was on a desperate executive talent search when he struck gold. The massive and far-flung holdings of GM included an interest in Douglas Aircraft of Santa Monica, California. It was founder Donald Douglas who offered up his own vice president of engineering, James Howard "Dutch" Kindelberger, to become managing director of North American Aviation. Mr. Kindelberger was two years older than Breech, and his impeccable credentials became obvious during their interview. Kindelberger's spine was forged of steel from working in the foundries as a teen. A stint at Carnegie Mellon Institute brought discipline to his thought process and bestowed credentials as an engineer. Election as class president confirmed budding people skills. A grasp of aeronautics, military thinking, and future powerful political connections resulted from pilot training with the Army Air Corps. The capstone of his impressive résumé was work experience with the Glenn L. Martin Company, followed by a nine-year apprenticeship reporting directly to an airplane-building legend—Donald W. Douglas.

A powerful team of people backed by the economic might of GM yielded an industrial marriage made in heaven. Manifesting the combined traits of competence, experience, and ambition, Kindelberger was destined for bigger things—but he would go nowhere without the deep bench of talented long-ball hitters assembled by Anthony Fokker. Some of these gifted young people assumed important positions and provided continuity in the challenging decades ahead. Finally, the contribution of General Motors was twofold: First, the melding of rigorous product development, aggressive marketing, and efficient manufacturing accompanied by disciplined internal business practices. Second, the operating cash needed to resurrect an enterprise floundering in the throes of a Great Depression.

Like a fledgling eagle, Dutch was restless at age thirty-nine. It was time to take wing and soar as the leader of his own aircraft company, thus ultimately earning for himself well-deserved lifetime recognition as a captain of industry. The deal was struck. Kindelberger took two associates with him: engineer John Leland "Lee" Atwood and manufacturing guru Stan Smithson. The salaries were set: Kindelberger got $17,000 (plus generous stock options); Atwood $6,000 and Smithson got $5,000. The trio arrived at Dundalk in the summer of 1934, when Dutch pulled his shiny Oldsmobile touring car into the long-vacant parking stall bearing number 1. Employees winced when the newcomers sold the mockup of a new airliner for scrap. North American would never again market an airliner. Kindelberger, trained as a World War I pilot, was close friends with Air Corps general Henry "Hap" Arnold; therefore, NAA products catered to that niche until the end of World War II.

Fearing the formation of vertical monopolies, Congress enacted the Air Mail Act of 1934. Despite loopholes, its intent was to dictate separate ownership of airlines, airframers, and engine builders. Freed from the consortiums, the various companies went their separate ways. Now, with the holding company gutted and defunct, the name "General Aviation" was retired on December 31, 1934. The surviving airframe company was renamed with the sexier moniker "North American Aviation, Inc.," effective January 1, 1935. Lawyers updated the corporate paperwork, a logo was crafted, fresh stationery was ordered, and new signs were posted at the Dundalk plant. The new signage was short lived, because unbeknown to anybody, a move to California was in the offing.

Ernest Breech and his entourage arrived at Dundalk with the project management, aggressive marketing, and cost-accounting disciplines demanded by GM. Each new project was assigned a number. For instance, the project to design and build a single medium-bomber prototype (which later evolved into the B-25) was assigned NA-40. NA-98 was a production run at Inglewood for exactly a thousand wartime B-25H models. Airplanes ordered in lots of a thousand was unimaginable during the Great Depression! Meanwhile, a government contract number is a long string of letters and numbers. The "NA" numbering scheme is a powerful form of shorthand, cost collection tool, and methodology for organizing the working papers of each department. Books by other authors (Norm Avery and Kevin Thompson, *North American Aircraft*, vols. 1 and 2) provide listings of each NA number and its assignment. Only rarely was a number assigned and then the project abandoned.

The earliest internal project numbers were prefixed with "GA," representing General Aviation. That became "NA" for North American with NA-16, the first design undertaken by the new team. With both Kindelberger and Atwood hunched over the drafting tables, work on this trainer airplane commenced in mid-1934. Others have mentioned similarity with the shape and other attributes of the Douglas DC-2 wing. This was true because both Kindelberger and Atwood had been assigned to the DC-2 project immediately prior to their exodus from Santa Monica. In any case, the small trainer airplane won an Air Corps contract, which boosted employee morale and yielded revenue for the income statement. With years of technical improvements and several iterations of renaming, this small trainer aircraft evolved from the BT-9 with fixed landing gear of 1935 and into the enduring AT-6 Texan of World War II fame.

Dutch Kindelberger covertly returned to California in search of suitable industrial sites, and a prioritized listing was prepared. He next called upon his considerable marketing skills to enlist Ernest Breech (followed by Alfred P. Sloan and then the entire GM board of directors) to fund $696,000 for a new factory to be located on real estate that is now the southeast corner of Los Angeles International Airport (or LAX). General Motors was one of the few entities on earth that could muster that amount of cash in the middle of a Great Depression. Dutch successfully argued three points:

- Better weather for test flying and outdoor work
- Back then: abundant and inexpensive real estate
- West Coast labor rates were lower

New signs were again posted on the real estate at Dundalk airport. This iteration said, "For Sale." The most-valuable employees were given a cash stipend to drive themselves from Maryland to California. Others were offered a job if they showed up, while employees deemed ineffective were left behind. The new Los Angeles plant, while big and modern by the standards of 1936, was expanded thirty-three times during the coming war.

Combat aircraft came of age during World War I, when it was quickly demonstrated that the airplane with superior speed, altitude, agility, and weaponry was more likely to win a dogfight. The arms race that began above the trenches of France a hundred years ago continues to this day. Each side seeks air superiority as protection from aerial attack for their own assets, including ground troops, ships, buildings, and other vital infrastructure.

America's investment in troops and military hardware during the 1930s was woefully inadequate. The Axis powers (Germany, Italy, and Japan) held qualitative and quantitative advantage over the Allies at the outset. Quickly, the vast but underutilized industrial might of the United States shifted from idle into overdrive, and a full-throttle wartime footing was achieved. America became not only the world's breadbasket but also a cornucopia of industrial production upon which Russia and the entire free world relied.

The World War II Era

Starting in 1940, the federal government expanded or built new plants in many cities—examples include Renton, Washington, and Marietta, Georgia. Akron, Omaha, Tulsa, Oklahoma City, Wichita, and obviously—Columbus—were on this list. Two of them, the Kansas City B-25 factory and a plant near Dallas, were to be operated by NAA. The Dallas site built eight hundred B-24 Liberators under license from Consolidated, along with all wartime AT-6/SNJ trainers, and most of the P-51D Mustangs. The Ford Motor Company undertook the most ambitious project of them all, at Willow Run, Michigan. A huge, L-shaped factory was constructed with the intent to build B-24 bombers (licensed by Consolidated Aircraft) at a pace of one per hour. Like most other World War II aircraft factories, the startup was challenging—but with over eighteen thousand built, the B-24 Liberator, a heavy bomber, was the most produced American aircraft of World War II.

A labor shortfall was created when traditional factory workers were drafted into military service, and other groups stepped forward to replace them. Women, both younger and older, capably filled this void and did their part to win the war.

A radial engine receives the attention of a mechanic. The war created an opportunity for people trapped in southern agriculture to leave sharecropping behind and find careers in the industrialized North or West.

Every airplane builder faced the same problem: a labor shortage. On short notice, how could the massive wartime workforce be hired, trained, and made productive? The term "learning curve" describes manufacturing efficiencies gained over time as employees internalize the workplace operating rhythm. Women were exempted from the draft, with the expectation they would fill in for the men gone to war. The typical ratio of women performing (for the first time) heavy industrial work was about 46 percent. Work in shipyards was even more demanding and dangerous. Breaking down complicated manufacturing processes into simpler steps that required less skill and training was one key to wartime success. Also, if special services including housing, enhanced cafeterias, and childcare were needed, then the federal government would provide them. However, the continued departure of skilled men working in critical defense jobs was slowing production; therefore, they too received draft board exemptions. When the war ended, a postwar baby boom ensued. Many women happily departed the workplace to tend their young families. The women who remained were mostly of retirement age by the mid-1980s; however, a foundation had been laid for their replacements to assume evermore responsibilities, including managerial and executive positions.

Unlike either Douglas, Grumman, or Curtiss, NAA held no primary wartime aircraft contracts with the US Navy. Yes, the Navy operated large fleets of both types (called SNJ and PBJ). The Air Corps B-25 Mitchell medium bomber bore the Navy designation of PBJ while the AT-6 Texan as a Navy trainer was called SNJ. Those aircraft were built under contracts administered by the Army on behalf of the entire US military. (*Note*: The Navy derived the letter "J" from predecessor Berliner & Joyce, and it was carried forward to NAA. The letter "N" was already assigned to the Navy-run airplane factory in Philadelphia.) Meanwhile, the Navy had their own set of contracts to administer—including the famous Norden bombsight.

After the AT-6 trainer, the second NAA wartime product was the B-25 Mitchell medium bomber. Kindelberger asked his mechanics to refurbish the first B-25 because it was worn out (sometimes called war weary) after extensive testing. NAA then acquired the medium fast-attack bomber on bailment (loan) from the Army and named it "Whiskey Express"—for reasons not fully understood. Kindelberger and other top executives rode it constantly between Los Angeles; Dayton; Washington, DC; Kansas City; and Dallas. Whiskey Express provided Kindelberger with an unprecedented management tool for span of control, effective customer coordination, and overseeing distant plants.

Almost ten thousand Mitchell bombers were built. Two-thirds of them emanated from the NAA-run wartime Kansas City B-25 factory. The B-25 was a bipolar airplane. Docile as a trainer or postwar executive transport, yet vicious during the Battle of the Bismarck Sea (March 2–4, 1943, near Lea, New Guinea), when credited for eleven of twenty-two sunken Japanese ships. It was the first battle where land-based

Family Day was scheduled on a weekend. It was often the only opportunity for family members to enter the secluded workplace. Employees could then showcase their vital niche within the factory. Normally, snacks, educational displays, and live entertainment were provided; however, cameras were banned.

bombers defeated a naval armada. Lt. Gen. George Kenney's Fifth Air Force earned the victory. The victims succumbed to skip bombing combined with withering gunfire from a bevy of fixed .50-caliber machine guns.

The final warplane introduced by NAA later into World War II was the iconic P-51 Mustang. Production peaked at nine hundred a month in January 1945, and roughly fifteen thousand were built. Their primary mission, up to 7.5 hours in duration, was to accompany the heavy-bomber formations from England deep into Germany, skirmish with the Luftwaffe, and return. The P-51D Mustang was an airplane the Navy tested and admired—but never purchased. Powered by a single Rolls-Royce Merlin engine, the Mustang fought hard in Korea and remains an air show attraction to this day. With a peak payroll of 91,000 wartime employees, North American produced over 40,000 warplanes between 1938 and 1945—which is more than any other US company.

The Truman Committee investigated, and found groundless, two allegations of impropriety at Dallas early

in the conflict. One was unfair promotion of supervisors, and the other was employee idleness. Dutch Kindelberger immediately flew there aboard Whiskey Express and did not depart until both issues were fully resolved. No other significant wartime lapses arose. NAA ended the war with a stellar reputation for quality of design and manufacture, cost and schedule performance, employee relations, and ethics. With the war winding down, representatives of the US Navy arrived at NAA eager to do business. Much of that work would ultimately find its way to Columbus.

In 1942, the Army Air Corps was renamed Army Air Forces. The inferior prewar military hardware gave way to a technical metamorphosis that placed the United States in the catbird seat by August 1945. The War Department became the Department of Defense (or DoD) on September 18, 1947. The designation of the Air Force as a new and coequal branch a mere month later escalated feuding with the Navy. NAA became an unintended beneficiary because it was gleefully selling new and improved warplanes to each. Meanwhile, with both GM and NAA solvent, prosperous, and growing, the GM ownership stake quietly ended in 1948 with the liquidation of its final shares of North American Aviation common stock.

Aircraft Piston Engines

Between the wars, two types of reciprocal aircraft engines existed. Liquid-cooled engines with pistons in-line offered a smaller frontal profile and less drag. Air-cooled radials (with metal cooling fins reminiscent of a lawn mower or chain saw) had pistons arranged in a circle about the crankshaft. Aviation experts debated endlessly and with passion the merits of each. William E. Boeing chose radial engines for his airmail planes because they were lighter. Dutch Kindelberger embraced the radial (Wright R-2600) for the B-25 Mitchell medium bomber while concurrently installing liquid-cooled engines (Packard-built Rolls-Royce Merlin) in the P-51D Mustang. The radial engine market

for aircraft was then dominated by Wright and Pratt & Whitney. Notable radial engines from Wright included the R-1820 (which powered the DC-3 and certain trainers), R-2600 on the B-25 Mitchell, and the R-3350, which started out on the B-29 but migrated to the DC-7.

The list of proven aircraft engines was shorter than the number of worthy airframes; therefore, reliable designs found their way onto multiple types of aircraft—both military and civil. The Curtiss SB2C Helldiver had a single R-2600 engine installed, which had a dry weight of about 2,000 pounds and produced 1,600 horsepower. A B-25 Mitchell was powered by a pair, while the Boeing Model 314 Clipper had four Wright R-2600 engines.

Allison, a division of General Motors, built the V-1710, an in-line, liquid-cooled engine found in the Lockheed P-38 Lightning, the Curtiss P-36 and P-40 fighters, and the earliest versions of the P-51 Mustang. Rolls-Royce of England built liquid-cooled engines utilized by multiple iconic indigenous airframes, ranging from the Supermarine Spitfire

Akin to a snowflake, the circular symmetry of a radial engine is better appreciated when not hidden behind sheet metal cowling. Liquid-cooled engines were the alternative, and experts passionately debated the merits of each.

Field service representative L. Rowe is typing a report back to NAA headquarters on his portable typewriter. An NAA sticker (bearing the wartime "E" for excellence) is attached to his satchel.

to the Lancaster heavy bomber. The Merlin was built under license by the Packard Motor Car Company of Chicago. But the fact always remained that a single bullet hole into the cooling system (engine block, hose, or radiator) causes rapid loss of coolant and a seized motor. Radials better endured battle damage to a cylinder head and often kept running long enough to get the aircrew to safety.

Wright adapted a British design for a jet engine, and it was designated the J65. As will later be seen with the FJ-3 Fury aircraft, it became problematic and constituted the last foray by Wright into jet engine building. Sadly, Curtiss-Wright, a company with a long and proud legacy both with airframes and engines, lost out in the marketplace for both.

Field Service Representatives

NAA demonstrated it could build excellent airplanes and support them with a wartime tradition of field service representatives serving shoulder to shoulder with the GIs. This small but important group was a two-way conduit of

Doing business with the Navy was new to NAA; therefore, a manual was created explaining proper shipboard etiquette for assigned employees. The goal was to avoid an embarrassing breach of etiquette. Missile-inspired inertial guidance systems from Autonetics Division were adapted for installation aboard slow-paced submarines. John Fredrickson

product sustainment information (training and troubleshooting) flowing into the field, while a simultaneous backward pathway for ideas related to product improvements or even new and better products. Field service reps were the eyes and ears of NAA that no other American company could match. Needed job qualifications included technical expertise, strong speaking and listening skills, and the ability to write effective reports. The legendary John "Jack" Fox was the prototype. At 5 feet, 4 inches in height, he was perfectly sized as a B-25 mechanic (factory-trained technical representative) aboard the first formation of four Mitchell bombers dispatched in February 1942 from California on an island-hopping adventure to Brisbane, Australia.

A college degree is useful for the better white-collar jobs. Field service representatives were employees with an engineering, maintenance, or manufacturing background. The NAA cadre were hand-picked, top notch, and invaluable as traveling goodwill ambassadors of the company.

With the Navy as a new and valued customer, NAA tech reps were now headed shipboard. Autonetics Division produced inertial navigation systems, and these systems were finding homes aboard submarines. Other field representatives found themselves aboard aircraft carriers. Always eager to put the best foot forward, NAA created an employee manual specific to joint service with the US Navy. It explained the rank structure, and the unique rituals and customs observed when boarding and aboard ships. The goal was to fit in and avoid embarrassing or awkward situations.

Shangri-La (CVA-38) Meets Seahorse

By the 1920s, the quest for a modern aircraft carrier was underway in three powerful countries, each surrounded by vast oceans. Japan, the United Kingdom, and the United States separately had projects underway to apply a "flat top" to one or more ships. Technical progress continued, and the climax came on December 7, 1941, with the devastating Japanese Imperial Navy attack on Pearl Harbor. Naval warfare was forever changed. Battleships, previously the naval symbol of national might, were henceforth obsolete. No further dreadnoughts were built after World War II. Aircraft carriers were thereafter the measure of projecting national naval power. An amazing number of countries dabbled with an aircraft carrier (or two), but it was only the United States that fielded significant numbers of these giant floating airbases and the flotilla of escorting vessels that protect them.

Three components of flight testing include a location, one or more pilots, and an airplane. Mustin Field (1926–

The Navy flight-tested a P-51 aboard USS Shangri La (CV-38) on a shakedown cruise out of Norfolk in November 1944. The Navy was warming to NAA. Pilot Bob Elder was never told the reasons, but he suspected that P-51s flying from aircraft carriers might be called upon to escort B-29s on their way to Japan. Instead, airfields for P-51s were established on suitable islands near Honshu.

1963) was adjacent to the naval aircraft factory at Philadelphia. The object under evaluation was a borrowed P-51 Mustang bearing the tail number 414017. The date was October 1944, and Allied forces were finally starting to make headway in a two-front global war. Areas on the runway were marked out, simulating the deck of an aircraft carrier. The simulation was made more realistic with installation of catapult and arresting cables. Unlike an aircraft carrier at sea, an airfield cannot maneuver into the wind (or accelerate) to gather additional headwind.

Seasoned Navy combat pilot Lt. Robert M. "Bob" Elder (1918–2008) was at the controls as over and over he rehearsed landings and takeoffs from the painted outline. Elder was born in Canada and attended the University of Washington in Seattle on a naval ROTC scholarship. Naval aviator wings were earned at Pensacola. Bob Elder became a champion of naval aircraft development, initially while still serving in uniform, and then as an aerospace executive later in life. His thumbprint remains on naval aviation to this day.

The ability of the B-25 Mitchell to take off from an aircraft carrier was demonstrated with Doolittle's audacious raid on Tokyo in April 1942. When asked about the source of the attack, President Roosevelt responded with his biggest grin and a whimsical reference to "Shangri-la." The warlords of Japan had picked the wrong Navy to embarrass in December 1941. By 1944, the US Navy fearlessly told the world the source of the Tokyo raid. Further, pending unconditional surrender, the empire of Japan should expect hell on earth, with ongoing mayhem on a massive scale.

Elder was not told of the purpose for this apparently dubious exercise. We know of it because of a typewritten report submitted to Los Angeles headquarters by the NAA Philadelphia factory field service representative. The event was further corroborated by photographs and an entry into the ship's log of *Shangri-La*—which was without air wing and on sea trials from Norfolk on November 15, 1944. Two aircraft participated. This time, the B-25 landed and brought a small team aboard the aircraft carrier. A tight-lipped Navy admiral observed the testing but said nothing. Ship's log—*Shangri-La*:

15 November 1944, 1220 hours
Lt. Robert M. Elder, USN, made the first carrier landing of P-51 type fighter plane #414017, followed by three landings and four takeoffs all successful.

The arresting cables were utilized for the gentle (low speed) landing. Takeoffs were without catapult assist. This Mustang, now dubbed "Seahorse" by the sailors, was taken below deck by elevator, and crew members were invited to take a closer look (Seahorse saw postwar service with the Pennsylvania Air National Guard).

An entirely new airplane, the ultra-long-range P-82 Twin Mustang, was in development at North American but behind schedule. Later in life, Elder postulated that the Mustangs aboard aircraft carriers were being evaluated to escort B-29 bombers over the Pacific on their way to Japan. This proved unnecessary, because close-in islands were captured and airfields hastily carved out; however, equipped with drop tanks and the aft fuselage fuel tank modification, the Mustang could fly unrefueled for 7.5 hours. Others speculate the Mustang was needed by the Navy because the early jets were fuel hogs lacking in combat range. In any case, as built, the P-51D Mustang was unsuited for service aboard an aircraft carrier.

The wings did not fold, a catapult connection was lacking, the airframe and systems were vulnerable to salt-induced corrosion, and the aft fuselage was insufficient to absorb arrested landings; however, after the deteriorating relationship with Curtiss, Navy brass were becoming enamored with a new provider. Jets were in the offing, and their Columbus-built solution was to be the FJ Fury.[1]

Other Aircraft Carriers

A slow march of innovations kept US aircraft carriers on the technical vanguard. A fully loaded FJ-4 weighs about 23,000 pounds, while an equally loaded Vigilante tips the scales closer to 63,000 pounds. Catapult-assisted launches boost aircraft off the deck, with the amount of force adjusted to handle heavier or lighter aircraft. Missions come to an abrupt halt when arresting cables snag the tailhook. An angled deck allows for concurrent landing and takeoff operations. The earliest jet aircraft arrived just in time for the Korean War—while nuclear power arrived later and obviated the need for frequent refueling at sea. Naval aviation has developed a list of needs and preferences for carrier-based aircraft:

- Twin engine jets provide a greater margin of safety at sea in case of engine failure
- A hyperextending nose gear provides a greater angle of attack when coming off the catapult
- Main gear and the entire airframe must withstand hard landings
- A sturdy tailhook attached to a robust airframe facilitates aggressive deceleration
- Folding wings save valuable space on deck or in the hangars below

Safely testing aircraft and weapons demands special equipment, technically inclined people, but, most of all—large acreage. Navy aircraft testing is typically accomplished at NAS Patuxent River, Maryland ("Pax River" in common parlance). Locations for naval weapons testing include

China Lake (California) and other designated naval bombing ranges. The Air Force operates multiple wind tunnels at Arnold AFB in Tennessee. Wright Field at Dayton was the primary home to Army Air Corps aircraft testing and procurement through World War II. Thereafter, USAF flight testing shifted to Edwards AFB in California. The desolate and lightly populated stretch from Edwards AFB to Mohave, China Lake, and Death Valley composes one of the few corridors in the United States where supersonic flight is routinely permitted.

When an aircraft is sold to the Navy, the contractor states that the airplane is, among other requirements, capable of landing on an aircraft carrier at a predetermined sink rate, usually expressed in feet per second. A Navy aircraft is often at a disadvantage as compared to an Air Force aircraft. Features such as the space-saving folding wings and the beefed-up structure necessary to cope with hard landings and abrupt stops add weight, cost, and complexity—while hard landings shorten airframe life. Early jet engines of limited thrust (and reliability) meant restrictions on either fuel or weapons loading.

The flight deck of an aircraft carrier appears expansive—except to a student pilot grasping for an arresting cable—to whom the deck appears the size of a postage stamp bobbing in the vast ocean. Antiaircraft guns were a legacy of World War II. US Navy

In addition, the contract specifies the required approach speed—the lower, the better. The airplane must survive the ultimate sink rate—21 feet per second. The static test is simple: Compute the necessary height. Lift the airframe and drop it suddenly. In the case of the Vigilante, the empennage broke off on the first try. Flight demonstration is performed by company pilots on land at Patuxent NATC or at NATF Lakehurst, New Jersey. This is more difficult than landing on an aircraft carrier because the ship generates a wake, which helps when lining up for landing. Further, the aircraft carrier can face exactly into the wind and then accelerate as needed to further boost velocity.

Four landing conditions must be demonstrated to the customer: landings off-center, the ultimate sink rate, landings with a roll or yaw maneuver, and landings where the hook is dragged across the arresting cable without touching the deck with the landing-gear tires. The tailhook snags the cable and brings the airplane down hard. If the airplane survives, the work of the test pilot is complete.

Combat Aircraft
Continue to Evolve

When the Air Force was created in 1947, the military services had a bevy of competing aircraft builders, each eager to deliver the best products. Inferior warplanes fell by the wayside. Sometimes, aircraft of equal utility were weeded out simply for being redundant. An effective new design from the Air Force might find its way into the Navy (or vice versa). Airplane designs were normally given a name. For instance, the Navy SB2C Helldiver was known as the A-25 Shrike when in service with Army Air Forces. Multisyllabic names such as "Vigilante" were sometimes shortened to "Vigi."

It was not until an edict from the Department of Defense (the "1962 United States Tri-Service aircraft designation system") that all US military aircraft were assigned common designations. Consistent with Army Air Corps standards, "A" was generally an attack airplane, bomber was "B," cargo "C," fighter "F" (replaced "P" for pursuit), helicopter "H," small liaison "L," observation "O," trainer "T," experimental "X," and "Y" was a prototype. Other standard prefixes were "K" for aerial-refueling tanker, "E" for electronics, "R" for reconnaissance, and "W" for weather.

Despite the best efforts of Robert McNamara to impose consistency on the military in 1962, the Navy and Air Force did their best to maintain their own ways of doing business. The Air Force tracks aircraft by "serial numbers," whereby the first two numbers are the fiscal year funded. Example: 71-1407 was applied to an E-3A airborne radar airplane funded in 1971. The Navy Bureau of Aeronautics

The Columbus wind tunnel was an invaluable tool for designing aircraft. A wind tunnel model is precise, complicated, expensive to build, and heavier than might be imagined.

(1929–1959, abbreviated BuAer) applied their own number. It is now called Bureau of Weapons and uses the abbreviation BuNo for "bureau number."

Breakthroughs in jet engine technology, better avionics (a term derived from "aviation electronics"), and weaponry advancements quickly rewrote the aerial-warfare playbook, as was vividly demonstrated during the Korean War. Television was the much-sought-after magic box of the

1950s. Dutch Kindelberger used it as a metaphor to describe the electrical systems within the P-51 Mustang as being simple, like a "doorbell," while the F-86 Sabre was more like television. The unreliable vacuum tube radios found in the P-51 gave way to solid-state technology packaged in "black boxes" (shoebox-sized plug-and-play modules).

With the arrival of swept wings and jet engines in the wake of World War II, some pundits incorrectly expected

The latest in computer technology was utilized in the weapon system, plus for plant-wide accounting, business, engineering, and inventory applications. Second-generation computers utilized round reels of magnetic tape for storage and processing.

extinction of propeller-driven combat aircraft. It was not to be. Some prop-driven "oldsters" were resurrected from retirement for service in Vietnam. Jungle warfare demands ruggedly built "low-and-slow" warplanes. As will be seen in chapter 8, an innovative new turboprop designated OV-10 Bronco was invented at Columbus for Vietnam and other wars of insurgency.

Human vision was extended by electronic eyes called radar. Offensive avionics are typically tied to the delivery of weapons. Defensive systems might consist of simple consumables, including strips of radar-confusing aluminum foil called chaff. A heat-seeking missile can become confused when a nearby flare emulates a jet engine. The initials "IFF" stand for "identification friend or foe," a system to help sort out other nearby aircraft. The list continues into items that deceive radar and perform other feats of apparent electronic magic.

The same technology that was enabling computers and advancing consumer goods also found their way into the equipment bays hidden beneath the skin of the sleekest aircraft designs. Those unreliable vacuum tubes (also the curse of early automobile radios) first gave way to transistors. Next, the transistors were repackaged onto tiny integrated circuit chips. Therein lies a dichotomy. Intel Corporation executive Gordon Moore (b. 1929) helped invent the integrated circuit. He coined "Moore's law" in 1965 by postulating that the number of transistor equivalents on an integrated circuit was doubling every eighteen months, and that trend would continue.

Meanwhile, a contemporaneous airplane (never sacrificed in combat) might have a useful life of twenty to forty years, with a major mechanical overhaul maybe every twelve years. Therefore, their avionics were perpetually becoming obsolete and in need of upgrade or replacement. The Apollo 11 moon landing, in 1969, was feasible only because once-room-sized computers had shrunk to the size of a shoebox. Weight and electrical demand also shriveled, while capability, durability, and reliability each escalated.

The Air War in Korea Heats Up

Pentagon leadership was in a state of near panic in December 1950, because 1950 had been a bad year. The North Korean dictator, Kim Il-sung (grandfather of current North Korean dictator Kim Jong-un), decided to invade the South during the summer of 1950. A United Nations sanction authorized allied countries (led by the US) to oust the invaders by using military force.

Caught by surprise, the US rounded up occupation forces from mainland Japan and the nearby island of Okinawa. The newest of weapons and the better-trained troops were stationed in Europe. On the initial response, US forces arrived on the Korean peninsula soft from garrison duty, undertrained, and bearing leftover World War II weapons. The F-82 Twin Mustang, having emerged too late for World War II, was rushed into Korea and scored the first kill. Otherwise, they were ho-hum and lasted until the inventory of spare parts ran out. The first-generation jets lacked the range to fly combat missions from Japan, and the runways in Korea were either too short or too riddled with potholes to permit forward basing. The P-51 Mustang earned fame in Europe as a long-range escort fighter. Having been renamed the F-51 when the Air Force was created in 1947, its new mission was now close air support. The radiator and other coolant plumbing left the Mustang (and pilot) very vulnerable to small-arms ground fire.

The battle ebbed back and forth. Seoul changed hands four times before hostilities ended. When Kim Il-sung suffered setbacks on the battlefield, he pleaded for help from his Russian friends. Air Force general Hap Arnold once commented that Joseph Stalin had a more detailed grasp of warplanes than some of his own generals. Stalin responded by sending nimble Soviet MiG-15 fighters into the fray. Western intelligence had no inkling such an advanced fighter was in the Soviet arsenal. American forces were caught agog and flatfooted. In his salty style, Dutch Kindelberger later commented:

It was difficult to tell where the skirmishes left off and the conflict began, but the Korean War was going full blast by June of 1950. The communist encroachment was opposed in the air only by prop oldsters and junior-grade jets. North American aircraft by nature of their exceptional longevity were fielded early in the war and served well. The P-82s outgrew their enginitis and succeeded in downing the first enemy aircraft. The P-51 was the standard operational fighter for United Nations forces and was an excellent vehicle for low[-]level bombing and strafing. They changed the designations to F-82 and F-51, [but] the old warhorses were little more than World War II products. Even the steadfast AT-6 trainer was mustered for ground spotting.

Then came MiG-15s barreling in and clearing the skies with their superior performance and firepower. "There is nothing sadder than a second-rate plane[,] at least to the boys who is [sic] flying it," Dutch mentioned. Saddest of all were the UN pilots manning the dozen or so types of Brand X jets of the time. These British and US planes were little more than trainers and were totally incapable of contesting the MiG-15. The state of Russian technology was convincingly demonstrated. Dutch said later, "Our conception of the Russian is crazy. We thought of him as a peasant with a cow, and his wife out pulling the plow—stopping only now and then to scratch. But Russia is building up and improving her industries all the time."

It takes a jet to stop a jet. The wizardry of engineering and manufacturing of North American had a jet in production to do the stopping. The F-86Es and Fs were rushed from flight test to Korea[,] and the kill ratio shifted decisively in favor the Americans.[2]

The MiG jets, initially flown by battle-hardened Soviet pilots, started arriving in November 1950. By February and March 1951, even with jet fighter escorts, the American daytime B-29 formations were forced to retreat from the skies over North Korea. In common with the Sabre, the Communist jets borrowed from Nazi World War II technology by melding swept wings with jet engines in a small package. Everything else in the deadly airspace over Korea was outclassed. The "trainer" Kindelberger referenced was the Lockheed F-80 Shooting Star. The Air Force bet heavily on the straight-wing jet. The Shooting Star was a dud in aerial combat but later redeemed itself as the beloved T-33 trainer.

Unlike Curtiss-Wright, North American Aviation (NAA) was overwhelmed with work that ranged from rehabilitating leftover World War II aircraft to building new cutting-edge airplanes. North American's facilities at Inglewood, Downey, Long Beach, and Torrance had become desperately crowded. In August of 1950, RAdm. A. M. Pride, then chief of the Navy's Bureau of Aeronautics, called North American chairman Dutch Kindelberger and suggested the assumption of Curtiss-Wright's lease at the Columbus Naval Weapons Industrial Reserve Facility. North American management acted quickly and was awarded occupancy on September 22. The urgency of the move was announced in *Aviation Week*:

> Transfer of the Curtiss-Wright Corporation's Columbus, Ohio, plant to North American Aviation Inc. will be effective November 25, instead of next April as planned. Operations should start by December 4, 1950.
>
> It's likely that the earlier date was decided on to clear NAA's main plant at Los Angeles for concentration on F-86 Sabre production. The Columbus plant would be available to handle orders from North American customers for Sabres and T-28 trainers. Orders for modernization of T-6G trainers can't be counted out either.[3]

As planned, Curtiss-Wright officially terminated activities on November 24, and North American moved in the next day. Kindelberger selected Charles J. "Chuck" Gallant, his personal assistant, to become general manager of the new location. Gallant's wartime performance at the Kansas City B-25 factory impressed Dutch; however, he remained an unlikely choice since he had no hands-on manufacturing experience. Intelligence combined with understanding Kindelberger's style of management won the prize. Plant workers were not the cause of the XP-87

Blackhawk debacle. Realizing the value of their experience, his first act was to offer positions to the entire Curtiss staff. This was a brilliant move. Gallant then convinced Reggie Clarke, a veteran NAA employee who had been responsible for B-45 production in California, to transfer to Columbus. Clarke was an excellent factory manager who possessed the manufacturing experience that Gallant lacked.[4]

The normal steps to create a new factory from scratch include real-estate acquisition, plans, permits, construction, hiring workers, and then training them. Years of delay were circumvented by obtaining the existing Columbus plant and then retaining the experienced workforce. The initial work at NAA Columbus was simply continuation of the overhaul and component fabrication contracts Curtiss-Wright left behind. This consisted of refurbishment of B-29s, assembly of F-84 tail surfaces, and spare-parts manufacturing for the C-46 Commando. The early workflow was hindered by malfunctioning government-furnished equipment and a series of unfortunate circumstances. The B-29 contract, for example, called for fifteen hours of flight time on each overhauled airplane, but the severe winter of 1950–1951 combined with the limited number of B-29-qualified flight crews immediately led to a "behind schedule" condition. Only four B-29 overhauls were completed by year's end.

Despite the bumpy start, the velocity of improvements at NAA Columbus was increasing. In 1951, the first full year of operation, four dozen B-29 overhauls were completed and a production line for F-86F Sabre Jets was established to relieve the backlog at the Inglewood plant. Columbus also completed thirty-nine T-6G upgrades, an urgent program to provide training aircraft for the Air Force and Navy. Postwar plans to develop new trainers had stalled due to interservice bickering and budget constraints. As a stopgap measure, Congress was forced to approve funds to modernize World War II–vintage AT-6 and SNJ trainers. The upgrade of these well-worn trainers consisted of raising the rear seat and installing a new canopy frame for improved visibility, installing a steerable/lockable tailwheel for more positive ground handling, updated avionics, increased fuel capacity, and improvements to the hydraulic system.

With the Korean War now in full swing, Columbus received new contracts in rapid succession. The Navy ordered the manufacture of eighty-two AJ Savage attack bombers and two hundred FJ-2 Fury swept-wing fighters. Even before volume production of the FJ-2 got underway, the Navy ordered 389 units of the FJ-3, an improved version of the Fury (ultimately the order would be increased to 538). The Air Force ordered a more powerful version of the Sabre Jet, the F-86H, and the Navy added to the workload yet again with a contract for the T-28B, a Navy version of the trainer. By end of 1953, the Columbus division had grown to 18,000 employees from the 1950 level of 1,600. Production lines were manufacturing a diverse mix ranging from light trainers and fighters to heavy bombers and reconnaissance aircraft for both the Navy and Air Force.

Girding the Columbus Plant for Cold War

With all of this going on, Gallant assembled an autonomous engineering department. He started by acquiring George Gehrkens, who had joined North American in 1937 and had served as project engineer on the iconic P-51 Mustang. In his new role at Columbus, Gehrkens attracted experienced engineers in the areas of trainers, fighter aircraft, and bombers. Most notably, he brought in Frank Compton as director of advanced design. This allowed Columbus to emerge as a fully integrated aircraft-manufacturing facility and undertake the complete design, development, and testing of the FJ-4, the most advanced variant of the Fury series. By the end of that year, the Air Force named Columbus as a second source for production of its most important fighter, the supersonic F-100 Super Sabre.[5]

NAA Park was established in 1953 and used for various recreational purposes, including baseball, jogging, picnics, trap shooting, and HAM radio operations. Initially consisting of 30 acres, the park was expanded to 67 acres when a new $400,000 activities building was established in 1963. Sources of funding included profits from the vending machines located in the plant. With a separate employee park already in California, NAA had a strong history of sponsoring recreational and family activities. The nonprofit Rockwell Recreational Foundation donated the land and improvements to the City of Whitehall on April 3, 1989.[6]

In the 1955 Annual Report to Stockholders, chairman Kindelberger announced record corporate profits due, in part, to the success of the Columbus Division. The pace continued into 1956, when Columbus won two prime Navy contracts. The first was for a carrier-capable jet trainer known as the T2J-1 Buckeye. The second was for a highly advanced Mach 2 attack aircraft with thermonuclear-weapon capability, the A3J-1 Vigilante. The attention of the entire aviation industry was centered on Columbus when the prototypes were rolled out in 1958. The T2J-1 passed its carrier trials in 1959 and was ready to begin service in the Naval Air Training Command, while the A3J-1 began an intensive test program at Patuxent River, Maryland, and Palmdale, California.

The second decade at the Columbus Division started with focus on T2J-1 and A3J-1 production. At the same time, the Air Force expressed interest in a counterinsurgency aircraft for use in Vietnam. Following French success with the T-28S Fennec used in Algeria, the Air Force launched a major program to upgrade its fleet of mothballed T-28A trainers into T-28D light-attack aircraft. The program covered 321 airplanes and lasted for eight years, but the results were disappointing. T-28D performance was inadequate in the hot, humid jungle conditions. Looking for enhanced performance, the Air Force evaluated a turboprop version, the YAT-28E, but decided not to order production after evaluating three prototypes. It wasn't until 1964, when Columbus received a contract for seven prototypes of a joint Navy, Marine, and Air Force light armed reconnaissance aircraft, the OV-10 Bronco, that a truly effective counterinsurgency solution was found. Also in 1964, after two years of study, production of the new twin-engine Buckeye was approved, and a contract was issued to convert twenty-seven Vigilantes to a new RA-5C standard.

As the NAA capacity for high-rate aircraft production in California atrophied, the Columbus plant temporarily remained an island of normalcy. The OV-10A Bronco experienced its first combat mission in July 1968 with the First Marine Air Wing. The following spring an OV-10A was flown to Europe for the 1969 Paris Air Show, where chief test pilot Ed Gillespie demonstrated the aircraft's capabilities, leading to an order for eighteen examples from Germany, the first international OV-10 sale. The Buckeye received further improvements with the selection of more fuel-efficient General Electric J85 engines for the T-2C model.

The third decade started with a celebration marking North American's twentieth anniversary in Columbus. Of the original 1,641 Curtiss-Wright employees hired by North American, 636 remained on the payroll. North American Rockwell was declared the winner of the huge Air Force B-1 Lancer bomber contract, and Columbus was expected to build portions of the airframe. But new aircraft orders were scarce, and it was revealed that Rockwell was in preliminary discussions to sell the Columbus plant. By the end of the year, the board of directors announced that the sale was scrubbed; instead, operations would be consolidated, and more than a million square feet of surplus plant space would be subleased to other manufacturers. New international orders were received from the Royal Thailand Air Force and the Venezuelan air force for Broncos and Buckeyes.

Vietnam War and Beyond

Finally, on October 18, 1972, a new aircraft development contract was won by the Columbus Division. The secretary of the Navy, John Warner, issued a $46 million contract for the prototype of a supersonic vertical-takeoff-and-landing aircraft known as the XFV-12A. NAA was famous for advanced research and development programs such as the XB-70 and X-15, but this was the first experimental project undertaken at Columbus. The mockup of the XFV-12A was examined and approved by Navy officials within a year, as work moved forward on B-1 bomber components. By September, Columbus shipped a complete tail-cone assembly to California in support of the first B-1 bomber—air vehicle number 1.

In February 1973, the shareholders of North American Rockwell approved a new corporate name: Rockwell International. The iconic name "North American Aviation, Inc.," adopted on January 1, 1935, was removed from the top of the marquee after thirty-eight years, portending a decline in the importance of aviation in a major corporation with far-flung reach. The moniker "North American" remained with the aviation division even as lucrative international aircraft sales continued as a source of business. Greece, Venezuela, and Indonesia placed orders for Buckeyes and Broncos.

Work progressed steadily on the prototype XFV-12A, and completion of the first article was projected for year's end in 1975, with the first flight in early 1976. After several delays (not unusual for such a radically new experimental aircraft), the rollout ceremony occurred on August 26, 1977. In November, the prototype XFV-12A was loaded aboard an aircraft and flown to NASA at Langley, Virginia, for hover tests. The dynamic hover testing was conducted in a special gantry, a remnant of Apollo space capsule development. The testing successfully demonstrated the precise maneuvering capability of the hover control system, but the desired lift from the unique Thrust Augmented Wing Concept was not fully achieved. Late in the year, the XVF-12A's augmenters were returned to Columbus for additional testing and development.

New aircraft orders were scarce in 1979, but a tooling contract was received from Boeing for work on the 767-200 commercial airliner. Separately, space shuttle parts consisting of forward fuselage, aft fuselage, and aft body flap (the control surface beneath the engines) for the small NASA fleet were manufactured at Columbus. The Navy issued a contract for upgrading OV-10As to the OV-10D standard by installing more-powerful engines with fiberglass propellers and forward-looking infrared radar (FLIR) night vision capability. These tasks were sufficient to keep the lights on—but barely.

The year 1980 marked the thirtieth anniversary of the Columbus plant under North American / Rockwell control. The Naval Air Systems Command announced a competition for VTXTS (next-generation total-training program). Columbus prepared a proposal based on a modernized T-2C Buckeye, but the contract was awarded to a McDonnell Douglas / British Aerospace partnership that produced the T-45 Goshawk. The Air Force took custody of the plant from the Navy for work on the B-1 bomber. McDonnell Douglas was the final aerospace tenant for assembly of parts for the C-17 transport—but only for a short while.

Working at the Airplane Factory: Hire to Retire

The state of Ohio remains home to vital manufacturing industries. As such, Columbus was the perfect location for a wartime airplane factory. Skilled workers, an excellent education system, the requisite infrastructure, and a friendly political/regulatory environment were already in place. As compared to automobiles, airplane manufacturing requires more acreage because airplanes have wings, which demand broad assembly bays (200 feet wide at Columbus), as well as outdoor parking ramps, measured in acres, and access to an airport runway. Moving aircraft assembly lines were a wartime standard and optional thereafter—depending on the needed production rate.

The mix of workers normally includes about two-thirds white-collar and one-third touch labor (hourly) workers, who often unionize—but not at Columbus. Employees can expect to be paid weekly on Friday. Pay in the aerospace industry is traditionally at the high end of prevailing wages because of the special skills needed. Work, as estimated and quantified by industrial engineers, is most often expressed as heads, head count, or FTEs—full-time equivalents. Job security can be "boom" (massive hiring) when a major new contract is awarded, or "bust" (wholesale layoffs) when the project ends. Despite the rollercoaster effect, a core cadre must remain as the repository of tribal knowledge needed for the next upswing.

A Monday-through-Friday work schedule was normal; however, forty-eight- or fifty-six-hour weeks (including weekends) were common for professional staff during "crunch" times. A white-collar career in the fast-paced aerospace industry demanded dedication to the task at hand. Wrecked marriages were sometimes a consequence. The Fair Labor Standards Act (FLSA) dictates hourly workers be paid overtime anytime the workweek exceeds forty hours. Most tasks were accomplished on first shift. Evening work was an option, to be invoked when the workload demanded. Third shift was a good time for repositioning work in progress, cleaning, painting, resupply of parts, and servicing the factory machinery.

Like other traditional aerospace companies, NAA offered an attractive suite of employee benefits, including employer-paid family healthcare, a company-funded pension, paid-vacation and sick-leave plans that typically grow with tenure, and a schedule of holidays. Potential employees can expect to be fingerprinted and investigated before hiring because involvement with classified weapons systems demands a government-issued security clearance. An occasional weekend "family day" allowed employees to bring guests into the workplace. There might be live music, snacks, and special displays to increase the "wow" factor; however, personal cameras were always banned within defense plants.

NAA General Managers of Columbus Plant, 1950–1988

Years	Name	Comment
1950–1958	C. J. "Chuck" Gallant	Hired in Los Angeles in 1935
1958–1968	W. H. "Will" Yahn	Joined NAA in 1950
1968–1970	R. F. "Dick" Walker	Hired in Los Angeles in 1939
1970–1972	W. F. "Will" Snelling	Joined NAA in Los Angeles in 1943
1972–1979	J. P. "John" Fosness	A-5 project engineer since 1955
1979–1981	V. R. "Hank" Hancock	Joined Columbus as a pilot/salesman in 1959
1981–1986	C. R. "Chet" Johnson	Factory manager, hired at Boeing Wichita in 1951
1986–1988	A. H. "Al" Smith	Another veteran of Boeing Wichita
1988–closure	J. A. "Jake" Borror	

For nearly five decades, all under ownership of the US military, the Columbus plant delivered airplanes. Signage changed as multiple plant operators came and went, but the name "North American Aviation, Inc." lasted the longest. It was a time of perpetual change not only to technology, airplanes, and the workplace, but also to society itself. A high-school education was sufficient for entry-level assembly-line workers, storekeepers, or in-plant transportation. That same diploma augmented with industrial math, mechanical aptitude, and blueprint-reading skills might be qualifiers for more-higher-graded aircraft assembly jobs, electrician, or quality control inspector. More highly compensated jobs include journeyman machinists, wind tunnel model builders, or skilled flight-line mechanics. An A&P (airframe and powerplant) license is generally not required by manufacturers but more often by airlines or aftermarket maintenance mechanics.

Engineering degrees always in high demand include electrical, mechanical, industrial, or aeronautical. Computers have made their way from the factories and offices and into the products. Like any industry, there is demand for lawyers, contract administrators, accountants, and human resource (HR) specialists.

Within a company the size of NAA, there are three groups of pilots: Engineering (or experimental) test pilots are at the top of the pecking order as measured by status, pay, esteem—but also job risk. Production pilots test-fly each airplane prior to delivery, and instructor pilots work with the customer to get their crews proficient and qualified. Robert "Bob" Hoover (1922–2016) was the most well-known NAA employee because of a thirty-six-year career (1950–1986) and postretirement stardom on the air show circuit. Both Hoover and his lifelong associate, Chuck Yeager, shared the attributes of World War II combat service, incredible flying skill, self-promotion, and longevity. Each autobiography remains a "must-read" for aviation buffs. Bob Hoover put an F-100 Super Sabre into a flat spin on July 7, 1955, and barely survived by ejecting at the last instant. That event changed his priorities. Like many other survivors, Hoover walked away from engineering flight test. The balance of his career was as salesman, demonstration pilot, and public-relations spokesman.

Edward A. Gillespie (1928–2015) was hired by Jim Pearce, director of flight operations, as an engineering test pilot. Ed was a graduate of the Navy Test Pilot School. He flew all the airplane types in production at the time— F-86s, FJs, T2s, T-28s, AJs, and F-100s. The US military was caught flatfooted and embarrassed when the Soviet MiG-15 arrived in the war-torn skies over Korea in November 1950. For the next decade, warplane development was full throttle, and it was test pilots who paid the price (with their lives) when corners were cut. When asked about the dangers, Ed responded, "Well, I started at North American Aviation in November 1956, and I was scared until November 1988, when I retired. I practically lived on adrenaline."[7]

The Columbus test pilot group had experience with flutter, carrier suitability, weapons delivery, flying qualities, spins, and structural demonstrations. By the time of a first flight, the pilot has sat in the cockpit many times and flown the best computer-aided simulators available. Wind tunnel data were discussed with the aeronautical engineers. Simulations inform the test pilot about how the airplane will perform under all conditions of designed flight. Generally, the chief test pilot will perform the maiden flight, primarily because of seniority. Test pilot was a dangerous occupation back then. Most who lived into their nineties did so because they stepped back and took safer jobs.

Despite an occasional strike, Dutch Kindelberger and the other executives at North American remained popular with the workforce. Kindelberger, a survivor of the Great Depression, had a propensity to leave his office for a smoke break and interaction with workers as he randomly wandered about the factory. On one instance, he encountered a young fellow cutting up a large sheet of aluminum. Dutch asked, "What are you doing?" "My supervisor told me to cut it up into small pieces before the 'old man' found it and decided to turn it into an airplane" was the response.

North American Aviation seized upon German technology at the end of World War II and over the next twenty-five years leveraged it to create a big company with a diverse product portfolio. By the 1960s, primary operating sites included the following:

Site	Business unit	Product
Anaheim	Autonetics	Guidance systems
Canoga Park	Rockedyne	Missiles and rocket motors
DeSoto	Atomics International	Small reactors
Downey	NASA space programs	Apollo and space shuttle
Inglewood	L.A. Division (LAX)	Headquarters
Columbus Division	Military aircraft	Various
Plant 42, Palmdale	Military airplanes	XB-70 and B-1B bombers
Tulsa/McAlester	Commercial airplanes	Parts and assemblies
Seal Beach	Space manufacturing	Saturn rocket, Stage 2

Along with Hollywood-style entertainment (motion pictures and television), the combined economic clout of the various aerospace companies hastened development of Southern California. Depending on the year and operating tempo, each of these divisions might have a payroll of ten, twenty, or even thirty thousand workers (a term called "head count"). Long after the demise of NAA, former employees were known to celebrate their collective history with an active retiree group called the "Bald Eagles." Columbus alumni, who assumed the mantra of high-rate aircraft builders, were a distant part of this family. Members were invited to craft and submit articles to a quarterly newsletter. These articles enrich this book because they are as useful as a face-to-face interview.

Periodic reunions were held. Authors Mark Frankel and John Fredrickson were invited to the final gathering of the "Bald Eagles" in May 2017. Both attended at a large venue in Long Beach, California, where they were honored to rub elbows, listen to stories, and break bread with the proud survivors of a career at NAA. Guest speakers included Dutch Kindelberger's grandson and various retired executives.

The disdain between nonaerospace Rockwell management and NAA alumni remains palpable. Some were still in the workplace when new employee badges marked "Boeing" arrived after the acquisition of December 6, 1996. A few rose to senior positions within Boeing. Separately, under the leadership of Ed Rusinek and Nolan Leatherman, the retiree group continues to fund fine-quality engraved granite benches that commemorate NAA and its products. So far, fifteen benches have been donated to various parks, educational institutions, and aviation museums; however, the name "Rockwell" never appears on any of them.

A Savage Story

The AJ-1 Savage was propelled by three engines—a pair of 2,000-horsepower Pratt & Whitney R-2800 radial engines augmented by a gasoline-burning Allison J33 jet engine hidden in the aft-center fuselage (where only the exhaust port is visible).

Naval aviation's most urgent project at the end of World War II was the development of a carrier-capable atomic-strike aircraft. It resulted in the North American AJ Savage—the world's first aircraft specifically designed to carry a weapon of mass destruction—and for a time, the world's largest and heaviest carrier-based aircraft.

The Savage's origin can be traced to the late months of World War II, before the existence of the atomic bomb was generally known. VAdm. Marc A. Mitscher, deputy CNO for air, and his successor, VAdm. Arthur W. Radford, ordered preliminary studies for a new class of postwar aircraft that could carry heavy payloads over long distances. These large aircraft would operate from a behemoth aircraft carrier with a flush deck—no island or other vertical obstruction to interfere with their operation. The "supercarrier," as it came to be known, was expected to displace 85,000 tons, with a deck length of nearly 1,100 feet giving it the ability to launch and recover 100,000-pound aircraft. Essex-class carriers of the time displaced approximately 37,000 tons with an 870-foot deck, handling aircraft of less than 20,000 pounds.

Handed novel requirements and a hectic schedule fueled by intense interservice rivalry, the people at NAA in California did their best—but came up short. Three Navy prototypes, designated XAJ-1, were rushed from design and into fabrication. Two of the first three crashed, at the expense of human lives.

Every airplane factory has a compass rose. It is the place where the magnetic compass gets calibrated. It is also a convenient place for the company photographer, because the lighting and camera remain static while the airplane is rotated in a full circle.

AJ Savage General Characteristics

Model	No. built	First flight	Length	Span	Empty lbs.	Gross	Max. mph
XAJ-1	3	1948	63 ft., 1 in.	71 ft., 5 in.	27,558	47,000	471
AJ-1	55	1949	63 ft., 1 in.	71 ft., 5 in.	27,558	50,964	471
AJ-2 / -2P	85	1953	63 ft., 1 in.	75 ft., 2 in.	30,000 (est.)	52,862	471
XA2J	1	1952	70 ft., 3 in.	71 ft., 6 in.	35,350	61,200	451

On August 13, 1945, one week after the first atomic bomb was dropped on Hiroshima, BuAer announced a design competition for a carrier-based attack aircraft capable of delivering a 10,000-pound bomb (the approximate weight of the "Fat Man" bomb dropped on Nagasaki). The atom bomb was a devastating weapon that changed everything. Getting that weapon into their arsenal was an instant obsession with the top Navy brass. Lacking a means of delivery, the Navy initiated a hasty design competition for a carrier-based attack aircraft capable of delivering an atomic bomb. If naval aviation were to remain viable, a carrier-capable atomic-strike aircraft was essential.

An RFP (request for proposal) was mailed to several experienced naval contractors specifying an aircraft with a 43,000-pound gross weight, a 29,000-pound landing weight, a maximum speed of 500 mph at 35,000 feet with 60 percent fuel, a service ceiling of 45,000 feet, a rate of climb of 2,500 feet per minute, and a stalling speed of less than 100 mph at maximum gross weight. The aircraft was expected to have a combat radius of 1,000 nautical miles with an 8,000-pound load but be capable of carrying a 12,000-pound load at the expense of range. Further requirements included in-flight access to the bomb bay (early atomic bombs were manually armed in flight) that could accommodate a 5-foot-diameter, 16-foot-long weapon. Cockpit pressurization was required, and the aircraft had to demonstrate takeoff capability from a 600-foot deck run.[1]

Responses were received from NAA, Consolidated Vultee, and Douglas. All three proposed composite propeller/jet designs using twin Pratt & Whitney R-2800 turbocharged reciprocating engines for primary power and one or more centrifugal-flow turbojets to boost takeoff and maximum speed performance. Consolidated Vultee's design specified two Westinghouse J34 turbojets, one in each nacelle, but the design lacked the necessary combat radius and exceeded the maximum landing weight—it was rejected out of hand. Douglas proposed Model D-566, a high-aspect-ratio wing design (long span, narrow chord), but it suffered from an unacceptably high empty weight.

North American's model NA-146 submittal was prepared by Howard Evans, Los Angeles Division's chief designer. NA-146 offered the shortest takeoff distance, lightest landing weight, best rate of climb, and lowest cost. The proposal was accepted by the Bureau of Aeronautics on June 24, 1946, with a contract for three flying articles and one static-test article designated XAJ-1. The design consisted of a tricycle landing gear, high-wing monoplane of abnormally large size for a carrier airplane (71-foot, 5-inch wingspan; 63-foot, 1-inch overall length; 20-foot, 5-inch height). To facilitate carrier operations, the outer wing panels and the upper half of the vertical tail folded manually. The J33 turbojet mounted in the fuselage received air from an inlet on the upper fuselage that would open when the jet was running, and close for drag reduction at other times. High-grade aviation gasoline was used to run all three engines, thus simplifying the fuel system (gasoline often fueled early turbojet engines).

Initially designed and developed at headquarters in Inglewood, California, it was produced by the Downey plant until 1951, when production was transferred to Columbus, Ohio. This aircraft was to be the first in a series of aircraft that would operate from the proposed 85,000-ton flush-deck aircraft carriers capable of launching and recovering oversized aircraft.

From the outset, the Navy's plan to develop an atomic bomber and a carrier from which it would operate faced several stumbling blocks—minor at first, but increasingly difficult over time. First, President Truman issued a memorandum in the aftermath of Hiroshima and Nagasaki preventing the military services from developing or employing atomic weapons without the specific approval of the president. Second, Truman asked Congress to pass legislation unifying the military services under one secretary of defense (SecDef) and establish an independent, but coequal, Air Force.[2] Nevertheless, Truman authorized the Navy to proceed with their plan for developing a nuclear-strike capability from sea. Initially three Midway-class carriers (CV-41, CV-42, and CV-43) were modified to accommodate unconventional ordnance. Carrier decks were strengthened; bomb-loading, handling, and stowage facilities were upgraded; and bomb elevators were enlarged.

With presidential approval in hand, the Navy assumed that the other services would acquiesce to their plan, but

Marking Time©
North American AJ / A-2 Savage

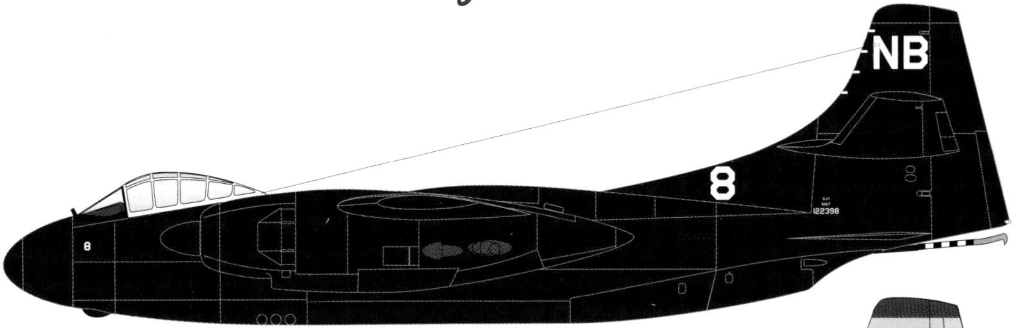

NB

8

AJ-1 BuNo. 122398
VC-5
NAS MOFFETT FLD, CA   FEBRUARY, 1950

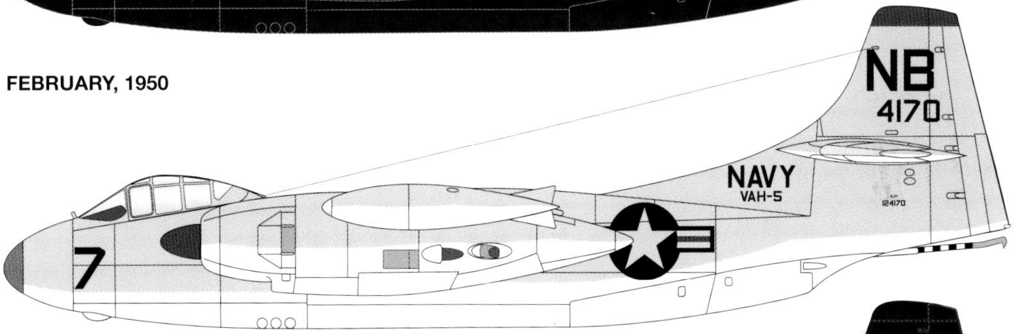

NB
4170

NAVY
VAH-5

7

AJ-1 BuNo. 124170
VAH-5, HATWING-1
NAS SANFORD, FL   MAY, 1957

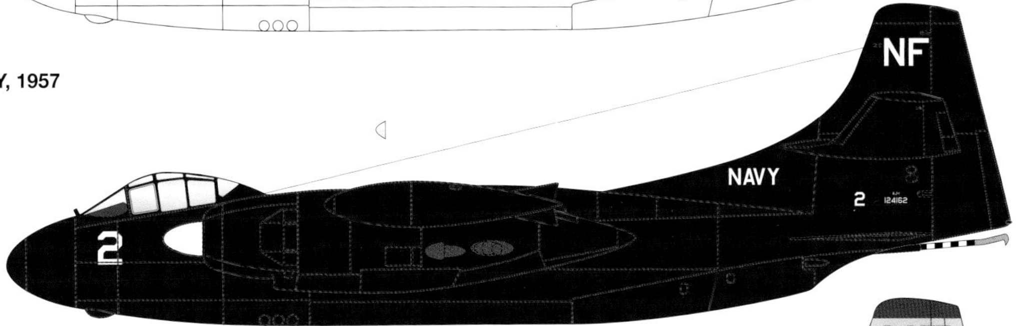

NF

NAVY

2

AJ-1 BuNo. 124162
VC-6, USS YORKTOWN (CV 10)
WESTPAC   OCTOBER, 1953

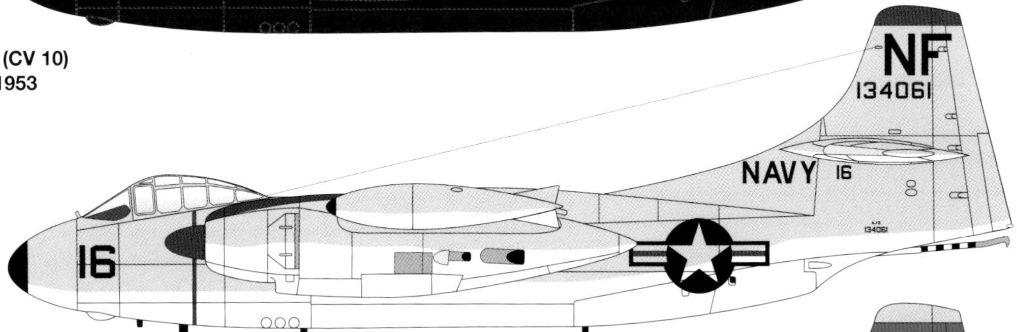

NF
134061

NAVY   16

16

AJ-2 BuNo. 134061
VAH-6
NAS NORTH ISLAND, CA   1956

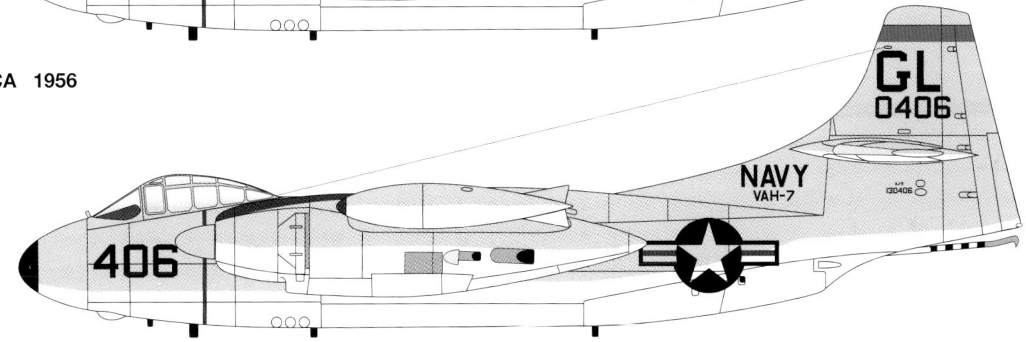

GL
0406

NAVY
VAH-7

406

AJ-2 BuNo. 130406
VAH-7, HATWING-1
NAS SANFORD, FL   1957

© JDMC Graphics 2018

41

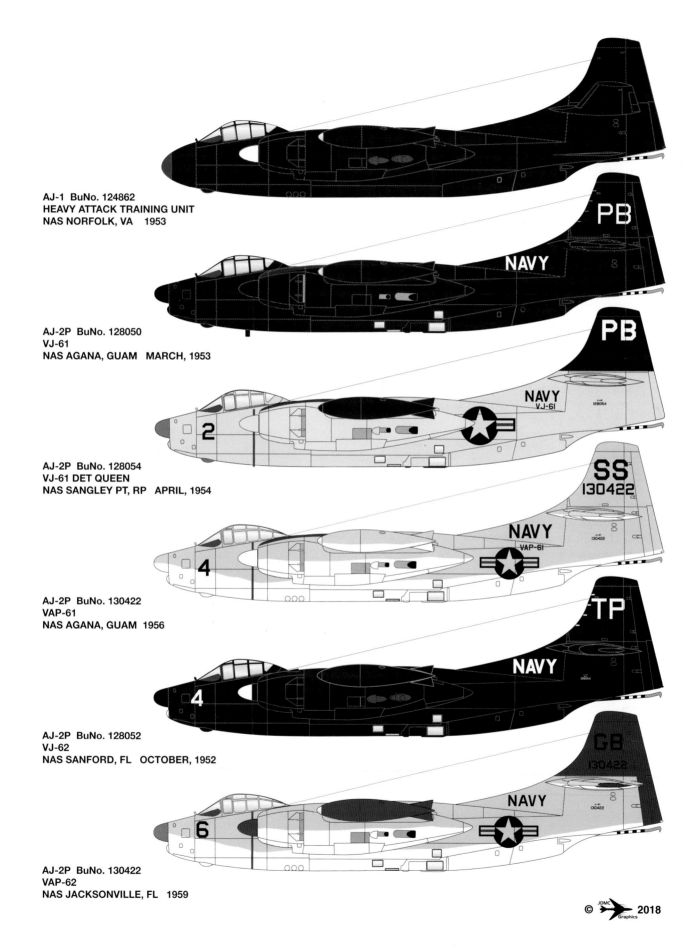

AJ-1 BuNo. 124862
HEAVY ATTACK TRAINING UNIT
NAS NORFOLK, VA   1953

AJ-2P BuNo. 128050
VJ-61
NAS AGANA, GUAM   MARCH, 1953

AJ-2P BuNo. 128054
VJ-61 DET QUEEN
NAS SANGLEY PT, RP   APRIL, 1954

AJ-2P BuNo. 130422
VAP-61
NAS AGANA, GUAM 1956

AJ-2P BuNo. 128052
VJ-62
NAS SANFORD, FL   OCTOBER, 1952

AJ-2P BuNo. 130422
VAP-62
NAS JACKSONVILLE, FL 1959

© JDMC Graphics 2018

instead a growing opposition was encountered. The opposition peaked in December 1947, when a classified memorandum written by RAdm. Daniel Gallery, assistant CNO (guided missiles), was leaked to the press, causing an uproar. Gallery proposed an atomic-weapon delivery system that employed a fleet of twelve expendable attack aircraft. The aircraft would have no landing gear, taking off from carrier decks on detachable trolleys. Once launched, the aircraft would have sufficient range to reach their targets and ditch at sea after the strike. The crews would be recovered by pre-positioned submarines. Weight savings from the reduced fuel load and the elimination of landing gear would yield higher performance over the target. Gallery reasoned that it made far more sense to fly an aircraft 1,000 miles to strike a target from a forward-deployed carrier than to fly a bomber 5,000 miles from a land base.

The Gallery memorandum was written in an environment of severe budget cuts and the growing belief that traditional land and naval forces had become obsolete with the advent of the atomic bomb. This represented an existential threat to the Navy, which faced the possibility of losing air assets to the newly formed Air Force. Attempting to resolve the matter, SecDef James Forrestal convened a conference of the service chiefs in Key West, Florida, on March 11, 1948. The conference resulted in the April 1948 "Key West Agreement," which gave the Air Force responsibility for strategic targeting of urban and industrial centers while granting the Navy tactical nuclear-strike responsibility for military installations. In briefing President Truman on the conference, Forrestal stressed that it had been agreed that the Navy was "not to be denied use of [the] A-bomb."[3] Instead of resolving the matter, the friction between the services grew more intense. In March 1949, President Truman, who had become increasingly frustrated with Forrestal's lackluster political support and his inability to curtail military spending, asked for his resignation.[4] Construction of the "supercarrier," USS *United States*, which recently had been approved by Forrestal, was summarily canceled by his replacement, Louis A. Johnson. The secretary of the Navy, John L. Sullivan, resigned in protest, and the debate over the Navy's nuclear role erupted into the notorious "Revolt of the Admirals."

The Revolt of the Admirals

The proposed supercarrier named USS *United States* (CVA-58), was the centerpiece of the Navy's postwar plan. It was to be the first in a series of four "supercarriers" that would carry a new generation of nuclear-capable naval aircraft. But the Air Force considered development of its enormous, intercontinental B-36 bomber to be essential to the national defense. Colliding with this dichotomy was President Truman's budget ceiling of $14.2 billion, leaving SecDef James Forrestal with a Solomon-like dilemma.

Forrestal favored balancing appropriations among the services, but he was challenged by the aggressive argument of the Air Force secretary, Stuart Symington. In a 1948 speech Symington asserted that the Soviet Union was America's most dangerous threat. Furthermore, it was the Air Force's mission to counteract that threat with a fleet of large, land-based strategic bombers. Appropriations should be allocated to best blunt the threat and not balanced among all the services. Symington's argument steadily gained traction with the public and Congress.

Funds for USS *United States* had been provided by Congress in the Naval Appropriations Act of 1949. Keel laying was scheduled to start on April 18, 1949, at the Newport News drydock. But Truman's increasing frustration with Forrestal resulted in his resignation. Louis A. Johnson, a staunch supporter of Truman's austerity policies, became the new secretary of defense. Unlike Forrestal, Johnson had little sympathy for the Navy. One of his first acts was cancellation of USS *United States* without even consulting either the secretary of the Navy or the CNO. Secretary of the Navy John L. Sullivan resigned in protest and was replaced by Francis P. Matthews, a former lawyer from Omaha, Nebraska, who famously quipped that his only naval experience was ownership of a rowboat. Navy leadership's morale plummeted as concern grew about its future. Meanwhile, the recently formed Air Force seemingly emerged as the lead service in the still-evolving national defense strategy. Another blow was dealt to the Navy on May 17, 1949, when SecDef Johnson announced his intent to transfer Marine Corps aviation assets to the Air Force. Congress considered this a step too far. Expressing outrage, they ordered the secretary to "cease and desist" until they could hold hearings on military unification and strategy.

As the hearings were being organized, an anonymous memorandum was circulated among members of Congress that alleged political and financial improprieties in the Convair B-36 procurement program committed by SecDef Johnson and Air Force secretary Symington. Congressman James Van Zandt (R-Pennsylvania) attempted to establish a select committee to investigate these allegations, but the chairman of the House Armed Services Committee, Carl Vinson (D-Georgia), fearing a challenge to his authority, took steps to bring the matter under his jurisdiction. Vinson hastily convened hearings on August 9, 1949, to investigate the merits of the anonymous memorandum. It was then discovered that the memorandum had been written by a civilian assistant to the undersecretary of the Navy, Cedric R. Worth. "The Worth Paper," as it came to be known, proved to be baseless, just a collection of rumors—Johnson and Symington were granted absolution while Worth was fired. By August 25, when this phase of the hearings adjourned, the Navy had suffered severe embarrassment.

The hearings reconvened on October 6 with focus on the proposed reduction of the Navy, expansion of the Air

Force, and cancellation of USS *United States*. Navy secretary Matthews opened the hearings with remarks that seemed barely supportive of the Navy's position. His statement was not well received by many of the naval officers in attendance and provoked guffaws on occasion.[5] Matthews's remarks were followed by the testimony of a forceful advocate, Adm. Arthur W. Radford, one of the original architects of the Navy's nuclear-strike concept. He questioned not only the usefulness the Air Force's atomic-blitz strategy, but also whether the B-36 was an effective weapon. A series of technical witnesses followed Radford, examining the capabilities and vulnerabilities of the B-36 in detail. Then a long list of Navy luminaries lined up to make strong arguments excoriating the B-36 program. They included Fleet Admirals Chester Nimitz, William Halsey, and Ernest King; Admirals Raymond Spruance and Thomas Kinkaid; Marine Corps commandant Gen. Alexander Vandergrift; and Captain Arleigh Burke. The Navy's closing argument was to be made by the CNO, Adm. Louis E. Denfeld:

> The CNO's appearance was eagerly awaited both by the proponents of naval aviation and by those on the other side of the fight. The latter were hoping (even expecting) that Denfeld would repudiate the views of the earlier Navy witnesses.[6]

In fact, Denfeld was quite conflicted over his testimony. As a member of the Joint Chiefs of Staff (JCS), he needed to be mindful of their support for the Air Force, and as a subordinate to Secretary Matthews, he needed to reflect his apparent support for the Air Force position. Yet, he was directly responsible for naval operations and the naval officers that he represented. On the afternoon of October 13, Adm. Denfeld presented testimony strongly in support of naval aviation. An opinion gaining ground on Capitol Hill was that the Navy held secondary importance in the atomic age. Denfeld stated unequivocally his intent to overturn that thinking. His forceful testimony shocked the secretary of the Navy, the secretary of defense, the JCS, and much of the country.

The Air Force rebutted the Navy's case point by point with only two witnesses: Air Force secretary Stuart Symington and Air Force chief of staff Gen. Hoyt Vandenberg. They were followed by the chairman of the JCS, Gen. Omar Bradley, who delivered a harsh rebuke to the Navy. He viewed the admirals as being "insubordinate, mutinous," and deserving of public censure. He summed up his remarks by saying, "This is no time for 'fancy dans' who won't hit the line with all that they have on every play, unless they can call all the signals."[7]

The hearings concluded on October 21, 1949, and seemed to be a devastating setback for the Navy. Secretary Johnson's cancellation of the supercarrier stood, Adm.

Denfeld was fired, and several other admirals were reassigned or opted for early retirement. But historian Jeffery Barlow argues that, in retrospect, the "revolt" was responsible for a turnaround in the fortunes of naval aviation. The hearings had the long-term effect of making Congress aware of the need to develop advanced carriers and aircraft, not merely modernize World War II–vintage Essex- and Midway-class carriers.[8]

Lockheed P2V Neptune: An Interim Solution

The Lockheed P2V Neptune, a large patrol bomber that evolved from a 1941 design, presented an interim solution. In September 1946, a modified P2V-1 named "Truculent Turtle" set a world distance record of 11,235.6 nautical miles by flying unrefueled from Perth, Australia, to Columbus, Ohio.[9] The Neptune's remarkable range, coupled with its large weapons bay that could be configured to carry a Mk. 1 atomic bomb (based on the "Little Boy" design), made it an obvious placeholder for the Savage.

The problems were many. The Neptune was a shore-based aircraft. As such, it lacked arresting gear and would be too heavy when fully loaded to catapult. Instead, it required eight 1,000-pound-thrust JATO (jet-assisted takeoff) rockets and 900 feet of clear deck for a takeoff run. The Neptune was a rocket-propelled beast, and its 100-foot wingspan cleared the carrier's island by a razor-thin 10 feet. It was a crash waiting to happen for aircrews unable to rehearse when at sea. This was because a satisfactory arresting system was never developed. Unless the Neptune could land at a friendly base, it would have to ditch near the carrier, making it a single-use weapon. Furthermore, its size made below-deck storage impossible. Nevertheless, two P2V-2s were modified to develop heavy-load takeoff techniques at NATC Pax River, Maryland. The feasibility was demonstrated by a series of heavy takeoffs flown from *Coral Sea* (CV-43) and *Midway* (CV-41). This led to the modification of twelve new Neptunes, designated P2V-3Cs, that were delivered to the three special-weapons units formed to operate them. The units were assigned to the largest carriers in the fleet, *Midway*, *Franklin D. Roosevelt*, and *Coral Sea*. Training was conducted at Kirtland AFB near Albuquerque, New Mexico. The first heavy-attack squadron, VC-5, established at Moffett Field in California on September 9, 1948, received the first P2V-3Cs in November 1948. In April 1949, after two months of JATO training at NAS Pax River, the Neptunes were craned aboard USS *Coral Sea* for exercises. The P2V's size made flight operations challenging because of the large deck space they required.[10]

A Lockheed Neptune propelled by JATO (jet-assisted takeoff) blasts away from the deck of USS Franklin D. Roosevelt (derisively known by the crew as "Swanky Franky"). Like the AJ-1 Savage, the Neptune could deliver a nuclear bomb; however, longer wings rendered it poorly suited for aircraft carrier operations.

The Neptune program demonstrated that Midway-class carriers could accommodate a 74,000-pound, 100-foot-wingspan bomber. The new Savage under development by North American was a substantially lighter and smaller aircraft, capable of operating from both *Midway* and upgraded Essex-class ships.

Savage Prototype Testing and Early Production

Extreme security shrouded the Savage program. In 1946, few North American employees knew that they were building an atomic bomber, and that hindered the design process. When Navy officials with the appropriate security clearance conducted a mockup inspection of the XAJ-1, they suspected a problem with the bomb bay. To ensure that the Savage could carry a Fat Man bomb, the inspectors needed a full-sized model of the atomic bomb. They asked NAA to produce a model shaped to specific dimensions, without revealing what it represented. About an hour later, an exact wooden copy of the Fat Man was delivered by the project engineer, Ray Gayner. It was an object that should have taken much longer than an hour to produce. When the inspection was over and it appeared that the Savage could accommodate the bomb, the North American people expressed surprise at the secrecy, since they had just gone through the same exercise with an Air Force team, fitting the Fat Man replica into one of their aircraft.

After the mockup approval, Gayner and two other NAA engineers received "Q" security clearances that authorized them to work on the weapons, but they were forbidden to generate any drawings or written material. They were forced to memorize the data and dimensions necessary for designing the bomb bay hardware. The components that they designed were manufactured by contractors located in distant corners of the country, so that each source had limited information.[11]

The Navy established an aggressive procurement

Factory workers assemble the first Columbus-built Savage. The Savage was the Navy's first attempt at a carrier-based aircraft designed to deliver a nuclear bomb. Its mission was later expanded to photography and then service as an aerial refueler.

schedule from the outset. The mockup was built and reviewed on October 15, 1946, less than four months after the development contract was awarded—remarkable time for such a large airframe. Nine months later, on the basis of the mockup inspection alone, twelve production Savages were ordered on October 6, 1947. Only eleven months after that, a second production order for twenty-eight units was issued on May 20, 1948. Even though the prototype had not flown yet, forty production articles were on order. This acceleration of the normal development/testing cycle resulted in a series of serious mishaps, but the Navy pressed ahead because of the urgent need to establish an atomic-weapon delivery capability.

The first XAJ-1 (BuNo 121460) was rolled out of the Inglewood plant in June 1948. North American had placed emphasis on weight reduction during construction, and the XAJ-1 was nearly 1,000 pounds under the design weight. Project test pilot Bob Chilton recalls the ceremony:

> The BIG SHOW was put on when the XAJ came out the door. The scene is very clear in my mind because it was the first of its kind I had ever seen—all previous first airplanes were just rolled out to the flight line and cranked up!
>
> This one was different! Big platform 50 yards out from the factory building, flags flying, PA system with speakers all over the place, and a whole mess of Navy uniforms and high brass. I was impressed.
>
> When the massive hangar doors were opened, and she came out behind a tow tug—lots of clapping and whistles and a few cheers—then it gradually faded away to absolute silence—that thing was ugly! I mean ugly! That squatty-looking beast had massive wrinkles—great big waves of wrinkles all across the side of the bomb bay, angled up from the front to the rear at about a 20/30-degree angle. It seemed like time had stopped. There was total silence. People on the platform just stood there and looked, first at the airplane, then at each other, then back at the airplane. And it was quiet! No one said a thing for the longest time—like forever!
>
> Finally, Dutch Kindleberger [sic] made some smart crack: "We had to keep it thin and light," and that broke the ice a little bit and they went through the routine. But, gad, what a long, long moment.[12]

The wrinkles, accentuated by the California sun glistening off the XAJ's polished aluminum skin, were caused by insufficient structure in the bomb bay area. Additional stiffeners were installed before Bob Chilton's first flight from Los Angeles International Airport on July 3, 1948. No significant problems occurred, but a postflight

Communications were vital to plant operations. Means included local and in-plant telephone, public address systems for factory paging, telex for electronic messages, and the weekly plant newspaper for updating employees.

The medical staff responded to industrial accidents by rendering first aid. Routine flight physicals for company pilots were also handled, but the primary mission was clearing employees returning to work after illness.

A segregated basketball team displays the NAA logo on their jackets. NAA was a leader in providing varied recreational programs, especially during World War II, when many younger workers were separated from family for the first time.

inspection revealed severely burned landing-gear doors. It was common practice to leave the landing gear extended on first flights, and the engine exhaust stacks were located too close to the gear doors. Chilton, a famous P-51 Mustang test pilot, flew the first twelve test flights but grew increasingly apprehensive with each flight.

Legend has it that after the twelfth flight, he climbed out of the cockpit, walked over to the dual-right landing gear, urinated on the tires, and resigned as test pilot (but remained as flight test engineer). Despite Chilton's misgivings, the first prototype performed well and survived the entire test program. However, disaster struck the second prototype, BuNo 121461, when the entire tail was ripped from the airframe during a maximum-rudder sideslip test. Chilton had been replaced by Al Conover and Chuck Brown; both were lost in the accident. Wing failure claimed the third prototype, BuNo 121462, at Edwards AFB during a service ceiling climb test. The aircraft was being flown by Dan Darnell and Bud Pogue. After a prolonged climb to reach the specified 45,000 feet, the left wing outboard of the engine nacelle came off. The aircraft snap-rolled violently, causing both engines to separate from their mounts, and the right wing also failed. Both pilots escaped from the tumbling fuselage and parachuted safely. The cause was traced to a fuel line leak from the left tip tank that sprayed fuel on the engine turbosupercharger. The resulting fire burned through the wing spar.

The Savage was oversized by the standards of a World War II aircraft carrier. With wings and tail folded, a Savage rides the elevator from flight deck to the hangar below.

A new role emerged for Savage: aerial refueling. The military designation of KXAJ-2 deciphers into K (tanker), X (experimental), A (attack), J (North American, née Berliner & Joyce), and -2 (model 2).

The rain squall has cleared as an AJ Savage taxis from the ramp to the runway. Tip tanks provide additional fuel capacity and the additional range needed for global force projection.

Savages and other aircraft share the rain-soaked ramp at an unknown naval air station. The US Navy maintains a domestic presence along every North American coastline, and at more inland locations than might be expected.

The rushed project to deliver the Savage was taking lives. Postwar flight testing was a dangerous job. The loss of Conover and Brown in the sideslip mishap coupled with the deaths of two other pilots in an XB-45 accident (also a tail failure) left NAA's test pilot staff sorely depleted. Jim Pearce, a former naval aviator, was hired from Grumman and appointed as the XAJ-1 project test pilot. Pearce recalls his impressions of the XAJ-1:

The early version of the AJ with the stick instead of a wheel for control, the super[-]high control-boost ratios[,] and the almost Bonanza-like dihedral horizontal stabilizer was a dream to fly. When everything was working properly—it handled like a fighter. The problem is that everything worked properly only about five percent of the time . . . various sideslip maneuvers were an experience unlike anything I ever experienced before or since, as the aft fuselage bent and buckled under the tremendous torque

The XAJ-1 was completed in September 1948. Pilots Al Conover and Chuck Brown were test-flying airplane #2 in February 1949 when there was a structural failure of the empennage (the tail broke). Navy hard-hat divers were brought in to retrieve the wreckage from the shallow Pacific waters just west of LAX.

loads imposed by the relative angles of attack of the left and right high-dihedral horizontals during sideslips.[13]

Pearce's XAJ-1 experience began on April 1, 1949, with a harrowing familiarization flight. Joe Lynch was selected to check out Pearce in the complex airplane, which had only one set of controls. Lynch explained that the Savage was easy to fly, provided its automatic systems— cowl flaps, intercooler doors, propeller synchronization, and hydraulic control boost—worked well. Unfortunately, this flight would demonstrate automatic system failures. Shortly after takeoff, the right propeller began surging between high and low rpm. Lynch attempted to deactivate the faulty propeller synchronizer but couldn't find the correct circuit breaker. Unable to stop the rapid surging, he killed the right engine and feathered the propeller. While pulling circuit breakers, he managed to disable the radio and the elevator trim. The XAJ-1 was at 800 feet over the dry lake bed, and Lynch decided to land. As he lowered the flaps in preparation for landing, the aircraft pitched down into a steep dive toward the ground. Without elevator trim, the elevator became impossible to move.

Separately from the salvage operations depicted, XAJ-1 #1 was being ferried from Edwards AFB to NAS Pax River on June 22, 1950, when it crashed in rural Virginia. Victims of this accident included a Navy uniformed pilot, a Navy civilian, and an NAA employee.

Pearce unstrapped himself from the copilot seat, grabbed the stick, and helped Lynch pull the Savage out of the dive. They were marginally successful, landing on the lake bed nosewheel first. The Savage rolled to a stop undamaged, and they were able to taxi back to the hangar, where Lynch told Pearce that he was now considered fully checked out.

After fourteen months of developmental flight testing, the Savage was deemed ready for formal demonstrations to the Navy at Pax River, Maryland. The demonstrations went well until August 9, 1950, when Pearce was required to fly a maximum-speed rolling pullout, which subjects the aircraft to extreme loads. The maneuver is commenced at full power with 428 knots of airspeed at 10,000 feet in altitude. The airplane is placed in a 45-degree right bank, followed by immediate application of full left stick. As the wings roll level, the aircraft is placed in a 4.8 g pull-up while still holding full left stick. The aircraft is expected to roll into a steep left climbing turn. However, this time the Savage continued to roll right when left stick was applied. Suddenly finding himself inverted, Pearce allowed the XAJ-1 to continue the right roll until he was upright, and he could reduce the power. He pulled out of the maneuver after losing nearly 9,000 feet. This "wrong-way roll" and the maximum-rudder sideslip test convinced NAA engineers to remove the dihedral on the horizontal tail.

Even though the XAJ-1 test flight program resulted in the loss of two prototypes, and serious design problems were still being uncovered, the Navy was determined to expedite delivery to the fleet. The first production article, BuNo 122590, was completed and flown in May 1949— less than a year after the maiden flight and only one month after Jim Pearce joined the flight test program. Considerable redesign and rework were being accomplished on the test aircraft even as production AJ-1s started rolling off the assembly line at the Downey plant. Production Savages were remarkably consistent with the prototypes. The most-obvious external differences were a heavily framed canopy replacing the earlier clear bubble canopy, manually folding wing and fin panels, and a third crew member station added to the cockpit. Wingtip fuel tanks could be installed for increased range. Modifications resulting from the test program, such as removal of the tail dihedral, were retrofitted to the production airplanes. Jim Pearce noted:

The Navy pilots were not happy with a big aircraft like the Savage having a control stick instead of a wheel to move the ailerons and elevators. They also were not happy with the fact that these controls had to be highly boosted hydraulically to allow the plane to fly like a fighter. These concerns brought about a change from a control stick to a wheel with which to fly the airplane and a reduction in the amount of hydraulic boost assisting the movement of the ailerons and elevators. The result of all this was the

AJ-1 Savage being converted from a bomber that flew like a fighter to a bomber that flew like a bomber.[14]

With only four months of contractor testing, the first production ship, BuNo 122590, was delivered to the NATC in Pax River, Maryland, on September 19, 1945. It and a second early production unit were used for the Board of Inspection and Survey (BIS) evaluation. Concurrently, VC-5, the squadron instrumental in developing the Neptune nuclear-delivery program, received six Savages. The testing and development cycle had become so compressed by the Navy's desire to get the AJ-1 into fleet service that VC-5 was forced to employ their AJs in a fleet indoctrination program while also performing flight test work that was usually accomplished at Pax River. VC-5 operated from NAS Moffett Field, California, until April 1950, when the squadron was transferred to NAS Norfolk, Virginia, in preparation for carrier trials.

On April 21, 1950, Capt. John T. Hayward, commanding officer of VC-5, made the first Savage takeoff from the deck of USS *Coral Sea*, flying BuNo 122600, but no arrested landing was attempted since the AJ was not yet cleared for it. The workup for carrier landings was conducted at Pax River by Lt. Cmdr. Don Runyon, flying BuNo 122594. In July, when additional AJ-1s became available, VC-5 pilots prepared for carrier qualification by completing at least thirty field carrier landings. By the end of August, the squadron was declared ready to qualify aboard ship, and on August 31 Capt. Hayward made the first two arrested landings aboard *Coral Sea*. He was so confident of the AJ's behavior that he carried VAdm. Felix B. Stump in the copilot seat for the first "trap," and J. F. Floberg, assistant secretary of the Navy, for the second. The entire squadron followed and qualified without incident. To the surprise of many, the Savage was adept at launching from (and landing on) aircraft carriers with considerable ease. During the first Savage operations aboard *Midway*, a total of 139 landings were made without incident.

But the AJ's unblemished record was lost several weeks later, when Capt. Hayward led his carrier-qualified squadron to Guantánamo Bay, Cuba, to train aboard USS *Franklin D. Roosevelt*. On the final day of deployment, BuNo 124163 dove into the water after takeoff. The probable cause was attributed to unintended control lock engagement. Several other safety-of-flight issues arose within the month, which caused the grounding of all AJ-1s. The Navy and North American worked feverishly to fix the problems, but as one modification was completed to cure the immediate problem, a new one would arise. From October 1950 to October 1951, the AJ fleet was grounded intermittently for eight months. On June 8, 1951, during a period when the grounding order had been lifted, a Savage from the naval aviation detachment at Kirtland AFB was lost due to an intense fire in the jet engine bay.

It was becoming obvious to everybody that the rush to deliver the Savage was now taking its toll. The old cliché of "haste makes waste" was now operative. NAA had previously demonstrated amazing results with a smaller and simpler product: the P-51 Mustang prototype (NA-73) went from conception to flight in 117 days. That instance of good luck was visible only in the rearview mirror.

At one point it was decided to convert the AJ's hydraulic systems to operate on Hydrolube, a nonflammable, water-based fluid to reduce the risk of fire from leaks in the high-pressure systems. But this served only to increase the number of problems, since the fluid was found to be incompatible with the hydraulic system. In addition to recurrent hydraulic, mechanical, and electrical problems, crews found deck handling of the Savage to be very cumbersome. Its large size had an adverse impact on other flight operations. Moving a recovered Savage out of the way required folding the wing panels and vertical tail, one surface at a time, by a crewman with a portable hydraulic pump—a time-consuming and treacherous process at sea. If a Savage launch aborted due to a mechanical issue (a frequent occurrence), it would disrupt the entire flight schedule because of the time needed to fold the panels and remove it from the staging area.

The rushed development and overly complex systems resulted in a rash of mishaps that blemished the Savage's reputation. A 1952 accident investigation noted that of the fifty-eight AJ-1s built (three XAJ-1 prototypes and fifty-five AJ-1 production articles), eleven had been lost, mostly due to mechanical failure. The accident rate was nearly four crashes per year from persistent hydraulic system failures and in-flight fires.[15]

In addition to its nuclear-strike role, the AJ-1 was also evaluated as an in-flight-refueling tanker by the NATC. The first XAJ-1 had its jet engine removed, allowing a refueling drogue to be extended out of the former jet exhaust. Initial tests involved refueling F2H Banshees and were later expanded to include aircraft such as F9F Panthers and F11F Tigers. Ultimately the tanker package was refined by relocating the refueling equipment into the bomb bay, allowing the Savage to retain its jet engine.

Photo Savage and Improved Strike Savage

In early 1950, the Navy investigated a photoreconnaissance role for the Savage. The forty-first production Savage, BuNo 124850, was modified at North American's Downey facility to receive a suite of cameras. At the same time, the Navy decided to incorporate extensive airframe and systems improvements to overcome the problems responsible for grounding the AJ-1 fleet. The new Savage was designated

AJ-2P. The original bulbous nose was replaced by a sharper one that featured a fold-down access bay for the forward-looking K-38 oblique camera. The bomb bay area was fitted with high-resolution side- and down-looking cameras and provisions for photoflash bombs to illuminate the target. Improved R-2800-48 reciprocating engines and an uprated J33-A-10 turbojet were installed. The empennage was redesigned by increasing the height of the fin, increasing the chord of the rudder, and eliminating the 12-degree dihedral angle of the horizontal stabilizer. The hydraulic system was simplified, and the internal fuel capacity was increased. The single nose-gear door on the AJ-1 was replaced by two-piece clamshell doors. In the cockpit, the pilot's stick was replaced with a wheel, and the third crew station was moved to a compartment forward of the bomb bay. In later AJ-2P production, a fourth crew station was added behind the pilot's seat, with that crew member facing aft.[16]

The Navy was delighted with the Downey conversion and on August 18, 1950, ordered twenty-three AJ-2Ps to be built at North American's new Columbus plant. This was the first "new-build contract" awarded to Columbus, which was previously used to remanufacture and upgrade existing aircraft. After successfully completing the initial batch of twenty-three aircraft, the Navy ordered seven more AJ-2Ps. The reconnaissance Savages were assigned to VJ-61 and VJ-62 (later redesignated VAP-61 and VAP-62),

On February 14, 1951, the Navy expanded the Columbus contract to include fifty-five new strike Savages, designated AJ-2, which would incorporate the improvements of the reconnaissance aircraft but retain the strike capability of the original AJ-1 Savage. The improvements allowed a maximum catapult weight of 54,000 pounds, with a maximum arrested-landing weight of 37,500 pounds. The cockpit changes included the substitution of a control wheel in lieu of the AJ-1's stick, and relocation of the throttles to the center console, allowing power control access to both pilots in the event of an emergency. The first AJ-2 was test-flown on February 19, 1953, and the last example was delivered by the end of that year. In service, the AJ-2 and -2P proved to be far more reliable than the earlier AJ-1. On August 14, 1952, the Navy ordered all forty-two surviving AJ-1s upgraded to approximate AJ-2 standards.[17]

The Stillborn Savage

In April 1948, three months before the first flight of the XAJ-1, the Navy ordered two flying prototypes and a static-test article of a twin turboprop derivative of the Savage. The designation A2J was assigned to the turboprop variant, which was intended to become the phase 2 heavy-strike aircraft in the Navy's nuclear strategy. It was expected

that engineering work already done for the AJ-1 could be leveraged to produce a higher-performance attack aircraft without the need for a completely new design.

Two years earlier, the power plant division of the Bureau of Aeronautics funded the development of a turboshaft engine that promised to provide substantially more power with less mechanical complexity than a reciprocating engine. The Allison Division of General Motors agreed to design an axial-flow turboprop, the T38, to produce nearly 3,000 shaft horsepower. This would be developed into the T40, a turboshaft power plant of 5,500 shaft horsepower. The T40 was essentially two T38s joined to a common shaft driving coaxial counterrotating propellers. The T40 generated so much enthusiasm that BuAer planned five new aircraft around it: the A2J, AD2, P5Y, XFY-1, and XFV-1.[18]

The "Super Savage," as it was nicknamed, started as a simple modification of the AJ-1. But substantial work was required when the Navy decided to optimize the airframe for the T40 power plant. This grew the gross takeoff weight to 72,000 pounds, nearly 25,000 pounds more than the AJ-1, which further complicated the design by the need for complex high-lift devices (double-slotted flaps and leading-edge droops). The burgeoning size and weight also called its ability to operate from Midway-class carriers into question. BuAer concluded that the size, weight, and complexity of the A2J should be reduced. NAA submitted a revised proposal of a smaller airframe, which eliminated the auxiliary turbojet engine and lightened the structure. This new iteration was expected to weigh 58,000 pounds, making it acceptable to the Navy. The revised Super Savage had integral-power folding wings and tail for improved deck handling, a remotely controlled tail turret for defensive purposes, and ejection seats for crew survival. The wings had leading-edge flaps to reduce the landing speed, the vertical stabilizer was swept back with a substantial increase in area, and pitch control was provided by an all-flying stabilizer. The new design promised a 40-knot increase in speed, a 5,000-foot increased service ceiling, and a combat radius extension of 330 nautical miles.

Allison, however, was having serious difficulty with T40 development. Engines for the first XA2J were expected before the end of 1949 but were not even flight-qualified until March 1951. As a result, the XA2J maiden flight slid behind schedule until January 4, 1952. Engine problems plagued the flight test program. By the end of July, the XA2J had flown only five times, averaging less than an hour per flight. By mid-1953, it was apparent that the Navy's enthusiasm for the Allison T40 was fading, and the turbojet-powered Douglas A3D was favored to become the Navy's next-generation heavy-strike aircraft. The Super Savage program was terminated before the second XA2J ever flew.

The Savage Contribution

The Savage was developed during a period of great uncertainty. Naval aviation was fighting the newly formed Air Force for its very survival. The NAA engineering staff was dramatically reduced by the postwar drawdown and competing priorities. The AJ design incorporated many advanced concepts—some producing problems that required years of operational experience to resolve, the most persistent being five separate 3,000 psi (pounds per square inch) hydraulic systems that were prone to failure. And the Navy insisted on abbreviated test and development cycles before placing the Savage in operation.

Even with the repeated aircraft losses and the frequent groundings, the Savage evolved into a reliable first-generation nuclear bomber and established the Navy's role in the atomic age. The AJ-2P Savage further matured with airframe and systems improvements. When those improvements were retrofitted to the AJ-2, the full heavy-attack potential was realized. New missions included reconnaissance and aerial refueling. The winners? The Navy gained valuable experience operating large aircraft at sea, NAA designers now better understood the aircraft carrier environment, and workers at the Columbus plant were again building sturdy aircraft for rugged duty aboard carriers.

A single AJ-2 Savage airframe (BuAer 130418) can be seen on display at the Naval Air Museum at Pensacola, Florida. Built in 1953 and with service on multiple aircraft carriers (*Bennington* and *Yorktown*), it was retired in 1960. Like many veteran sailors, it found a new civilian occupation, first in 1962 as a forest fire fighter, and later as an engine test platform for Avco Lycoming Corporation. It was again retired and flown to the museum on May 9, 1984.

T-28 Trojan: The First Modern Trainer

An early version of the T-28A is captured in flight over the shoreline. Updated with tricycle landing gear, it was intended to replace the ubiquitous SNJ/AT-6 Texan as the primary trainer both for Air Force and Navy.

During World War II, the development of new trainers was low on the national priority list. Available funding and engineering resources were dedicated to tactical aircraft. Trainer development was, for the most part, neglected, resulting in a fleet of training aircraft designed in the 1930s still in use at the war's end. As jets were introduced into frontline service after the war, it became apparent that the training commands were handicapped by equipment from another era.

The Navy acted first to correct the problem by promulgating its "New Training Plan." The goal was two new airplanes—one for the primary and basic training and the other for more-advanced student pilots. According to the plan, the venerable World War II–vintage SNJ would be phased out by 1950. An RFP was released on April 26, 1945. Fairchild was selected to develop the primary/basic trainer, which the Navy designated XNQ-1. North American won the competition for the advanced trainer with its NA-142 design and received a contract in September 1945 for two prototypes and a static-test article.

XSN2J: A False Start

The prototypes were designated XSN2J and assigned BuNos 121449 and 121450. The XSN2J was similar in appearance to the SNJ that it was intended to replace; however, it was larger, heavier, and much more capable in the training role than the SNJ. It was equipped with dive brakes on the upper surface of the wing and could drop bombs and fire rockets. There were also provisions for two .50-caliber machine guns, one in each wing, and a Mk. 8 gunsight.

Two types of aircraft gun mounts were common starting in World War I. A wing-mounted weapon was rigidly

The Texan and the T-28 are seen side by side in flight. Aviation luminaries Dutch Kindelberger and Lee Atwood stooped over the drafting table in 1934 and designed the legendary NAA trainer, a tail dragger designated SNJ when in Navy service.

The aborted XSN2J was a precursor to the T-28. It looks like a hybrid between the SNJ and T-28. Two of the tail draggers were built. Unlike on the SNJ, the empennage was built sturdy for arrested landings.

attached to the airframe and called a "fixed gun." A gun that could swivel and be aimed by an airborne gunner was called a "flexible" gun. Sometimes photographs of guns installed on trainer aircraft can be misconstrued as combatants of last resort. In fact, they are used to prepare pilots for the fixed guns they will later encounter. Other crew members honed their aerial marksmanship skills by live-firing the flexible guns.

Thousands of SNJ aircraft were built in tandem with Air Corps AT-6 aircraft at Dallas during the war. To avoid production line complexity (and the resulting slowdowns), the Army-managed contract was insensitive to the Navy's need for a sturdy tailhook; therefore, the Navy performed its own tailhook retrofit with improvised aft-fuselage reinforcement and provisions for a rope release mechanism.

This time, carrier-landing features and strength were incorporated in the original XSN2J design. It was also designed to be catapulted if needed—another capability the SNJ lacked.

Because of its growth in size and weight, the XSN2J required a more powerful engine, the Wright R-1820 Cyclone. The instructor in the rear seat was to have the ability to "upset" instruments in the student's cockpit. This innovative feature for instrument flight instruction enabled simulating in-flight emergencies. The XSN2J's first flight was achieved on February 10, 1947, by accomplished NAA test pilot George "Wheaties" Welch at NATC Pax River.

Unfortunately, shortly after the XSN2J evaluation began, the Navy decided that it failed to provide sufficient training benefit to withstand the severe austerity measures imposed by the Truman administration in 1948. The vast fleet of SNJs that survived the war would suffice for now. After all, the level of pilot training had been dramatically reduced after the hostilities, and the reduction in the operational fleet requirements provided a steady supply of obsolescent airplanes for the advanced phase of flight training, thus further mitigating the need for a modern trainer. The XSN2J-1 program was canceled, and the SNJ would continue—for the time being—which turned out to be several years. Nevertheless, the XSN2J-1 program, while soon forgotten, would be the genesis for the first new trainer design intended for use by both the Air Force and Navy training commands.

T-28A Trojan

Approximately six months after the XSN2J program was abandoned by the Navy, the Army Air Forces became the Air Force, a separate and independent branch of the military. One of the first acts of the newly formed Air Force was the release of preliminary requirements for a new basic trainer under the XBT (experimental basic trainer) program. The requirements emphasized maintenance access and a "tricycle" landing-gear configuration, which dictated a new design competition. The nosewheel arrangement provided better directional control on the takeoff and landing roll. The tricycle landing-gear configuration had become standard on jet aircraft, since they lacked the "prop wash" to help raise the tail for acceleration to takeoff speed.

An RFP for the new trainer was released in 1948. In the process, the Air Force simplified its designation practice for trainers, eliminating the use of the prefixes *P* for Primary, *B* for Basic, and *A* for Advanced. The numbering for new trainers was to begin with twenty-eight, since the highest number reached in the P/B/A series was the PT-27. Fourteen companies submitted a total of twenty-eight designs. The two finalists in the competition were North

American and Douglas. Their winning proposals were designated XT-28 and XT-30, respectively. Both were powered by the 800-horsepower Wright R-1300 radial engine. In its proposal for the XT-28, North American placed particular emphasis on maintainability in addition to meeting all the other specific requirements. Frank Compton, NAA's lead designer of the XBT, noted:

In June 1947 my boss, Howard Evans, chief designer of NAA's Los Angeles division engineering department, received an advanced copy of the newly established requirements for the Air Force XBT trainer. At this point preliminary design activity was informally initiated. It is important that a proposed design not only characterize the published requirements but also feature, through clever design or diverse approach, a particular element of the requirements felt to be uppermost in the mind of the user, in this case the Air Training Command.

As for the XBT, the priority was superior maintainability. The requirement stated that "the aircraft will demonstrate a high rate of readiness." Sorting everything out[,] it was further determined that the maintenance index must be comparable to the T-6 (Air Force version of the SNJ). Considering the increased complexity projected for the XBT configuration, this would be a difficult act to follow. By early August 1947, a designed-in maintenance concept featuring superior accessibility, component interchangeability[,] and a plan to increase subsystem reliability was presented to the chief designer. Following scrutiny of the cost and weight trade[-]offs, Evans approved the approach and the NA-159 design concept jelled.[1]

Compton's design featured easily opened doors that provided access to system components. Engine accessories mounted on the rear of the engine were accessed through the nosewheel well, and an access door in the firewall that was reached with an integral ladder. The engine cowling was quick opening and self-supporting.

The Douglas XT-30 proposal, on the other hand, was far more unusual. It seemed to emphasize the Air Force requirement for good over-the-nose visibility and the possibility of converting the reciprocating engine to a jet engine in the future. Its Wright R-1300 was located behind the rear cockpit, with an extension shaft driving the nose-mounted propeller and a cooling fan drawing air in from a nose-mounted inlet. Douglas claimed that there was no maintenance penalty associated with the submerged engine arrangement. Excepting the Bell P-39 Airacobra and P-63 Kingcobra, there were few examples of airplanes with engines buried in the fuselage, and even fewer had been carried forward into production.

The Air Force evaluation favored the North American proposal for its maintainability features but expressed

Hidden behind this sheet metal nose cowl is a Wright R-1820 Cyclone engine, capable of producing 1,425 horsepower. The airplane has a 40-foot wingspan and carries a crew of two—normally a student and instructor pilot.

some concern about the airplane's rollout directional stability and turnover angle (potential to tip over). A nosewheel-configured airplane with a radial engine was forced to be relatively short-coupled (tail positioned close to the wings) because of center-of-gravity considerations. This reduced directional stability during rollout, particularly in crosswinds. Raising the cockpit to provide the requisite visibility over the nose resulted in a relatively high center of gravity. If a student pilot lost control on rollout and ran off the runway or landed hard on the nosewheel, the nose landing gear could fail. The result might be the airplane flipping over onto its back—a bad landing outcome worse than ground-looping a T-6/SNJ.

The Air Force issued a letter of intent dated April 5, 1948, authorizing construction of two flying prototypes and one static-test article. The first XT-28, 48-1371, flew on September 24, 1949, at the Los Angeles International Airport, piloted by NAA test pilot Jean "Skip" Ziegler. Even before the test flight program was completed, 266 T-28As were ordered and the nickname "Trojan" was

assigned. But development problems slowed production, and budget austerity forced a delay in funding the contract. As a stopgap measure, the government ordered an upgrade of the T-6/SNJ fleet to the T-6G standard. Selected Texans were refurbished by completely stripping and cleaning the airframe, overhauling the engine and propeller, and updating the avionics.

When the T-28A finally entered service, the steerable nosewheel configuration significantly improved the visibility forward when taxiing. The over-the-nose visibility requirement in flight was provided by a high seating position under a large canopy. The canopy segments over the front and rear seats were opened by hydraulic power. The canopy sill was relatively low; with the canopies open, much of the pilot's torso was exposed, an advantage for entry/exit and, more importantly, for bailout (during taxi with the canopy open, it has been likened to riding an elephant). The T-28's wings attached to the fuselage with 8 degrees of dihedral, a notably large amount, which ensured excellent lateral stability. There were significant features related to initial cost and maintainability. For example, the outer wing panels could be removed without disconnecting the aileron cable system. The horizontal stabilizers were identical. Two men could remove a horizontal stabilizer or the vertical fin in ten minutes. The left and right elevators and trim tabs were also interchangeable. The T-28A had a gross weight of 7,800 pounds, making it 2,600 pounds heavier than the T-6 it replaced. The seven-cylinder Wright R-1300 engine, swinging a two-bladed Aeroproducts A422-E1 propeller, provided 800 horsepower, an increase of 200 horsepower over the T-6. Although the power-to-weight ratio remained about the same as the T-6's, the T-28A performance was noted for being anemic, particularly on takeoff.

The two XT-28As were equipped with speed brakes, but these were later deleted for production.

The rollover pylon (called a "turnover truss" by North American engineers) that had been incorporated to guard against potential flips on landing proved unnecessary and was deleted. As a result, after evaluation on 49-1709, the canopy was lowered 4 inches effective with 51-3763. The windscreen angle was increased by 2.5 degrees. These changes improved the instructor's visibility forward and were a slight benefit to speed and range.

The first production T-28As were delivered in April 1950 and the last in 1953. In all, the total production was 1,194 units spread among the Inglewood, Downey, and Columbus plants. Together with the T-6G, they provided all the Air Force standard flight curriculum training prior to the students' transition to the Lockheed T-33 jet trainer. However, in November 1952, initial screening in light airplanes such as the Piper PA18 Cub, a practice used

The Columbus repertoire included an eclectic mix of airplanes ranging from simple trainers (T-28 assembly line—seen here) to the supersonic Vigilante. The assembly line concept was adapted from the automobile builders as America prepared to enter World War II.

Factory documentation photograph of the aft cockpit instrumentation of a T-28C, dated March 23, 1956. The instructor and the student each had their own set controls and flight instruments.

during World War II, was started again to provide an early and inexpensive means of weeding out student candidates with a fear of flight, airsickness, or poor coordination.

The T-28A's modest power, particularly evident on takeoff, produced sluggish acceleration, which seemed to mimic the takeoff characteristics of early jets. The Wright engine, in addition to sounding rough, had to be handled with care to prevent actual failure of a cylinder. While early problems with crankshaft failures were subsequently eliminated, the engine remained unpopular. For one thing, it was difficult to tell the difference between a Wright R-1300 running normally and badly. Student pilots, particularly in formation flying and aerobatics, tended to treat the engine roughly. This shortened its life and occasionally justified the emphasis in flight training on quickly locating an alternative landing site in the event of an engine failure.

The aircraft was pleasant to fly, with light control loads and an excellent roll rate. The incipient stall was clearly heralded by significant buffeting. Accidentally spinning a T-28 was unlikely; if forced to spin, it did not resist recovery. It was fully aerobatic except for "snap rolls," which were prohibited. The snap roll was initiated from level flight at a speed well above stall by jerking full back on the stick and kicking rudder. The result was a spin, in effect, but with the airplane traveling forward during the first turn rather than downward. The maneuver imposed high loads on the T-28's aft fuselage, which was weakened by the large structural opening aft of the wing for a baggage compartment. A snap-roll entry that was overly enthusiastic would result in a permanent twist of the fuselage between the wing and the empennage, requiring an expensive structural repair or, more likely, the early retirement of that airframe.

The T-28A went on to a successful but brief training career, cut short when the twinjet Cessna T-37A entered service in 1957. An experimental all-jet training syllabus produced encouraging results, so the Air Force decided to eliminate its propeller trainers. The last T-28A departed the training command unit at Bainbridge Air Base, Georgia, in January 1958. Since these were relatively new, low-time airplanes, many soldiered on in other roles for proficiency and utility flying. At the same time, several Air National Guard units, forced to retire their F-51s as they finally wore out, received surplus T-28As to fly until jets were assigned. Most T-28s, however, were placed in desert storage at Davis-Monthan AFB (Tucson, Arizona).

T-28B

By 1952, the Navy also needed a replacement for its aging SNJ fleet. It evaluated two T-28As as advanced instrument trainers, assigning Navy BuNos 137636 and 137637 to the Air Force trainers. But the Navy was interested in a more powerful engine, so North American installed a 1,425-horsepower, nine-cylinder Wright R-1820 in a larger cowling with a three-bladed Hamilton Standard propeller to absorb the additional 625 horsepower. The Navy conferred the designation T-28B on the reengined Trojans, and noted North American test pilot Robert A. "Bob" Hoover made the first flight of the prototype, 137636, on April 6, 1953.

It is evident this airplane will hit the deck hard when the hook snags a cable. The Navy specified an airframe capable of absorbing a sink rate of 21 feet per second, and an airframe sufficient to absorb instantaneous deceleration.

Marking Time©
North American T-28 Trojan

Part 1: USAF Trainers and Hacks

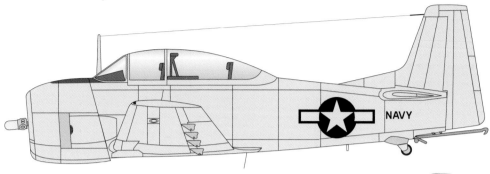

XSN2J-1 BiNo.121449
NORTH AMERICAN AVIATION
MINES FLD, CA 1947

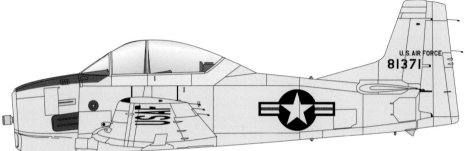

XBT-28-NA 48-1371
FLIGHT TEST (MATERIEL DIV)
WRIGHT-PATTERSON AFB, OH 1949

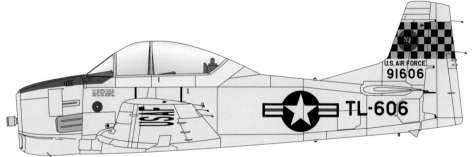

T-28A-NA 49-1606
  th PTS, 3595th PTW (ATRC)
NELLIS AFB, NV 1951

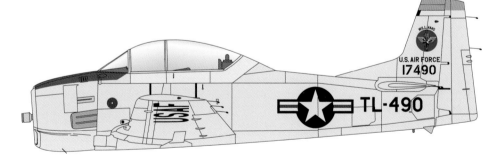

T-28A-NT 51-7490
PTS, 3525th FTW (ATRC)
WILLIAMS AFB, AZ 1953

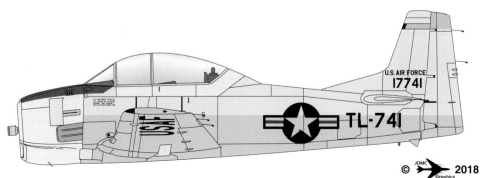

T-28A-NT 51-7741
3650th PTW (ATRC)
COLUMBUS AFB, MS 1953

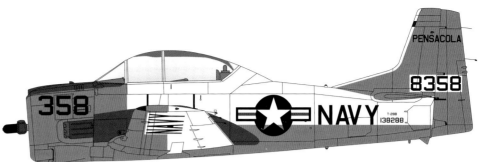

T-28B BuNo. 138358
STATION FLIGHT (AIRPAC)
NAS PENSACOLA, FL AUGUST, 1962

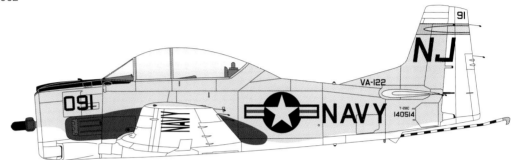

T-28C BuNo. 140514
VA-122, RCVW-12 (AIRPAC)
NAS LEMOORE, CA 1969

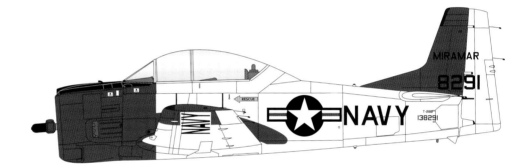

T-28B BuNo. 138291
STATION FLIGHT (AIRPAC)
NAS MIRAMAR, CA 1974

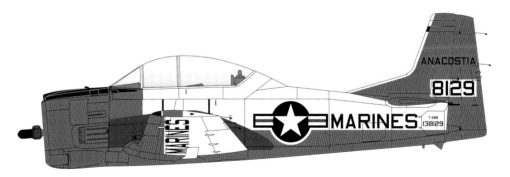

T-28B BuNo. 138129
MARDET ANACOSTIA (USMC)
NAS ANACOSTIA, DC 1958

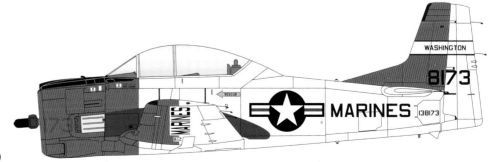

T-28B BuNo. 138173
MARDET WASHINGTON (USMC)
NAF WASHINGTON, MD 1968

© JDMC Graphics 2018

Whereas the T-28A trundled aloft on its 800-horsepower Wright R-1300, the T-28B leaped into the air behind the more powerful engine. Although the B had a 20 percent higher gross weight, 8,095 pounds, it was more than offset by a 78 percent increase in power, resulting in a weight-to-horsepower ratio of 5.8. The engine was mounted with 5 degrees of downthrust, twice that of the T-28A, because of the higher power of the big Wright engine driving that three-bladed propeller. The service ceiling increased by 50 percent, a significant improvement, largely provided by the single-stage supercharger of the R-1820. This was a mixed blessing because the pilot was required to manually shift the blower speed at about 10,000 feet (the critical altitude) to increase power available at higher altitudes. This was accomplished like shifting the manual transmission in an automobile, by first reducing the power with the throttle, changing to the higher blower setting, and then pushing the throttle back up.

Mismanagement of the shift risked overboosting the engine, which shortened its life, as did forgetting to change back to the lower blower setting when descending through the critical altitude and then adding power. The speed brake installation, which had been deleted on production T-28As, was reinstated on the T-28B. Although unnecessary in a propeller-driven airplane that already had a built-in speed brake (the propeller), it served to familiarize the student with the function of the speed brake, which was a necessary feature on jet airplanes. It came with a flight-manual caution, however, because it caused a nose-up pitching moment when deployed, which increased with speed. It was therefore not to be extended above 250 knots of indicated airspeed. There were also other minor changes from the T-28A—such as a free-swiveling (castering) nosewheel and relocation of the battery to help offset the heavier engine.

The first production T-28Bs were delivered to Navy advanced-instrument-training squadrons beginning in 1954. The production run of 489 units also replaced the SNJs for all basic training except for carrier qualification, which remained the province of the SNJ-5Cs. Most T-28Bs were built in Downey, California, but production was shifted to Columbus, Ohio, in 1952, where the final forty-nine units were produced. At one point, there were eleven Navy training squadrons operating T-28Bs—nine in the Pensacola, Florida, area and another two at Meridian, Mississippi. The T-28Bs served far longer in the Navy training command than the T-28A trainers of the Air Force.

Capt. William B. Nevius, USN (Ret.), was a flight instructor in T-28Bs with ATU-803 (air training unit) in 1955, when his daughter Colleen was born. The day he brought his wife and daughter home from the hospital, he had been flying BuNo 137648. Many years later, Colleen attended Purdue University in the naval ROTC program, which was just opened to women. Upon graduation in 1977, she was accepted for naval aviation training, which was also now available to women. She soloed in 1978 in the actual T-28 that her father had flown twenty-three years earlier.

VT-27, based at NAS Corpus Christi, Texas, was the last squadron to provide training in the T-28B. The final T-28B training sortie occurred in early 1984. BuNo 137796, the command's last T-28B, was ferried to the Naval Support Facility at Anacostia, Virginia, on March 14, 1984, for static display. Even after retirement from the training syllabus, T-28Bs remained on the active inventory as station hacks and chase planes. Some were modified to become T-28BD drone directors (later designated DT-28B after 1962).

T-28C

During World War II, the trainer for carrier qualification was the SNJ-3C, -4C, or -5C, with the *C* suffix indicating that it was equipped with a Navy-installed tailhook for carrier landings. It was sturdy and had the added advantage of not requiring the student to check out in a different, more powerful airplane for carrier qualification. But the fleet of carrier-capable SNJs was not going to last forever, particularly given the wear and tear of high-sink-rate touchdowns and high loads in the aft fuselage, inevitable in arrested landings aboard aircraft carriers. The logical replacement was the T-28. The first T-28C was modified from a T-28B and flew for the first time on September 19, 1955. (In this case, the *C* no longer stood for carrier compatibility but was simply the next revision letter alphabetically.) The lower aft fuselage and rudder were notched to accommodate a tailhook, the landing gear was modified for greater oleo stroke to absorb even-harder touchdowns, and the propeller was shortened to provide an additional 5 inches of ground clearance to avoid pecking the deck after a tailhook engagement (the blades were slightly widened to maintain their strength). The changes resulted in a gross weight increase of about 250 pounds—which slightly reduced speed, rate of climb, service ceiling, and range—but not by enough to compromise its training effectiveness.

The NATC accomplished at-sea carrier compatibility testing of the T-28C (in fact, a T-28B BuNo 138187, modified to the carrier configuration) in November 1955 aboard the Essex-class aircraft carrier *Tarawa* (CVS-40). Lt. Cmdr. W. F. Tobin and Lt. Robert R. King accomplished fifty landings during the at-sea evaluation, which had been prEceded by the usual and extensive shore-based testing.

Introduction of the T-28C for carrier qualification was delayed until April 1957, when an Essex-class carrier with an angle deck, USS *Antietam* (CVS-36), became available to replace the smaller, more challenging, straight-deck CVL (light aircraft carrier). At that point, the days of the

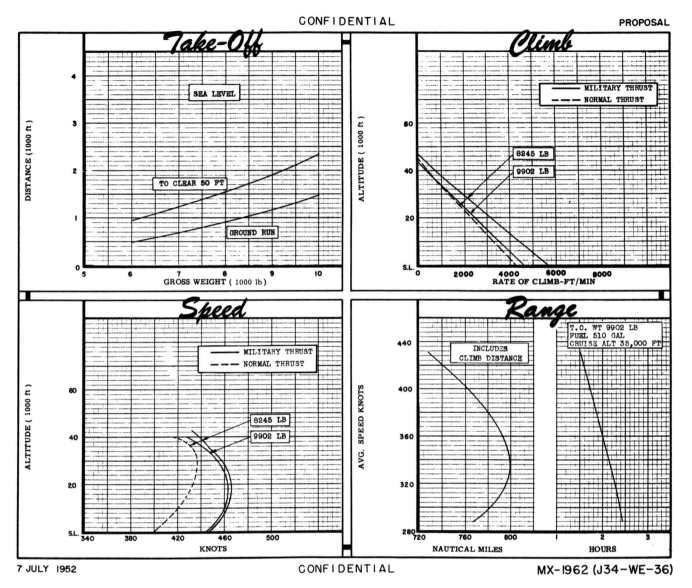

Take-Off

DISTANCE (1000 ft)

SEA LEVEL

TO CLEAR 50 FT

GROUND RUN

GROSS WEIGHT (1000 lb)

Climb

ALTITUDE (1000 ft)

—— MILITARY THRUST
- - - NORMAL THRUST

8245 LB
9902 LB

S.L.   2000   4000   6000   8000
RATE OF CLIMB-FT/MIN

Speed

ALTITUDE (1000 ft)

—— MILITARY THRUST
- - - NORMAL THRUST

8245 LB
9902 LB

S.L.   340   380   420   460   500
KNOTS

Range

AVG. SPEED KNOTS

INCLUDES
CLIMB DISTANCE

T.O. WT 9902 LB
FUEL 510 GAL
CRUISE ALT 35,000 FT

720   760   800
NAUTICAL MILES   HOURS

T-28 performance metrics are plotted in a series of four boxes. The pilot's job is to always remain within the boundaries of the box; however, engineering test pilots get paid to probe the edges of the box—sometimes at their own peril.

SNJ as a carrier trainer were numbered. The last training flight in one was completed on May 21, 1958, and the last SNJ was retired from the Navy in February 1960. The Columbus plant produced 299 T-28Cs between 1955 and 1957. They were operated by four training squadrons in the Pensacola, Florida, area: VT-2, -3, and -6 at NAS Whiting Field and VT-5 at Saufley Field.

From the outset, all variants of the T-28 could be configured for armament training. A gun pod with one .50-caliber M3 machine gun could be installed under each wing. Early T-28As used the A-1CM sighting system, while subsequent Trojans used the N-9-1. Bomb pylons with type S-2 racks carrying practice bombs or rocket launchers could also be installed. A few T-28Bs incorporated a two-pod system for streaming a tow target, the line being carried in one pod and the banner in the other. However, it was

The date is November 1955. The location is aboard USS Tarawa (CVS-40), where the Naval Air Test Center (NATC) conducted carrier suitability testing on the T-28C aircraft. US Navy

Pulled from storage at Davis-Monthan AFB, the first T-28D rolls forth from the Columbus plant. The Columbus crew was equally adept at building new aircraft and refurbishing or repurposing old ones. John Scott collection

determined during qualification testing in late 1956 that the aft fuselage and rudder modification required for the tailhook on C models resulted in unsatisfactory spin recovery when armament was carried. NACA wind-tunnel spin tests established satisfactory spin recovery with underwing stores by installing strakes on the T-28C's cowling.

Ed Gillespie was called on to write a portion of the handbook. High-altitude flying was required to gather the data. One mission found him in a T-28C at 36,000 feet. It had taken almost three long hours to make the slow climb. He said, "I was frozen; it was icy cold up there. An Air Force guy from Wright-Patterson came by in an F-86D," recalled Ed. "He did a 360 turn and came back to have a look-see. I don't think he believed what he saw. He looked at this little yellow prop plane and then flew on."[2]

Nomad, Fennec, and T-28D

The T-28A's training career with the Air Force was brief—only seven years. But shortly after retirement, several events converged to give the T-28A a new lease on life,

first as a civilian transport and then as a counterinsurgency combat aircraft. In 1956 the Trojan's lead preliminary designer, Frank Compton, was named director of plans and programs at Columbus. In his new role, Compton was responsible for developing marketing opportunities for NAA products. His frequent trips to Washington, DC, and various naval aviation installations justified the use of a company airplane. Division manager C. J. Gallant warmed to the idea but insisted it be a North American aircraft.

At the same time, the plans and programs received several inquiries about the availability of T-28Bs for commercial use. It occurred to Compton that mothballed T-28As could easily be upgraded to the T-28B standard and certified for civilian use, making it an ideal company plane and prototype for the commercial market. Compton hired a former Marine test pilot with an engineering degree, J. Lynn Helms, who was tasked with investigating the certification matter under CAA regulations (the CAA—Civil Aeronautics Administration—was the forerunner of the FAA—Federal Aviation Administration. Helms would head the FAA later in his career). The dual-purpose T-28 plan was presented to Gallant, who approved the project and assigned the company designator NA-260. Recalls Compton:

> We were off and running. The first order of business was to find a technician/mechanic to spearhead the modification effort. The person we were looking for had to possess A1 [top-notch] credentials, have intimate knowledge of the T-28B, the cunning of a supply sergeant[,] and the drive and persistence of a ramrod foreman. Our search narrowed down to one person—a flight line operation technician named Bill Nichols. Bill had the R-1820 engine overhaul and repair experience and displayed genuine interest in the project.[3]

Helms rummaged through the Air Force boneyard in Tucson, where he found two suitable T-28As for the project, but his search for surplus R-1820 engines proved more elusive. The entire R-1820 inventory was controlled by the Navy and a Wright engine rebuilder, Pacific Airmotive Corporation. As luck would have it, Pacific Airmotive was aware of NAA's plans to convert a T-28A into a big-engine T-28B demonstrator, since they were preparing a light-attack proposal based on the T-28B for the French government. Pacific's interest in the project led to a joint venture with NAA that would license the conversion of more than two hundred reengined T-28As for the French. By mid-summer 1958, negotiations among North American, Pacific, and the French were wrapped up, and modification of the first NA-260 was started. In exchange for NAA's work on the airframe, Pacific Airmotive agreed to provide a complete Wright R-1820-56S engine rated at 1,350 horsepower, with a Hamilton Standard Hydramatic three-blade propeller.

An underwing gun pod is attached to the wing of this resurrected T-28 as the role of the T-28 shifted from retired pilot trainer into jungle warfare. The typical Air Force T-28 had a relatively short life as a trainer, which meant the airframe flight hours were low.

Refurbishing weary trainers was an ongoing activity by NAA Columbus. The T-28 is a trainer airplane that was successfully adapted to combatant duty when it handled Vietnam War close-in sorties with aplomb. Hangars of Lane Air Service are visible in the top right.

T-28 Trojan General Characteristics

Model	No. built	First flight	Length	Span	Empty lbs.	Gross	Max. mph
T-28	1.949	1948	33 ft	40 ft., 1 in.	6,424	8,500	343
YAT-28E	2	1965	35 ft., 7 in.	40 ft., 1 in.	8,375	15,500	360

The T-28 had demonstrated an excellent history of structural integrity in Air Force and Navy training command service, but there were some fatigue and structural deformations on highly stressed aircraft. After studying the airframe, Bill Nichols concluded that he could strengthen NA-260 significantly by adding only 10 to 12 pounds of reinforcement. He also realized that the added weight of the big engine and structural reinforcements justified the use of the T-28C's carrier-capable landing gear, increasing the design limit descent rate from 10 to 16 feet per second. But CAA certification was not as effortless as Compton imagined:

We anticipated that the certification testing would be completed without a hitch since the T-28 series had undergone thousands of hours of flight and operational development testing at contractor, USAF, and Navy levels. This was not the case as civil and military standards are frequently divergent. The job turned out to be tedious and time consuming.[4]

A preliminary type certificate meeting was convened on May 17, 1958, and the nickname "Nomad" was assigned to the project. The CAA seemed impressed, but at the following meeting, sixteen items were identified that needed either compliance or approved deviations before flight demonstrations could begin. The most serious was an excessive stall speed, which would require weight reduction, wing modification, or both, setting the project back by months and adding substantial cost. Taking into consideration the T-28 cockpit's 40 g impact resistance, the docile flying qualities, and the low military-training-accident history, the CAA agreed to issue the deviations.

According to Compton, Bill Nichols accomplished a miracle by wrestling the Nomad demonstrator to flight status very quickly on a limited budget. It was obvious that CAA certification would be expensive. A plan was approved to conduct certification flights outside normal work hours, using as test pilots Lynn Helms, Lee Miller, and Frank Compton. The plan was organized in a manner needed to minimize the number of flights while gathering the maximum amount of data.

The first flight of the Nomad occurred on June 2, 1958, with Lynn Helms at the controls. Only two discrepancies were reported: excessive aileron heaviness and the engine surging at slow airspeeds. Further testing identified rapid throttle movements as the cause of the engine surge, but aileron linkage adjustments produced overly light stick forces, which resulted in "stick snatching." Improved control harmony over the Navy's T-28B was considered necessary for the civilian market, and Compton's team finally achieved it in the next few flights. The test phase for certification took nearly eighteen months to complete. Finally, on July 29, 1960, the Nomad's type certificate 1A18 was issued.

It became apparent a year earlier that Pacific Airmotive was considerably behind schedule in delivering three Nomads to the French for evaluation. To prevent the French from balking, NAA agreed to sell Pacific the prototype Nomad. Furthermore, the services of Bill Nichols would be provided to expedite the conversion of the two additional Nomads, as required by the contract. This effectively killed NAA's plans to market the Nomad as a civilian aircraft, but it allowed Pacific Airmotive to meet its obligations.

The Nomad prototype was transported to the Sud Aviation factory in Saint-Nazaire by the French aircraft carrier *Bois Belleau* in July 1959. After modifying the wing store stations to accept French ordnance, the Nomad (now named Fennec, or "desert fox") was flown to Algeria for test and evaluation in a strike-reconnaissance role. On April 16, 1960, near the end of the test phase, the prototype Nomad/Fennec was destroyed in a quirky accident. A rocket failed to launch in flight but was jarred from its pylon after a normal landing. It ignited on contact with the ground and caught up with the Fennec as it rolled out, penetrating the wing, igniting a fuel cell, and resulting in a total loss of the aircraft. Pacific Airmotive Nomads 2 and 3 were shipped to France in October 1959, where they were converted into Fennecs to complete the test program.

Pacific retained a fourth Nomad as a demonstrator for the civilian market, but it was placed in storage after the program dwindled.

The French ultimately acquired 145 Trojans (T-28As) from the US Air Force stockpile at Davis-Monthan. They installed the R-1820 engine, beefed up the wing, adapted it to French ordnance, added armor plate, installed French military communication-navigation equipment, and modified the air induction system for desert operations (Fennecs can be identified by an additional air scoop on the top of the cowl). Now designated T-28S, the Fennec equipped four squadrons in the Algerian campaign. They performed effectively and became popular with flight crews and maintainers. But their service was short lived because an armistice was declared in late 1961. The Fennecs returned to France, where they were used for training and reserve duties through the late 1970s.

In the early 1960s, the US government searched for an effective counterinsurgency (COIN) aircraft for its growing involvement in Vietnam. France's success with the Fennec served as a template for an expedient solution. Between 1961 and 1969, 321 T-28As arrived at NAA Columbus for conversion to the T-28D configuration. This time, a trainer airplane with the attributes of "low and slow" was adapted to become a jungle fighter. The guns and munitions hardpoints were no longer for training. Henceforth, the planes were combatants.

The entire supply of Air Force T-28As in desert storage was withdrawn. Privately owned aircraft were then conscripted by repurchase from their owners. The conversion consisted of installing an R-1820-56 engine (rated at 1,425 horsepower), strengthening the landing gear, adding cockpit armor plating, installing self-sealing fuel cells, and adding hardpoints under each wing (now totaling six), and some aircraft received an ejection seat for bailout. Robert Genat describes the system:

> This was an improvement over the previous method of abandoning an aircraft in flight that was recommended on the As, Bs, and Cs: diving out of the cockpit toward the trailing edge of the wing. Limitations to this bailout method were speed (you had to be moving less than 120 knots) and altitude. Dangers included the possibility of smacking into the horizontal stabilizer. The T-28 extraction seat or "Yankee extraction seat" was originally developed for the Douglas A-1 Skyraider. It had zero-zero capability[,] which meant you could sit in the aircraft on the runway and punch out at zero airspeed, zero altitude. The seat featured a solid-propellant rocket. Pulling the handle activated a detonation cord, commonly called a det cord[,] that blew away the Plexiglas in the canopy. Ejection was initiated with the canopy closed; otherwise you'd hit the frame on the way out.

The Columbus conversions were designated T-28D-5. Fairchild Hiller modified 72 T-28As, which were designated T-28D-10s. Unfortunately, even with additional strengthening, the heavy ordnance loads, a hot and humid operational environment, and rough, pierced steel plank runways contributed to a number of structural failures. By 1964, the T-28D was replaced by the Douglas A-1 Skyraider.

YAT-28E

By 1962, the Air Force was aware that the T-28D was, at best, an interim solution to the COIN fighter requirement. In September 1962, a $735,000 contract was awarded to NAA Columbus for a one-plane prototype of a turboprop T-28A conversion. A Downey-built T-28A, serial number 51-1242, was retrieved from desert storage and arrived at Columbus shortly after the contract was awarded. Since much of the design work had been done in advance, the conversion started immediately. A Lycoming YT-55-L-9, a turbine engine designed for helicopters, was selected as the power plant. It was a free power turbine (*Note*: A free power turbine is a form of turboprop engine where the power is extracted from the exhaust stream of a gas turbine). Rated at 2,445 shaft-horsepower, it dwarfs the

1,425-horsepower output of the Wright R-1820 radials used in the T-28D. A Lycoming press release describes special features of the engine:

A split[-]power propeller reduction gear developed by Lycoming, which distributes the loads on the gearing and improves the life of the gears. Lighter, more compact, and more efficient than standard two-stage planetary reduction gear trains, the system transmits approximately one-third of the input power to the propeller through the first stage reduction gear, while two-thirds are transmitted by the second[-]stage reduction gear.

The new gear has been designed to be compatible with advanced versions of the engine with power exceeding 3,000 shaft horsepower.[5]

Complete rework of the T-28A's nose was necessary to enclose the new engine, vertical tail area was increased to accommodate the torque from the engine, and an enormous 11-foot, 6-inch Aero Products Allison four-blade propeller was necessary to absorb the power of the engine. A large opening for the turbine exhaust was placed on the port side of the fuselage above and ahead of the wing root, a pair of .50-caliber machine guns were installed in built-in pods under each wing, six pylons were installed under each wing, and provisions

The AIM-9 Sidewinder was an enduring 1950s invention of the China Lake naval weapons laboratory and a mainstay air-to-air missile ever since. Here, it seen attached to the wingtip of a T-28 variant. When sensing a target, the heat-seeking mechanism warbles a tone into the pilot's headset, yielding the phrase "I've got the music!"

The quest for a sturdy counterinsurgency warplane yielded the turboprop-powered YAT-28E: Y (for prototype), A (for attack), T (for trainer), and -28E (the variant). A fresh design, the OV-10 Bronco, obviated the need for the turboprop Trojan.

Weapons intended for tropical warfare are ironically arrayed in the snow. A dozen hardpoints are available to mission planners. The payload will be dictated by variables including target attributes, distance to target, and weapons inventory on hand.

for wingtip-mounted AIM-9 Sidewinder air-to-air missiles were added. The air brake was modified, and the flap system enhanced to deal with a 3,500-pound weight increase and higher airspeeds.

The COIN fighter, originally designated RA-28 by the Air Force, was redesignated YAT-28E before its first flight. The first ship was rolled out of the hangar on January 30, 1963, bearing the tail number 50-1242, nearly thirty days ahead of schedule. It flew on February 15, piloted by the Columbus Division's chief test pilot at that time, George Hoskins. A North American press release reported that the initial flight lasted approximately one hour and was trouble-free. The flight demonstrated flying qualities, including power stalls, takeoff and landing characteristics, and ground handling. Aside from a slight aileron overbalance and a light vibration, Hoskins considered the flight "a complete success." The initial flight was witnessed by Air Force officers from the Aeronautical Systems Division of Wright-Patterson AFB and the Special Air Warfare Center of Eglin AFB. Before the end of February, the YAT-28E completed five contractor test flights, demonstrating slow-speed flight characteristics, full-power takeoffs, rate of climb, and 15-degree full-power dives from 20,000 feet. Since this represented completion of 19 percent of the contract flight test obligations ahead of schedule, North American predicted that the testing would be completed approximately one month early and the aircraft would be delivered to Eglin AFB, Florida, for Air Force evaluation by late April. But in late March, on the fourteenth test flight near Logan, Ohio, the aircraft was lost:

> Following two dives from 20,000-ft with 3g and 4.5g pullouts, the airplane had entered the third maneuver on the test flight: a diving right-turn with a 30-degree nose-down attitude and a 45-degree bank that was to end with a rollout and pullup at a maximum 3.5 g. Instead, the bank steepened to 60-degrees, then 90-degrees, and finally the airplane went over on its back. Pieces began coming off the tail and the airplane entered what appeared to be a flat spin.
>
> Only one aircraft was built in the program, and the program's future was not clear in the wake of the crash.[6]

With no ejection seat, George Hoskins was unable to escape the crippled aircraft and perished with YAT-28E number 1. But the Air Force was convinced that the aircraft was showing promise, and authorized North American to build another prototype. T-28A serial 51-3786 was shipped to Columbus for conversion in June 1963. Significant reinforcement was added to the horizontal stabilizer—thicker skins and heavier attach fittings provided a 250 percent increase in strength to the tail, an area that had been historically weak in all T-28 variants.

The vertical tail area was increased and a North American LW-2C ejection seat was installed in the front cockpit (since the rear cockpit carried test instruments, no seat was installed). Ship number 2 was completed in five months and received tail number 0-13786. It was flown by North American test pilot Don McCracken on November 15, 1963. A mechanical problem shortened the first flight, but a full-length test flight was made on November 21. Shortly after that flight, the Air Force took possession of YAT number 2 to begin its Category I evaluation. Maj. A. T. Iddings and Capt. R. L. Regan were assigned to the evaluation and flew sixteen sorties from the North American Columbus facility between February 14 and 25, 1964. Iddings and Regan investigated taxi, takeoff, climb, cruise, maneuvering flight, stalls, trim changes, bombing and strafing runs, and landings.

They reported that at idle, the power plant produced excessive residual thrust, causing a high taxi speed and undue brake wear. Likewise, full power at takeoff was considered excessive—a reduced power setting for training and transition was recommended. Also, excessive "g" loadings were encountered in maneuvering flight at several weight and airspeed conditions, and unacceptably high aileron forces were experienced. Trim changes due to airspeed were unacceptable, making the tracking of bombing and strafing runs difficult. Residual thrust from the power plant made the landing rollout unnecessarily long. The engine suffered from compressor stalls during engine acceleration, and rpm surges during engine deceleration. Finally, the battery was considered inadequate for reliable turbine starts. Nevertheless, the Air Force decided to ferry the YAT to Edwards AFB for Category II testing, where the entire aircraft and all systems were to be evaluated in an operational environment. North American's support crew would be replaced by Air Force personnel preparing, operating, and maintaining the aircraft in a realistic service environment. During Category II testing, the issue of excessive control force continued to plague the program. Weapons delivery evaluation started on March 13, but it became apparent that the YAT was unsatisfactory for delivering ordnance. NAA Columbus urgently addressed the control problems and succeeded in improving the Air Force classification to "acceptable, although less than desired."

Meanwhile, a third T-28A, serial number 51-3788, was being converted to YAT-28E status at Columbus. This aircraft represented the production standard, with a rear cockpit LW-2C ejection seat, an enlarged canopy to provide clearance for the rear seat, further elongation of the vertical tail to compensate for the destabilizing effect of the larger canopy, the addition of fuel capacity, and additional armor plating. Ship number 3 was rolled out on June 10, 1964, with tail number 0-13788. It flew on June 30, making a total of twelve contractor flights before it was conditionally accepted by the Air Force on July 17. The Air Force considered ship number 3's flying qualities significantly improved, and delivered it to the user command—the Special Air Warfare Center at Eglin AFB, for Category III testing.

Category III testing is the evaluation of the entire integrated system operating under field conditions. Operational tactics, refinement of logistics, personnel, maintenance, and training requirements are established during this step. At Eglin, sixty-four sorties were flown over 65.5 hours of flight time, including two simulated combat missions with a cursory examination of hot-weather operations. A maximum ordnance load totaling 6,000 pounds was carried, using all twelve stations. Carrying this load, performance was degraded but still considered acceptable. The takeoff roll was 3,500 feet, the rate of climb was 1,500 feet per minute, and attack speeds of 240 to 260 knots were easily attained. However, the roll response at landing speeds was considered unacceptable. The overall impression was that the YAT showed promise as an attack/trainer.

Ship number 2 was returned to Columbus to improve its flight control system. Several misalignments were found in the airframe, which accounted for some of the difficulties. After correction, it was ferried to Eglin, where it joined ship number 3 until the conclusion of Category III testing. By January 1965, the Air Force, faced with the costs of additional engine development, redesign of the exhaust system, and static testing, decided to discontinue the YAT-28E program. By then a new, more capable COIN fighter, the OV-10 Bronco, was in development at Columbus. Both YATs were returned to the factory for storage.

The Navy, however, was looking to replace their aging T-28Bs and Cs, and a turboprop T-28 seemed like an attractive choice. In early 1965, the Navy entered into a bailment agreement with the Air Force to conduct a limited flight evaluation of the YATs (bailment is a type of loan). On January 24, 1966, ship number 3 began a test program conducted by pilots from the NATC and the Basic Air Training Command. All flights originated from the NAA Columbus facility. A total of twenty-seven sorties totaling 40.1 hours were flown. The aircraft was modified from its Air Force strike configuration to a Navy trainer configuration by deactivating the armament circuits and limiting the engine output to 1,900 shaft horsepower. A three-axis electric trim system was installed, as was a rudder shaker stall-warning device from a T-28C.

On his second flight in the YAT, then lieutenant Gary Wheatley suffered a total engine failure at 20,000 feet after a series of compressor stalls. He elected to perform a dead-stick landing at Lockbourne AFB, 30 miles away. Arriving over the field with 3,000 feet of excess altitude, he commenced a rapid decent with landing gear lowered in maximum side slip, and crossed the threshold with 1,000 feet of altitude and 170 knots of airspeed. Fortunately, he touched down at the runway midpoint and used 6,000 feet to stop. Wheatley summarizes his impression of the YAT as "a combination of the highest performance intermixed with some of the worst flying qualities I have ever seen. It was an exciting airplane to fly, and we all treated it with respect from takeoff to final landing."[7]

On May 3, 1966, the Navy declined further interest in the YAT-28E, concluding that it was not suitable for their training purposes. The performance exceeded training requirements even with reduced power, the climb angle was excessively steep, the stall warning was inadequate in accelerated stalls, the flight controls were excessively heavy, and the massive ejection seat blocked the instructor's visibility from the rear cockpit. While the Navy continued to use T-28Bs and Cs in their training syllabus well into the 1980s, for the first time in over eighteen years NAA's T-28 programs were at an end.

FJ Fury Series and Columbus Sabre Jets

A pair of Marine FJ-3 Fury Jets are in formation as they break right and the camera captures their sleek lines. One carries external fuel tanks, while BuNo 136134 is "clean."

The Navy's venture into jet aviation began on January 7, 1942, when it issued a small design study contract to the Westinghouse Electric Company for the development of an axial-flow gas turbine. Westinghouse, with no prior aircraft engine experience, was chosen because of their credentials in steam turbines and the hope that they would not be constrained by reciprocating engine technology. One year later, on New Year's Day 1943, the Navy invited McDonnell Aircraft, a recently incorporated airframe manufacturer in St. Louis with limited design experience, to develop a carrier-capable fighter aircraft that would be powered by two of the Westinghouse turbojets. The Westinghouse engine was successfully run three months

later, on March 19, 1943, and McDonnell's fighter, the XFD-1 Phantom I, flew less than two years later—on January 26, 1945.[1]

The urgency for jet fighters was apparent well before the McDonnell Phantom's first flight. A massive two-stage invasion of Japan code-named Operation Downfall was evolving. The first stage, Olympic, was set to begin in November 1945, followed by Coronet in the spring of 1946. It was feared that Japan, with the aid of German technology, was developing jet fighters to defend their homeland. This caused the Navy to accelerate their jet development efforts. On September 5, 1944, the Navy Bureau of Aeronautics (BuAer) issued an RFP to eight companies for jet-propelled carrier-based fighters. Four companies responded: Grumman, McDonnell, Vought, and North American. Grumman was eliminated out of hand since the company's resources were stretched thin by a large F6F Hellcat production commitment and the development of two new fighters (the F7F Tigercat and F8F Bearcat). Vought, highly regarded by BuAer because of their successful F4U Corsair series, was awarded a contract for three prototype XF6U-1 Pirates. McDonnell, already selected to build the XFD-1 Phantom, which would become the first American jet to operate from a carrier, was issued a contract to develop an improved version, the XF2D-1 Banshee.

FJ-1 Fury

As the preeminent American military aircraft manufacturer, NAA was awarded a contract to build three XFJ-1 Furys. Designers had pondered the possibility of developing a jet version of the Mustang but, recognizing the importance of jet propulsion, instead opted to propose a "clean sheet" fighter. Assigned NA-134 for company purposes, the proposal was delivered to the Navy. A second proposal, NA-140, was submitted to the Army Air Force (AAF) at almost the same time. These were similar but not identical designs. Both employed a low-mounted, laminar-flow, straight wing derived from the P-51 Mustang. Armament for both consisted of .50-caliber machine guns mounted within the fuselage sides near the air intake. Both had a cylindrical fuselage enclosing a 3,820-pound-thrust General Electric TG-180 turbojet (later built by Allison and designated J35) with a single undivided inlet duct to maximize engine performance. However, the Navy design

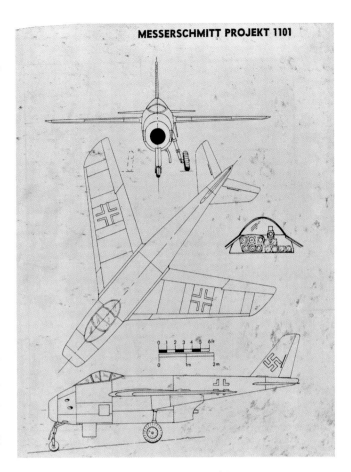

This German-designed Messerschmitt Project 1101 appears remarkably akin to an FJ Fury. With early jet engine thrust limitations, airframe designers were forced to accept small but nimble designs.

An FJ-2 Fury bearing USMC livery taxis away from the Navy-owned Columbus plant operated by NAA. BuNo 132032 bears the markings of Marine squadron VMF-232. The FJ-Fury put Marine pilots, mostly flying from fixed bases, on a par with their Air Force counterparts.

had a wider fuselage cross section for additional fuel capacity, and the cockpit was placed on top of the circular inlet duct. The AAF version used a curved inlet duct that snaked over the nose gear and under the cockpit, reducing the fuselage cross section, and the wings used a thinner airfoil. Although work on the Navy proposal preceded the AAF proposal, the Air Force was first to issue a contract. On August 30, 1944, North American received a letter contract under the designation XP-86. The Navy contract was issued four months later, on January 1, 1945, ordering two flying prototypes and one static-test XFJ-1.

On June 20, nearly ten months after North American received the AAF contract, the straight-wing XP-86 mockup was approved. But the program was halted when wind tunnel data predicted that the design would not meet the speed requirement of 600 mph (it appeared that the straight-wing XP-86 would be no faster than Republic's F-84). Nevertheless, the XFJ-1 program progressed rapidly, since top speed was less important to the Navy than the stability at low speed necessary for carrier operations. On May 28, 1945, more than fifteen months before the prototype XFJ-1 would fly and preparations for Operation Downfall were

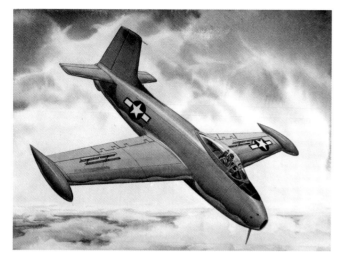

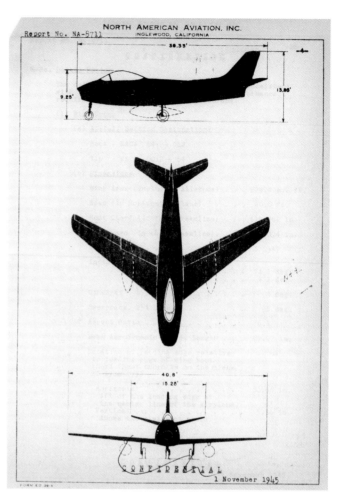

NORTH AMERICAN AVIATION, INC.
Report No. NA-5711
INGLEWOOD, CALIFORNIA

This historically significant sketch is dated November 1, 1945. NAA had already obtained Army Air Forces buy-off to proceed with a straight-wing F-86. On the basis of Nazi wind tunnel data from Völkenrode and on their own initiative, NAA reworked the design from straight wing to swept wing.

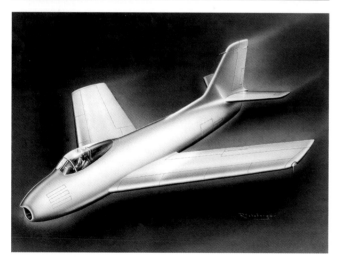

Three sketches document the evolution of the FJ Fury. Sketches and wooden models helped aircraft designers communicate their ideas to others. The first is dated 1944, then we see the straight wing give way to swept wing.

gaining momentum, the Navy ordered a hundred FJ-1 production units (this number would be reduced to thirty after the surrender of Japan).

Meanwhile, North American submitted a new proposal to the Army Air Force for a swept-wing XP-86, which was accepted on November 1, 1945. It was the first completely new swept-wing design to be embraced by a customer—several months ahead of the MiG-15 or the Boeing XB-47. It became the basis for the iconic F-86 Sabre.

The Navy's first XFJ-1 (BuNo 39053) was completed only one year after the contract was issued at the North American Inglewood plant in January 1946, but its General Electric TG-180 engine was not available until June. Taxi tests were conducted from late July to early August, and a successful maiden flight was made by Wallace Lien on September 11, 1946. The second prototype (39054) flew one month later, followed by the third prototype (39055) in February 1947. The preliminary flight test report stated a top speed of 542 mph at 16,000 feet, a service ceiling of 47,700 feet, and a rate of climb of 4,690 feet per minute. In early 1947, the first prototype reached Mach 0.87 in a shallow dive, the fastest recorded speed in America at that

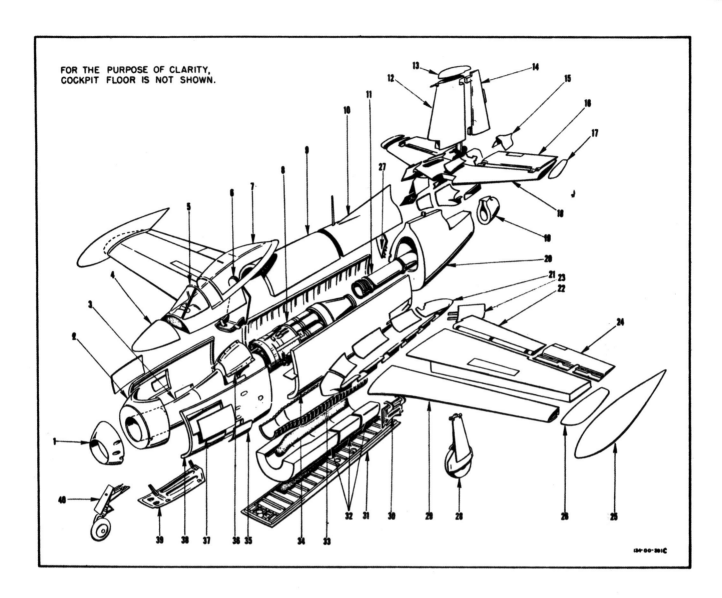

FOR THE PURPOSE OF CLARITY,
COCKPIT FLOOR IS NOT SHOWN.

134-00-301C

1. Engine Air Intake Duct Leading Edge·
2. Fuselage Front Section
3. Engine Air Intake Duct
4. Ammunition Access Door
5. Windshield Installation
6. Pilot's Seat
7. Sliding Canopy
8. Power Plant Installation
9. Engine Access Door (Front)
10. Engine Access Door (Rear)
11. Tail Pipe Installation
12. Vertical Stabilizer
13. Vertical Stabilizer Tip
14. Rudder
15. Tail Fillets and Dorsal Fin Installation
16. Elevator
17. Horizontal Stabilizer Tip
18. Horizontal Stabilizer
19. Fuselage Tail Cone
20. Fuselage Rear Section

21. Wing-to-Fuselage Fillets
22. Wing Flap
23. Speed Brake
24. Aileron Installation
25. Droppable Wing Tip Fuel Tank
26. Wing Tip
27. Speed Brake
28. Main Landing Gear
29. Wing Assembly
30. Main Landing Gear Wheel Fairing Door
31. Fuel Tank Access Door
32. Fuselage Fuel Tanks
33. Engine Shroud
34. Fuselage Center Panel
35. Radio or Battery Access Door
36. Engine Accessory Access Door
37. Gun Access Door
38. Fuselage Front Panel
39. Nose Gear Wheel Fairing Door
40. Nose Gear

Like a human anatomy chart at the hospital, this exploded view of the FJ-1 helps everybody from factory workers to procurement specialists and Navy maintainers better understand the internal components of an airplane.

Utilizing a tiny shop-sized wheel, the FJ-1 designers designed a kneeling nose in lieu of folding wings. Also, the fuselage top was removed to access the engine. Neither feature worked out well, and both were dropped from subsequent Fury versions.

The role of the FJ-1 established precedents for the next generation of jet aircraft that followed them onto aircraft carriers. Thirty were built and half of them were crashed. Some of the experimental innovations were later abandoned.

time. The summary of the flight characteristics concluded that the XFJ-1 handled well but that a lack of neutral dynamic stability (snaking or weaving) occurred above 325 mph. The condition was cured by the addition of turbulators (devices that add turbulence to the air flow) to the trailing edge of the rudder. The addition of wingtip fuel tanks had little effect on handling characteristics.[2] North American completed their contractor test flights by the end of the summer, and the three XFJ-1s were turned over to the NATC for acceptance trials in September 1947.

The XFJ-1 employed several unusual features. Speed brakes were mounted on the wings rather than on the fuselage. This precluded wing folding—a common feature on carrier aircraft to conserve space. To compensate for the rigid wings, the Fury's nose gear could be folded, allowing the aircraft to "kneel" and permit several Furys to be stacked. Engine access was provided by a removable upper fuselage section running from aft of the canopy to the vertical stabilizer. These features proved to be troublesome. During an early test flight, the speed brakes on one wing failed to deploy. After snap-rolling violently, the pilot forced the retracted panels to extend. He was able to control and land with both sets of speed brakes open, but witnesses reported that the rate of descent was impressive. The kneeling nose leg required a cumbersome hand pump to fold the strut and was rarely used at sea. In usage, this feature saved minimal deck space, and the hydraulics frequently malfunctioned. The removable fuselage section required a hoist to lift the large panel, which made hangar deck maintenance difficult.

The first production FJ-1 was designated NA-141 to distinguish it from the prototype (NA-134). It was delivered

from Inglewood to the Naval Air Test Center on October 5, 1947, and by January 1948, six more had been delivered. Production aircraft differed from the prototypes by a relocation of the speed brakes from the wings to the lower rear fuselage and by the addition of a leading-edge wing fillet to smooth the airflow at the wing/fuselage intersection (the prototype XFJ-1s had a straight leading edge). Like the prototypes, production Furys had no ejection seats, no pressurization, and no cockpit heat. Service testing at NATC confirmed that the Fury would perform well under operational conditions, although a canopy failure during a spin test and an elevator loss during an extended dive were concerns.

In November 1947, one month after the first FJ-1 was delivered to NATC, sixteen Furys were delivered to VF-5A (redesignated VF-51 in August 1948), a fighter squadron based at NAS North Island in California. Commanded by Evan "Pete" Aurand, VF-5A was assigned the task of taking the Fury to sea, an assignment so important that the commander was permitted to hand-pick the squadron personnel. But first, to display the potential of a Navy jet, Aurand scheduled a series of land demonstrations. A spectacular triple speed record run was flown on February 29, 1948, when three Furys took off from Seattle and headed south. One Fury, piloted by squadron executive officer Lt. Cmdr. Robert M. Elder, peeled off from the three-ship formation and landed at San Francisco after one hour and twenty-four minutes at an average speed of 492.6 mph. A second, piloted by Pete Aurand, repeated the maneuver at Los Angles in one hour, fifty-eight minutes, and seven seconds at an average speed of 521 mph. The third, piloted by Lt. Cmdr. John J. Magda, landed at San Diego in two hours, twelve minutes, and fifty-four seconds at an average speed of 511.8 mph. All three Furys established travel time records between Seattle and their California destinations.

An FJ-1 Fury, bearing the stenciled name of Lt. Ritchie, rides the elevator to the hangar deck below. Human hands pushing on the leading edge provide the propulsion.

Commander Pete Aurand smiles and chomps on a cigar as he sits in the cockpit of a Fury jet. Both Aurand and Elder performed pathfinder roles by integrating jets into naval service.

Bob Elder flew the P-51 Mustang on and off aircraft carrier USS Shangri La on its shakedown cruise. Bob Elder remained an accomplished naval air innovator for the balance of his long career—both in uniform and in a leadership role with industry. Image courtesy of Aldrich

Aurand started an extensive pilot familiarization program shortly after the first Fury arrived in November 1947. In addition to combat maneuver practice and cross-country flights, VF-5A pilots practiced simulated carrier landings on a runway configured to represent a carrier deck. Anxious to make VF-5A the first jet squadron at sea, Aurand and his executive officer, Elder, made over two hundred practice carrier landings on a simulated deck painted on a North Island runway. On February 27, 1948, two days before the California speed runs, Aurand received authorization from the CNO to perform limited carrier operations at sea, even though the Fury had not undergone customary carrier trials by the NATC. The CNO authorization prohibited catapult launches, or the installation of tip fuel tanks, thus limiting the landing weight to 11,300 pounds, takeoff weight to 11,600 pounds, and recommended minimum wind over the deck of 35 knots. On March 10, 1948, Pete Aurand and Bob Elder flew their Furys to USS *Boxer*, steaming 75 miles off the coast of San Diego, where they landed without incident. This was not the first successful carrier landing of a jet—that was accomplished nearly twenty months earlier by Lt. Cmdr. James T. Davidson on July 21, 1946, in a McDonnell XFD-1 Phantom aboard USS *Franklin D. Roosevelt*[3]—but it was the first time that an operational squadron landed jets aboard a carrier. Aurand's landing technique was described in the March 22, 1948, issue of *Aviation Week*:

> In approach to the carrier the FJ-1 entered its lineup with the deck approximately 200 yards further away than is customary with propeller aircraft, which continue on their banked turn to the left until almost upon the carrier's fantail. The jet technique is indicated by a longer glide, without the braking effect of the propeller, and the necessity for having the aircraft lined up for the signal officer's "cut" or wave-off while still some distance from the deck. Upon receiving the signal officer's "cut" at an altitude of approximately 35 feet above the deck level, the jet pilot retards the plane's throttle to its idle thrust block, retaining a turbine speed of 3,200–3,500 rpm, and delivering somewhat less than 50% thrust.
>
> At the same time the nose is dropped, and a partial flame-out is affected [*sic*] just above the deck with the result that the tail hook engages an arresting cable just as the plane lands solidly on its main gear and then pitches forward on its nose wheel.

In a subsequent review of the tests, Cmdr. Aurand gave a pilot's reaction to the characteristics of the FJ-1 in carrier operation:

> The visibility is what impresses you the most. For the first time I not only knew what I was doing, but I actually saw what I was doing in my landing approach. Usually by the time you're down to the deck with a propeller plane[,] you are busy lining up the deck by looking out the side. It was almost frightening to look ahead from the FJ and see the barriers for the first time. The jet is the easiest plane to land . . . You just fly it down and there you are.[4]

The CNO authorization precluded catapult launches, so Aurand's first takeoff after the successful carrier landing was a free deck run. Witnesses report that the Fury's acceleration was so gradual, it was not certain if Aurand could get airborne before plunging over the bow. The entire 880-foot length of USS *Boxer*'s deck was used, and Aurand's Fury settled noticeably as it lost lift from the ground effect provided by the deck as it cleared the bow. It is uncertain whether Elder followed with another deck run, but at some point Aurand made a command decision or received authorization to use catapult assistance. Twenty-four takeoffs and landings were executed that day. *Aviation Week* magazine reported that by the end of the session, the jets were consistently airborne with 700-foot deck runs.

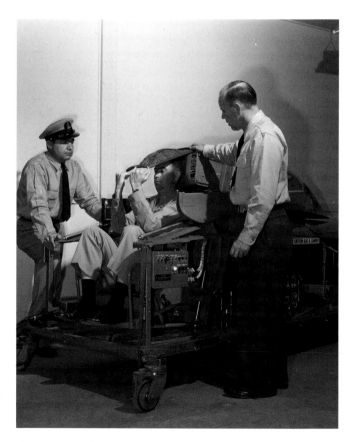

An ejection seat familiarization tool allows the pilot to rehearse the steps necessary for successful bailout. Some are activated by pulling the face protector down; the face protector helps retain the helmet and oxygen mask.

After further onshore workups, Aurand flew his entire squadron (now designated VF-51) to USS *Princeton* on May 3, 1948, for carrier qualifications. Three days earlier, an East Coast squadron, VF-17A, based at Quonset Point, Rhode Island, hoisted sixteen FH-1 Phantoms aboard USS *Saipan* and put out to the Atlantic. By May 5, VA-17A had logged over two hundred landings (with one minor mishap), becoming the first jet squadron to achieve full carrier qualification. VF-51's qualification did not go as well. The fourth Fury aboard USS *Princeton* experienced a hard landing and broke the left wing off at the root. The fuselage, pilot, and right wing skidded off the deck, while the severed wing remained on the deck. The pilot was rescued but the aircraft was stricken. During the next two days, several other Furys crashed into the barrier, ending the qualification early. USS *Princeton* returned to San Diego, where the damaged aircraft were craned ashore.[5]

On August 10, 1948, the customary NATC carrier suitability trials for the Fury were finally performed aboard USS *Princeton*, using two VF-51 aircraft painted with photo reference markings and carrying special instrumentation to measure arrestment and launch forces. One Fury was damaged in a hard landing and stricken after only two months in service, but the other completed the trials, and the FJ-1 was deemed carrier suitable. The next month, Aurand took several FJ-1s aboard USS *Tarawa* (CV-40) for jet-familiarization operations. In January 1949, he conducted squadron-size operations aboard *Princeton*, and aboard *Boxer* in February.

Less than a month after the carrier suitability trials, Aurand was provided with another opportunity to display the FJ-1's performance. The Bendix Trophy Race originated in 1931, when Vincent Bendix, president of the Bendix Corporation, established a trophy for the fastest cross-country flight. Aviation notables including Jimmy Doolittle, Roscoe Turner, and Jackie Cochran had previously won the race, and the distinction of being the fastest humans on the planet. Racing was halted in 1939 due to the impending war, but it was revived in 1946 by a group of Cleveland businessmen, with a new class for military jets. Army Air Force jets dominated the class in 1946 and 1947 with the new Lockheed P-80 Shooting Star, but in 1948, SecDef James Forrestal decided that the race would be an all-Navy event. At that time, the Navy was in an existential battle with the newly formed Air Force for government funds.

The FJ-1 Fury was the Navy's only jet assets on the West Coast, so it fell to Cmdr. Aurand to prepare six of his VF-51 pilots and Furys for the race. In prior years, the trophy had been won by military aircraft stripped of all combat gear, but Aurand, confident of the FJs' performance, entered his jets carrying full ammunition loads, with enlarged tip tanks carrying twice as much fuel as standard tanks. Taking off from Long Beach, California, the FJs headed for Cleveland, Ohio, with only one fuel stop. Four

Fury jets finished the race in just over four hours, winning the top three places, but those that landed in Cleveland had little or no fuel. Elder flamed out from fuel exhaustion 50 miles from the airport and glided dead-stick to the runway (failing to cross the finish line). Ens. F. Taylor Brown, the most junior pilot in the group, recorded the fastest official speed of 489.526 mph but flamed out while taxiing in and had to be towed to the parking ramp. Two Furys did not finish. One incurred a mechanical problem at takeoff, and the other made an emergency landing in Ohio. While not officially entered, an Air National Guard P-80C completed the race more than one minute sooner than Ensign Brown's winning time of 4 hours, 10 minutes, 34.4 seconds.[6]

After providing jet familiarization to several carriers in the Pacific, VF-51 prepared to transition to a second-generation jet, the Grumman F9F Panther. The FJ-1s were turned into the overhaul and repair center at Alameda, California, where they were refurbished and assigned to four Naval Air Reserve stations (Oakland, Los Alamitos, Olathe, and Dallas). There they served as jet familiarization trainers for "weekend warriors" being recalled to duty for Korea, serving in this role from 1950 to 1953, when they were reassigned to the Naval Air Technical Training Center, NAS Jacksonville, Florida, and the service and maintenance pool at NAS Willow Grove, north of Philadelphia, Pennsylvania. By 1954, with spare parts becoming scarce and newer jets entering service, the last airworthy FJ-1s were retired. Of the thirty production FJ-1s delivered to the Navy, at least seventeen were stricken due to crash damage.[7]

In retrospect the Fury presented many headaches, while providing invaluable early jet experience. The Allison J35-A-2 engine was rated at only ten hours between overhaul, which meant an engine removal every fifth or sixth flight. This was a time-consuming task requiring removal of much of the fuselage top with a crane—an operation not easily done at sea. After considerable experience, the overhaul interval was expanded to thirty-five hours, but early jet operations were still impractical. Unnecessary taxiing was forbidden to avoid accumulating engine time. Furys were towed whenever possible. The "kneeling" storage feature was rarely used because of the difficulty in using a hand-operated hydraulic pump to fold the nose strut. And many onboard systems became inaccessible for maintenance when the Fury was sitting on its nose. To add insult to injury, the extra hydraulic connections necessary for the kneeling feature often leaked, making the entire landing-gear system unreliable. It became rare to find a Fury without a landing-gear failure noted in its maintenance logbook.

The Fury cockpit was unpressurized and unheated and had no ejection seat. Lack of pressurization meant that pilots risked incurring the "bends" and had to breathe pure oxygen on the ground for thirty minutes before takeoff. Lack of heat

Marking Time©
North American FJ/F-1 Fury

FJ-1 BuNo. 120350
VF-5A, CVG-5
NAS LONG BEACH, CA   MARCH, 1948

FJ-3 BuNo. 135829d
VF-51, CVG-5
NAS MIRAMAR, CA OCTOBER, 1955

FJ-3M BuNo. 135844e
VF-51, CVG-5, USS BON HOMME RICHARD (CVA 31)
WESTPAC CRUISE JULY-DECEMBER 1957

FJ-3 BuNo. 135862d
VF-21, CVG-2
NAS OCEANA, VA OCTOBER, 1955

FJ-3 BuNo. 136128g
VF-21, ATG-181, USS BENNINGTON (CVA 20)
WESTPAC CRUISE OCTOBER, 1957

© JDMC Graphics 2020

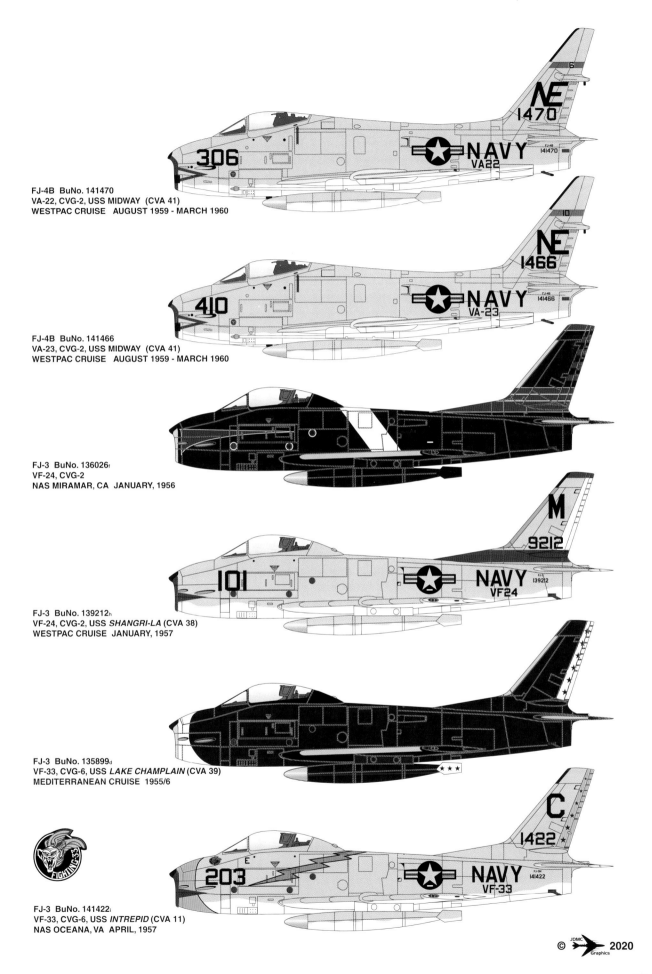

FJ-4B BuNo. 141470
VA-22, CVG-2, USS MIDWAY (CVA 41)
WESTPAC CRUISE   AUGUST 1959 - MARCH 1960

FJ-4B BuNo. 141466
VA-23, CVG-2, USS MIDWAY (CVA 41)
WESTPAC CRUISE   AUGUST 1959 - MARCH 1960

FJ-3 BuNo. 136026$_f$
VF-24, CVG-2
NAS MIRAMAR, CA JANUARY, 1956

FJ-3 BuNo. 139212$_h$
VF-24, CVG-2, USS SHANGRI-LA (CVA 38)
WESTPAC CRUISE JANUARY, 1957

FJ-3 BuNo. 135899$_d$
VF-33, CVG-6, USS LAKE CHAMPLAIN (CVA 39)
MEDITERRANEAN CRUISE 1955/6

FJ-3 BuNo. 141422$_i$
VF-33, CVG-6, USS INTREPID (CVA 11)
NAS OCEANA, VA APRIL, 1957

© JDMC Graphics 2020

meant that the pilots had to wear electrically heated flight suits that were inadequate at altitude even in the summer. And lack of an ejection seat meant that pilots had to depart a doomed FJ-1 by brute force—a feat that was possible with a 300 mph propeller-driven aircraft, but virtually impossible with a 500 mph jet. Only one man was lost being unable to depart from a Fury, and another did manage to parachute from his stricken jet; therefore, dead-stick or belly landings were preferred in case of trouble.

FJ-2 Fury

After completing his historic tour as commander of VF-51, Cmdr. Evan "Pete" Aurand was assigned to the Naval Bureau of Aeronautics as the assistant head of the fighter design branch. Lt. Cmdr. Bob Elder, Aurand's executive officer at VF-51, was transferred to the tactical test division of the NATC. Both Aurand and Elder, with their substantial jet experience, were keenly aware of the limitations of the FJ-1 Fury, and both admired the performance of the Air Force's swept-wing F-86, a North American stablemate developed in parallel with the FJ-1.

At the outset, both aircraft were remarkably similar, but the Air Force insisted on swept-wing aircraft when wind tunnel tests predicted mediocre performance from the straight-wing version. The redesign was tedious, fraught with many unknowns that set the Air Force program back by more than a year. Initially, North American's project aerodynamicist, L. P. Greene, studied German reports on swept wings that had been retrieved after the war. While it was clear that wing sweep delayed and reduced the drag rise associated with transonic flight, it also introduced certain stability problems.

Greene felt that leading-edge slats could overcome the stability issue, but it was essential that they operate automatically. In late August 1945, NAA's chief engineer, Raymond Rice, approved wind tunnel testing of a large-scale model of the swept-wing design. The model, which was 23 percent of full size, used a piece of bent metal to simulate the extended slat. It confirmed adequate stability and a reduced stall speed when it was in place, but with the makeshift slat removed, the sweep conferred considerable high-speed benefit. Additional wind tunnel work was done to determine the optimum aspect ratio of the wing (the ratio of the wingspan to the chord). Initially a ratio of six was proposed, which gave the best range, while a ratio of five yielded the best stability.

Encouraged by these data, North American submitted its new proposal to the Army Air Force, which was approved on November 1, 1945. The aspect ratio was revised to 4.79 in March 1946, when it was discovered that the stability problems with the high-aspect-ratio wing were too great. A sweepback angle of 35 degrees with an airfoil thickness of 11 percent at the root and 10 percent at the tip was decided upon. The leading-edge slats were actuated automatically, extending under their own weight at low airspeeds and retracting to a flush position at high airspeeds. Early XP-86 slats were rigged to open fully at speeds below 130 knots and retract fully at speeds above 290 knots, but this was changed to a range of 115–180 knots to reduce slat deployment during maneuvering. The extensive design, development, and testing invested in the XP-86 project by NAA yielded enormous dividends. With total production exceeding nine thousand (including licensees), the F-86 was finest fighter of its era.

Adapting the USAF F-86 Sabre into the Navy's FJ-2 Fury

Though the F-86 was 100 mph faster than the FJ-1, the Navy remained apprehensive about swept-wing stability for carrier applications. The new generation of jets being developed for the fleet—the F9F Panther, F2H Banshee, and F3D Skyknight—all had straight wings. Bob Elder was frequently assigned to fly the F-86 as chase plane at the NATC. He developed data showing that a swept-wing aircraft could be adapted to carrier operations. On the basis of Elder's data, North American proposed an F-86 adapted for duty with the Navy. On January 30, 1951, a presentation was made to Cmdr. Aurand by NAA vice president Alex Burton, joined by Howard Evans (chief designer), Ed Horkey (chief of the technical section), and Frank Compton (engineering designer).

The Navy's need to counter the nimble MiG-15 over Korea was urgent, and NAA presenters emphasized that the company's well-established F-86 production line would give the Navy a competitive fighter in the least amount of time at the least expense. The program proceeded with unusual urgency. NAA issued a formal production proposal on February 6, and the Navy responded with a letter contract for three hundred production aircraft on February 10. On March 8, two prototypes, designated XFJ-2, were ordered under proposal NA-179.

These were simply F-86E-10 airframes modified for carrier operations. The standard J47-GE-13 engine was replaced with a J47-GE-2. The windshield was reworked to improve visibility for carrier landings. The seat and canopy were strengthened to withstand a 40 g deceleration. The landing gear was strengthened, and the nose gear was lengthened to provide a 3-degree, 50-minute positive deck stance (the nose gear strut could also be extended by hydraulic pressure, providing a positive angle of 7 degrees, 30 minutes). Catapult bridle hooks, a catapult holdback, a barrier guard, a barrier pickup, a retractable tail bumper, and a V-frame tailhook were installed. No armament or wing-folding system was installed, but the XFJ-2s were ballasted to approximate the weight of these features.[8] A third prototype was ordered on March 19 under contract number 51-756. It was designated XFJ-2B under proposal NA-185, for the sole purpose of serving as an armament test bed.[9] This was a minimally modified F-86E, with four 20 mm Colt Mk 12 cannons replacing the original six .50-caliber machine guns (a weapon system upgrade already in work for the Air Force). A detailed specification and formal contract were issued on May 29. Cmdr. Aurand was appointed project officer, and he conducted the mockup inspection on June 26–28, 1951, at the NAA Inglewood plant.

While the XFJ-2B was ordered last and carried the highest serial number, BuNo 133756, it required the least work and was completed first. Newly hired test pilot Robert "Bob" Hoover was in the cockpit when it took off from Los Angeles International Airport on December 27, 1951. Hoover, as peer to Chuck Yeager, had established a stellar reputation at the flight-test division of Wright Field. Hoover ended his military service at the end of 1948 and commenced a civilian test pilot career with the Allison Division of General Motors. He next joined North American in May 1950, when NAA was having difficulty recruiting test pilots after a series of mishaps with the XAJ-1 Savage. Hoover's earliest NAA test assignment was the F-86, which also prepared him to fly the similar Fury.

Shortly after Hoover's maiden flight, the XFJ-2B was detached to the Naval Ordnance Test Station at Inyokern, California, where its 20 mm cannon system was assessed. Inyokern is located 70 miles from the Inglewood plant, allowing North American's engineering and technical staff to respond immediately to any issues arising during evaluation.

The carrier-capable prototypes, BuNos 133754 and 133755, followed in early 1952. Hoover flew 754 on February 14, 1952, declared it ready for preliminary carrier assessment, and ferried it to Inyokern for evaluation. Bob Hoover recalled in his autobiography:

I was the first pilot to fly the Navy XFJ-2. Part of the flight testing involved carrier suitability, catapult take-offs[,] and arrested landings.

We tested the FJ-2 at Inyokern [sic] Naval Air Station and at the north base at Muroc. One test was to determine the airplane's capability to withstand enormous side loads on the landing gear.

To perform the test, I landed on a simulated carrier deck. On one occasion, the A-frame tail hook of the FJ-2 grabbed the arresting cable at 135 knots while I was executing a twenty-seven-foot off-center engagement that could be encountered on an aircraft carrier.

The seven-eighths pierced steel [cable] snapped and danced across the simulated carrier deck like an electric snake. I scrambled out of the cockpit, all the while thinking, "How many people have I killed?[10]

The snapped cable caused several injuries but no fatalities. By June 11, 1952, the XFJ-2 had completed tests at Inyokern and was flown to NATC Pax River, Maryland, for its full carrier suitability trials. Four hours after flying cross-country, Hoover's Fury was already making its first catapult test. RAdm. Thomas S. Combs, chief of the Bureau of Aeronautics, expressed pleasure with the progress of the test program with a telegram:

The performance of North American Aviation in accomplishing the carrier suitability demonstrations of the XFJ-2 at Inyokern and Patuxent River so expeditiously and successfully is considered commendable. This is especially true in view of the fact that this is the first time any contractor has attempted such a demonstration. Well done!

The second carrier-capable prototype, 755, joined the program on July 4, 1952. Together, the two XFJ-2s performed 113 field-catapult launches from a runway-installed H4B catapult; 127 field-arrested landings; twenty nighttime, nonarrested landings; and ten Davis barrier engagements at speeds ranging from 45.6 to 99.7 knots. Upon completion of the field tests, sea trials were conducted aboard USS *Midway*, whereby thirty-three launches with an H4-1 catapult and thirty-one arrested landings were accomplished. Other than 6 to 14 feet of altitude lost on minimum-airspeed launches, the Furys performed satisfactorily. Likewise, arrested landings, using an approach speed of 115–118 knots, were considered satisfactory; however, excessive flare upon landing caused tail bumper strikes, with some damage. The XFJ-2s were found to have "excellent slow[-]speed handling characteristics in the carrier approach and after the cut," thus dispelling BuAer's apprehension about swept-wing slow-flight behavior. Recommendations included improving the low-airspeed catapult characteristics to prevent excessive loss of altitude at the deck edge, improving the view of the carrier deck during the approach, and making the tail bumper retractable for catapult launching.[12]

The second prototype, 755, was lost to a crash in July 1952 during a routine ferry flight from Pax River to the Columbus plant. Carrier suitability trials were completed on December 17, 1952, using the remaining XFJ-2, 754. Meanwhile, production of FJ-2s was already underway at Columbus under contract number 51-642. The first production FJ-2, BuAer 131927, was accepted by the Navy in November 1952—a month before the XFJ-2 carrier tests concluded. Initial production was slowed because of the large Air Force F-86F commitment. Only seven FJ-2s had been delivered by the end of the Korean War. On April 30, 1953, the Navy amended the contract to reducing the order to two hundred aircraft (from the original three hundred), with delivery to be completed by August 1954.

Production FJ-2s differed from the prototypes, with increased wing flap deflection from 38 to 45 degrees, increasing the horizontal tail area from 35 to 47 square feet and removal of the dihedral, rework of the nose to improve forward visibility, installation of a Martin-Baker ejection seat with height adjustment, arching the canopy rails to provide better visibility with the canopy closed and clearance for the pilot's helmet with the seat raised, incorporation of a wing-folding system, increasing the main landing-gear track by 8 inches, and installation of the XFJ-2B four 20 mm cannon armament system.

Before the FJ-2 was assigned to frontline service, the Navy Board of Inspection and Survey commenced acceptance trials for the FJ-2 in compliance with naval regulations. Eleven Furys were deployed to the NATC, where each division carried out a full battery of tests. Carrier suitability, armament, engine performance, stability and control, electronics, and service suitability were examined in exhaustive detail.

The results were troubling. While the FJ-2 substantially met or exceeded its performance guarantees without wing tanks, it could not achieve the necessary range or duration without them. Yet, the installation of wing tanks deteriorated performance to an unacceptable level. Separately, the maintenance required for flight readiness was excessive, a distinct handicap in carrier operations (the aggregate time required to remove and replace some components was 189 percent of the contract allowance). Also, the landing gear and arresting system were found to be structurally deficient.

But most damning was the armament system, which was deemed unsatisfactory for service use. Early tests revealed empty shell casings impacting the lower fuselage, wing skin, and tail surfaces. North American devised a storage bin to capture the spent shells, but accumulation of dangerous gun gases and gun jamming remained a concern. Gun alignment was a more intractable problem. The cannons converged below the aircraft roll axis, intending to make aiming in high-g situations easier, but the opposite effect was achieved. It was impossible to cure this defect without reworking the fuselage design, so the FJ-2 remained hobbled by chronic target acquisition and tracking problems.[12]

From the outset, the FJ-2 was intended to equip Marine squadrons in Korea, but the F-86F backlog at Columbus delayed Fury production until after the truce. When FJ-2 Fury was finally available in January 1954, it had become apparent that it was only marginally suitable for carrier operations. As a result, almost all were assigned to Marine units as air superiority fighters flown from land bases. The assignments were split between three Atlantic and three Pacific squadrons. The first unit to receive Furys was VMF-122 at Marine Corps Air Station (MCAS) Cherry Point, North Carolina, in January 1954. Maj. Johnny Vance,

Like a kit bash, the FJ-1 Fury featured the wings of a P-51 Mustang attached to a jet airplane, yielding an excellent interim naval air transition tool from propeller-driven aircraft to swept-wing jets. Swept wings and wings that folded followed on the FJ-2 Fury.

squadron commander, developed an intense flying schedule that committed a quarter of his pilots to be constantly aloft. His goal was to amass a thousand flight hours per month, with each pilot flying at least one sortie per day. In short order the squadron became highly proficient and, in March 1955, took their Furys to sea aboard USS *Coral Sea* for a six-month Mediterranean cruise. In the Pacific, VMF-235, based at MCAS El Toro, California, acquired FJ-2s to replace their F4U-4 Corsairs in the spring of 1954. They participated in steam catapult trials aboard USS *Hancock* that June (CVA-19 *Hancock* was the first carrier fitted with C-11 steam catapults) and deployed to Atsugi, Japan, where they flew their FJ-2s until 1957. VMF-232 acquired FJ-2s in 1955, operating them from MCAS Kaneohe Bay, Hawaii, until early 1957. VMF-312, VMF-334, and VMF-451 also flew FJ-2s, but frontline service for the FJ-2 was cut short by its numerous limitations. By 1957, FJ-2s were relegated to naval reserve units in Columbus and St. Louis.

The FJ-2 disappointment was predictable in hindsight. After demonstrating the feasibility of jet carrier operations with straight-winged FH-1 Phantoms and FJ-1 Furys, the Navy was rushed to develop a swept-wing fighter in response to the appearance of MiG-15s in Korea. The Air Force's successful F-86 seemed a ready-made solution; however, adapting a shore-based aircraft for naval service has always been difficult and often unsuccessful (the F-111B comes to mind). Several mistakes were made in the Navy's haste that ensured marginal performance. The Fury airframe gained nearly 1,000 pounds with the addition of wing-folding and arrestment systems, while retaining

A formation of Marine Fury jets fly by Mt. Fuji in Japan. The US military (Army, Navy, and Air Force) has maintained a ongoing presence and symbiotic military relationship with Japan since the ending of World War II.

the existing 6,000-pound-thrust J47 engine (in common with the F-86). Internal fuel capacity was limited to the extent that drag-inducing external fuel tanks were mandatory for most missions—thus deteriorating Fury performance even further. Cannon alignment problems yielded an inaccurate armament system. In sum, the FJ-2 joined the FJ-1 as little more than a technology demonstrator, by proving that a swept-wing jet could reliably operate from an aircraft carrier—while only rarely doing so.

FJ-3 Fury

Even before volume production of the FJ-2 was underway at Columbus, the Navy knew more performance was needed from their swept-wing fighter. In 1950, the Wright Aeronautical Corporation obtained a license to build the promising British-designed "Sapphire" turbojet engine, which produced 7,800 pounds of static thrust at sea level. Since the FJ-2's General Electric J-47 engine yielded only 6,000 pounds of thrust, the Navy became interested in evaluating the Wright engine in a Fury. After two years of delay, early examples of the license-built Sapphire, now designated J65, became available. In March 1952, the fifth production FJ-2, BuNo 131931, was taken from the

assembly line, fitted with a Wright J65-W-2 engine, and given North American designation NA-196. This FJ-2 remained stock in all respects except for the engine. The Navy was so certain that the Wright engine would overcome the weight penalty of carrier equipment that they issued contract number 52-987 for 389 units fifteen months before this reengined FJ-2 flew. When it finally flew on July 3, 1953, no significant problems emerged other than the need for increased mass airflow to the engine. The first production example, BuNo 135774, came off the assembly line five months later, in December 1953. Production units featured enlarged air inlets, additional cockpit armor, increased ammunition capacity, a J65-W-4 engine of 7,650 pounds' thrust, and a new designation—FJ-3.

Meanwhile, BuAer adopted a new procurement program named FIRM (fleet introduction of replacement models), intended to accelerate the introduction of new aircraft. The FJ-3 was the first plane to be developed under the plan. Under FIRM, experimental prototypes were eliminated and low-rate production was started immediately. When sufficient airplanes were available, they were assigned to four separate test programs, all conducted simultaneously. The first were assigned to the contractor for investigation of the flight envelope and safety-of-flight demonstrations. Any modifications found necessary during these contractor

Navy Fury fighters in the Columbus factory. The airframes ride individual carts that are hitched nose to tail and move forward in unison on a "pulse" assembly line. On the periphery, a few Air Force F-100 Super Sabres have been squeezed in for mechanical work.

tests were incorporated in the production line. Subsequent aircraft were assigned to the Board of Inspection and Survey (BIS) trials to ensure that contract guarantees were met, and that the aircraft was suitable for fleet operation. Other aircraft were assigned to the NATC for stability and control, engine performance, armament, electronics, and service test evaluations. The final group was assigned to the fleet introduction program (FIP), where the aircraft were operated by fleet personnel in a squadron environment.

Twenty-four FJ-3s had been produced by July 1954—enough to start the evaluation at Pax River. Two aircraft were assigned to the service test division for acceptance trials, using test pilots from the NATC, while six others were assigned to the fleet introduction program, using pilots from VC-3 and VF-173. The fleet introduction cycle was conducted over six weeks, during which two FJ-3s were lost from causes unrelated to aircraft defects. One suffered an engine explosion from foreign-object ingestion, while the other ditched in the Pax River because of fuel exhaustion. Together, these eight test airplanes accumulated 1,326.4 hours of flight time, allowing the NATC to conclude that the FJ-3 was a promising day fighter. The Wright J65 provided the thrust needed to make it outperform other fighters in the fleet at the time (it was compared to the F7U-3 and F9F-8), but the performance came at a cost—engine reliability. During trials, the seventeen engines were installed in the test airplanes. A history of oil seal

leaks in the front main bearing, resulting in numerous engine seizures, compressor and turbine blade rubbing, and difficult air starts above 25,000 feet were the primary problems. Each of these issues was either resolved or minimized, but even after the FJ-3 entered fleet service, grounding orders were frequent. Whenever one problem seemed solved, another arose. Some deficiencies, such as cannon alignment, were inherited from the FJ-2 and were impossible to correct without a major redesign. Capt. Robert Dreesen, USN (Ret.), a NATC test pilot, recalled:

[The FJ-3 was] a lively, comfortable, very smooth-flying aircraft that could take almost anything else in the air at the time in a dogfight situation. It could fly rings around the F9F-8, for example. But it was a lousy aircraft for air-to-air combat because of a design innovation in the FJ-2 carried over to the FJ-3. Someone in BuAer had decided that it would be a big advantage if the gun fire line were adjusted downward so that under a specified set of flight conditions, the gun line would correspond to the actual aiming point. The problem was that for all other combinations of flight conditions, the gun line was way below the roll axis. This made tracking a moving target very difficult. Testing the FJ-2 at Patuxent had established this problem[,] but by the time the report was in it was too late to make a change for the FJ-3. . . . Every aircraft in the fleet could outshoot the Fury against target banners.[13]

The FJ-3 continued to evolve as production accelerated. Early airplanes were delivered to the fleet with the slatted wing inherited from the F-86F. But improved F-86 performance was being reported from Korea with a new wing that eliminated the movable slats and replaced them

The Soviet MiG-15 arrived in Korea in November 1950 as a complete surprise to Western intelligence. Nothing could match them in a dogfight until the arrival of the NAA F-86—and even then, piloting skills were critical. Museum of Flight

with an extended leading edge. This fixed leading-edge wing, known as the "6-3" wing, was extended 6 inches at the root and 3 inches at the tip. It provided high-speed benefits and greater maneuverability but also created low-speed handling characteristics that seemed unacceptable for carrier operations. To determine whether the wing could be adapted to the Fury, the third FJ-2, BuNo 131929, was modified to receive the "6-3" wing with a full-chord fence at midspan, intended to improve low-speed behavior. The wing displayed an abrupt stall with sudden yaw-and-roll tendencies. A second full-chord fence was installed near the tip, but it produced equally disappointing results.

Finally, in October 1954, after a year of tests, 131929 was fitted with midspan and wingtip fences that extended only over the leading edge. The result was benign stall behavior in all conditions, with adequate stall warning. But the problem of excessive stall speed remained. NAA

engineers at Columbus, led by Pete Marshall, studied NACA airfoil research and experimented with a drooped (cambered) leading edge that reduced the stall speed to an acceptable level. NATC tests found that the cambered leading edge provided considerable improvement in turning performance, which increased with altitude. Airspeed was maintained better in a high-g turn, the 1 g buffet at 48,000 feet was eliminated and the limit g was increased, and the new wing provided an additional 14 square feet of wing area and carried 124 gallons of additional fuel—all highly desirable benefits from a tactical standpoint. The cambered "6-3" wing was employed on all FJ-3s from BuNo 136118 onward, and it was retrofitted on earlier FJ-3s.[14]

Even before the cambered leading edge was adopted, five miniature fences were installed on FJ-2 and -3 leading edges. These had no aerodynamic effect but instead acted as barricade engagement devices to prevent restraining

Hinged wings were installed on the F-86 Sabre–inspired Fury design. The FJ-2 Fury was then easier to park on a crowded aircraft carrier; however, the trade-off was increased weight, cost, and complexity.

straps from sliding along the leading edge and yanking the airplane to one side or the other during barricade impact. One fence was mounted inboard of the slat, while four others were mounted on the slat. These "barricade guards" were carried over to the "6-3" wing after the elimination of slats.[15]

Starting with the 345th production airplane, BuNo 131681, four additional underwing pylons were installed to increase the FJ-3's ordnance capability. In this configuration, the Fury could carry 500-pound bombs or rocket pods on the inner stations, 1,000-pound bombs or AIM-9 Sidewinder missiles on the intermediate stations, and 200-gallon fuel tanks on the outboard stations. These late production Furys (194 units) were designated FJ-3M and became the Navy's first aircraft to employ Sidewinder missiles operationally and were considered the most capable air-to-air fighters of the time.

During flight testing the high Mach characteristics of the FJ-3 were found to be identical to the FJ-2, which was considered undesirable. Between Mach 0.93 and 0.96, a rudder buzz made tracking extremely difficult. North American corrected this discrepancy with a "splitter plate" rudder that was installed on all production aircraft from BuNo 139230 onward. A similar "splitter plate" elevator was installed on some aircraft but didn't seem to be a production change.

In September 1954, VF-173, which had participated in the FIP test cycle two months earlier, became the first squadron to receive the new Fury. By May 1955, after a period of intense workup, the squadron qualified and deployed aboard USS Bennington (CV-20) for the FJ-3's first cruise. Another notable FJ-3 squadron was VF-51, the same squadron that achieved fame under Cmdr. Pete Aurand with the first Fury, the FJ-1. VF-51 became responsible for developing much of the FJ-3's tactical usage and displayed its effectiveness in the 1957 Naval Air Weapons Meet at Naval Air Station El Centro, California, where the commanding officer, Cmdr. Alex Vraciu, achieved the highest individual score.

A second Fury squadron, VF-211, achieved fame in August 1956 with the deployment of the first Sidewinder-equipped FJ-3Ms aboard USS Bon Homme Richard (CV-31). That same month, slightly more than two and a half years after the first FJ-3 rolled off the Columbus production line; the 538th unit was delivered, marking the completion of FJ-3/3M production.

Between 1954 and 1958, the FJ-3 and -3M served with twenty Navy and six Marine frontline squadrons,[16] but its career was short. By 1958, newer and more-capable fighters such as the Vought F8U Crusader entered service, and the FJ-3 was relegated to utility and reserve squadron duties. FJ-3 service was bracketed by the Korean and Vietnam Wars. While never firing a shot in anger and along with the Grumman F9F Cougar, it established routine carrier operations for swept-wing fighters. Two carrier milestones were established: On August 22, 1955, Cmdr. Robert G. Dose, the officer over Air Development Squadron 3 (VC-3), made the first "deck mirror landing system" arrestment flying an FJ-3 aboard USS Bennington (CV-20). The mirror system was devised by the British for their angled-deck carriers in 1954. It proved very precise and eliminated the need for manual signals from a landing signal officer (LSO). Less than five months later, on January 3, 1956, the commander of Air Task Group 181, Cmdr. Ralph L. Werner, flying an FJ-3, made the first landing aboard USS Forrestal (CVA-59), a new supercarrier designed expressly for jet operations.

Controlling the Regulus

In addition to serving as a frontline fighter with twenty-six squadrons, the FJ-3 played an important role in one of the most significant defense programs of the Cold War—the Regulus cruise missile. Regulus was a fighter-sized missile powered by an Allison J33 turbojet that could be launched under its own power from a runway or boosted into flight with JATO bottles from the deck of a carrier, cruiser, or submarine. It had a range of over 500 miles at near-sonic speed, and it could carry a nuclear warhead, striking with great accuracy for that time. However, it required guidance from a piloted aircraft to direct it in flight. Several aircraft types were modified to direct the Regulus, but the Fury, under the designation FJ-3D (DF-1C after September 1962), served as the missile's most successful director.

Origins of the Regulus program can be traced to a 1943 study by Chance Vought for a missile with a 300-mile range carrying a 4,000-pound payload. World War II priorities caused the study to be shelved until 1947. It was revived in response to a Navy requirement for a missile that could be launched from a submarine carrying a 3,000-pound warhead over 500 miles at Mach 0.85. Vought was awarded a contract to build five test articles, and the first flew on November 22, 1950. After a successful runway takeoff and climb to 3,500 feet, the test vehicle crashed due to a control system failure. Eighteen weeks later, on March 29, 1951, a second Regulus was successfully flown, followed by a string of thirteen successful test flights over the next eight months. During early development, Regulus test missiles were directed by Lockheed TV-2D jet trainers carrying two pilots—one to control the missile (the "able" pilot), the other to fly the jet (the "baker" pilot). As the Regulus flight envelope expanded, the TV-2D was hard pressed to keep up with the speedy missile. The twin-engine, straight-wing McDonnell F2H-2P Banshee was the first carrier-capable aircraft converted to Regulus controller, but its performance was still inadequate to effectively guide the missile. The swept-wing Grumman F9F-6D was modified for the job, but it also struggled.

The SSM-M-8 Regulus was a ship- and submarine-launched, air-breathing nuclear cruise missile active from 1953 to 1960. It is seen here on public display. Various Navy jets of the era flew chase missions. Mike Machat

So, it fell to the FJ-3, the hottest fighter of the day, to direct the Regulus. Converted from stock and redesignated FJ-3D, the Fury received an AN/ARW-55 radio control system in place of its standard AN/APG-30 radar. Knobs and switches mounted on the instrument panel and left cockpit wall provided full control of the Regulus (roll, pitch, yaw, throttle, and landing gear). The pilot flew the Fury with his right hand while commanding the Regulus with his left. The first FJ-3D was delivered to GMGRU-1 in May 1956 and proved to be a significant improvement over the other missile controllers.

According to F-86 historian Duncan Curtis, some FJ-3s were converted to the FJ-3D configuration immediately after production, while others served in tactical squadrons before being converted. The oldest aircraft to be converted was the seventh Fury, BuNo 135780, which was assigned to NAMC

A solid-fuel booster from Rocketdyne gets the Regulus into the air and underway before the air-breathing jet engine takes over for the cruise portion of the flight. The concept of cruise missiles derived from the World War II–era Nazi V-1 "buzz-bomb." Mike Machat

Point Mugu, California, where it was written off in 1957. Others such as 139244, the 423rd Fury and possibly the last FJ-3D conversion, entered service directly as a missile/drone controller.[17] FJ-3D missions included controlling the Regulus as a flight test vehicle, as a fleet-training missile, as a tactical missile, as an assault missile, and as a target drone. FJ-3D pilots also directed Regulus surrogates such as the F9F-2KD and F9F-5KD Panthers for initial training and to further build proficiency during equipment readiness exercises.

In 1956, Regulus I was superseded by a dramatically improved Regulus II capable of Mach 2 speed and 1,200-nautical-mile range. Regulus II was designed for an inertial guidance system and didn't require a constant radio command link, but early test flights still used a chase aircraft (TV-2D) for takeoff and landing control. There is no record of FJ-3D use in the Regulus II program. The missile's performance required the use of an F8U-1 Crusader during the cruise portion of the test, but even the Crusader had difficulty keeping the missile in sight.[18] Forty-eight test flights of Regulus II were conducted before the project was canceled on November 19, 1958. By then, Vought had delivered twenty missiles, with twenty-seven more on the production line.

The fleet of FJ-3D and FJ-3D2 Furys, which historian Curtis estimates at sixty aircraft, continued to fly as Regulus I controllers. In total, 514 Regulus I missiles were built, and they averaged 3.5 flights per missile. It remained in service as a target drone and training missile until June 6, 1966.[19] The FJ-3D2 was specifically configured to control F9F-6K Cougars and KDA target drones. The last two FJ-3D2 Furys operated by the Navy were retired from VU-5, Detachment B, Naha (Japan) Naval Air Facility, in 1963. By then the FJ-3D was redesignated DF-1C and the FJ-3D2 became DF-1D under the Department of Defense Tri-Service designation scheme of 1962.

FJ-4 Fury

On June 5, 1953, one month before the prototype FJ-3 made its maiden flight, Lee Atwood, president of North American, submitted a proposal for an even more advanced variant of the Fury. The proposal, titled "Improved FJ-3," was in response to the Navy's requirement for a Mach 0.95 interceptor with two-hour endurance on internal fuel, with fleet delivery to begin within two years. This requirement arose from the sudden cancellation of McDonnell's F3H Demon program due to its flawed Westinghouse J40 engine. Frank Compton, North American's chief of preliminary design, started to work on the proposal in February 1953, five months before it was submitted to the Navy.

The improved Fury would use the same 7,700-pound static-thrust Sapphire turbojet that powered the FJ-3, but in aerodynamic terms the FJ-3 was not far removed from the 1947-vintage XP-86. The improvement, therefore, was expected from extensive airframe refinements to reduce weight, increase range, provide a higher combat ceiling, increase maximum speed, and improve mission cycle time. The proposal promised a flying prototype in only ten months, with delivery of the first production article eight months thereafter. The deadlines were particularly risky since this redesigned Fury represented the first complete aircraft project—from concept to delivery—ever undertaken at the Columbus Division. The Navy viewed the proposal favorably and issued a limited approval on June 12. North American assigned project designators NA-208 to the two prototypes while reserving NA-209 for the production models. Work on the prototypes progressed rapidly, and on October 16 the Navy ordered forty-three production examples with the official designation, FJ-4. Another 107 units were added to the order on July 26, 1954.

Because of the tight schedule, Compton's group planned to rely heavily on the FJ-3, but the internal fuel requirement alone dictated a new design. Aside from the engine ducting, much of the FJ-4 became a new airplane. The wing was entirely new, featuring increased area (over 36 additional square feet) with a reduced thickness ratio (40 percent thinner.) The 35 percent wing sweep of the earlier Furys was retained, but the wing became more tapered (the tip was much shorter than the root), which required 4 degrees of washout (twist) for lateral stability.

Six .50-caliber machine guns were built into the forward fuselage of initial batches of Sabre jets. The Korean War demanded more firepower, so they were replaced with four 20 mm cannons. Aircraft guns are boresighted and then test-fired.

Highly educated and creative people have devoted entire careers to machining airplane parts. Most aluminum purchased by the aerospace industry is recycled as scrap before the airplane rolls out. Milling machines grind it away, using bits and tools of various size. More metal is lost to drilling. Punches might make holes for airliner windows. Seat leg and other castings are ground smaller, creating voids called "lightener." Wings are no exception. For centuries, people have known that acid will eat away at metal. The aircraft industry calls this chemical milling. The exact time that metal is exposed to the harsh chemicals determines the amount of metal removed. It is one of the techniques used to achieve the optimum thickness of wing parts in the perpetual trade-off among weight, shape, and strength.

The thinner wing required a redesigned main landing gear, resulting in a "trailing beam" shock-absorbing leg. The footprint (distance between the right and left tires) was increased by nearly 3 feet. The thinner wing also

This three-view line drawing depicts the FJ-3 Fury. Line art is an enduring tool for documenting the dimensions and outline of an airplane.

necessitated midspan ailerons, which limited the area available for landing flaps, so a "gipper" slotted flap system was developed by Paul Titus, which was coupled to a droopable leading edge, providing adequate lift and drag without diminishing internal fuel volume.[20] Tail surfaces were also thinned and increased in area while retaining the sweep of the FJ-3. After early test flights, the vertical fin, which was already taller than the FJ-3's, received another 10 inches of height to increase directional stability. The fuselage was deepened, with a dorsal spine running between the canopy and the vertical fin to provide volume for a 50 percent increase in internal fuel. To save weight, the forward cockpit armor was deleted, and the ammunition capacity was reduced to 576 rounds from the 648 rounds carried in the FJ-3. Cannon alignment was depressed only 2.5 degrees from the fuselage datum line rather than the 6.5 degrees used on the FJ-2 and FJ-3, resulting in much-improved gun tracking. Four wing stations were provided, all capable of carrying Sidewinder missiles. The inboard stations could also carry drop tanks or 2,000 pounds of stores, while the outboard stations could carry 500 pounds.

While prototype construction was underway, vice president of engineering George Gerkins assembled a flight test group for the Columbus Division. Jim Pearson, who had been prominent in the XAJ-1 Savage test program at Inglewood, was appointed manager of flight test and chief pilot. One of Pearson's early hires was Dick Wenzell, who had graduated at the top of his class from the Navy's Test Pilot School. Wenzell's first assignment was the FJ-4 program, where he flew the prototype, BuNo 139279, on October 28, 1954. A slight directional instability was the only problem he encountered, which was fixed by adding a 10-inch extension to the fin. Describing the FJ-4's flying qualities in *Approach* magazine, Wenzell writes:

Tremendous engineering design efforts have been expended on the FJ-4[,] and a continuous stream of development flights have followed the first flight in October 1954, to provide a sturdy, capable, comfortable, and easy handling airplane. . . . The airplane is much easier to maneuver on the ground because of the wider landing gear and less weight on the nose than the FJ-3. . . . [In the air] the FJ-4 has excellent maneuvering characteristics at combat gross weights due to the relatively low wing loading, the cambered airfoil section, washed out wingtips[,] and stall fences.

Because of these features, the buffet boundary is high and accelerated stalls are characterized by an increase in airframe buffet intensity as the stall is approached and a mild porpoise with no marked tendency to roll off or yaw if stalled. Recovery is easily affected by easing the stick forward toward neutral. Considerable maneuvering ability exists at combat ceiling.

The airplane exhibits very good landing characteristics. However, like any modern high-performance airplane, airspeed and sink rate must be kept under positive control for consistently safe landings (use engine thrust to regulate sink rate and pitch attitude to control airspeed).

Landings in 90-degree, 30-knot crosswinds have been executed with relative ease, crabbing to correct for drift. The wing-down method may result in damage to a wingtip in a severe crosswind.[21]

During 1955, the first seventeen FJ-4s were produced, followed by 113 more in 1956. By the end of March 1957, all 150 aircraft had been delivered. Seven of the early production aircraft were assigned to the NATC for preliminary evaluation.[22] The test program, which ran from December 15, 1955, until April 30, 1957, revealed several deficiencies in the new Fury. Ineffective speed brake operation, pitch oscillations at various airspeeds, asymmetrical wheel braking on landing rollout, excessive tailpipe temperatures above 45,000 feet, and excessive engine vibration between 60 and 85 percent rpm were some of the vexing problems. But overall, the test program concluded that FJ-4 was superior to any other nonafterburning jet then in service. With a top speed of 680 mph at sea level and 631 mph at 35,000 feet, rate of climb of 7,600 feet per minute at sea level, and a combat ceiling of 46,800 feet, the Fury outperformed its contemporaries; however, range was its most impressive attribute—1,485 miles on internal fuel and 2,020 miles with 200-gallon drop tanks.

Most of the 152 FJ-4s produced were distributed to eight different Marine squadrons (VMA-212, -214, -223, -232, -235, -323, -334, and -451), starting with VMF-451 in September 1956. They were considered a vast improvement over the FJ-2s that most Marine squadrons had operated. Drop tanks were seldom needed since range on internal fuel was adequate for most missions. An exception was the historic VMF-323 nonstop, non-air-refueled flight of sixteen FJ-4s from NAS Cubi Point, Philippines, to NAS Atsugi, Japan—1,940 miles distant. While five aircraft were forced to land short at Iwakuni due to external fuel tank problems, eleven Furys completed the record-setting trip.

FJ-4B: The Improved "Improvement"

The FJ-4 achieved nearly all the performance goals promised in the June 1953 "Improved FJ-3" proposal, and it was regarded as the best nonafterburning fighter of its time. But there were still shortcomings, and the Navy fighter community rejected it in favor of the supersonic F8U Crusader.[23] Simultaneously, the advent of smaller and lighter ordnance made carrier attack aircraft the perfect delivery vehicle for the Navy's nuclear ambitions. Initially

the Navy modified existing fighters such as the F2H-2 Banshee and F9F-8 Cougar to carry tactical nuclear weapons, but new aircraft were needed to take full advantage of this breakthrough. Douglas Aircraft Company (DAC) proposed a light (15,000 pounds gross weight) airplane, which evolved into the A4D Skyhawk. In mid-1954, North American chose to rework the FJ-4, giving it the attributes of an effective attack aircraft. Columbus engineers started working on "the improvements for the improved Fury."

Upgrades included stiffening the wing structure for two additional underwing ordnance stations, bringing the total to six, doubling the speed brake area with the addition of two ventral panels, and adding a low-altitude bombing system (LABS) for tactical nuclear-weapon delivery. The LABS delivery technique, developed by the Air Force in 1952 (where it was called "toss bombing"), consisted of a high-speed, low-altitude approach to the target followed by an abrupt pull-up into a half loop. The bomb was released during the vertical climb, slinging it in an arced trajectory to the target. The aircraft continued the climb into a half loop, rolled upright, and escaped from the blast zone in the opposite direction from its entry.[24]

From the outset the Navy was eager to place the new attack Fury in fleet service and ordered twenty-five production units on July 26, 1954. The order was increased by forty-six units on November 2, 1954, and again by 151 units on April 5, 1956. Total production orders reached 222 aircraft eight months before the first FJ-4B (BuNo 139531) was flown by Dick Wenzell on December 3, 1956 (some sources list December 4). Testing and early production went smoothly, with fleet deliveries beginning in 1957. The fleet indoctrination program for the FJ-4B was performed by VA-126 and VMF-223 at Moffett Field in California, where emphasis was placed on perfecting the LABS techniques for the delivery of tactical nuclear weapons. In service the FJ-4B never delivered a live nuclear weapon, but the feasibility

This side view of the FJ-4 demonstrates the steep angle of attack imparted by the longer nose gear and fuselage dorsal unique to the final version of the Fury.

of the concept was proven in the early 1960s when a Fury carrying a dummy Mk. 28 bomb and external fuel tanks flew from NAS Quonset Point, Rhode Island, to NAS Mayport, Florida, delivered the ordnance from treetop level, and returned to Quonset Point, a combat radius of more than 820 nautical miles.

FJ-4B production was completed by May 1958, with ten Pacific Fleet squadrons (VA-55, -56, -63, -116, -126, -146, -151, -192, -212, -216) and three West Coast Marine squadrons (VMA-212, -214, -223) receiving the new Fury. The FJ-4B (and the earlier FJ-4) was also assigned to numerous test and utility squadrons. Some were equipped to direct missiles and drones, but unlike the FJ-3D and FJ-3D2, they never received a "D" designation.

The FJ-4B was also equipped to carry up to five ASM-N-7 Bullpup air-to-surface guided missiles on its underwing pylons. The guidance transmitter pod was mounted on a sixth pylon, on the inner starboard. The Fury pilot visually guided the missile to its ground target through a radio link, using a small control stick, keeping it aligned through his gunsight. The system proved highly accurate during testing by VX-4 at Point Mugu, California, in late 1956. A total of eighty-five missiles were launched during the evaluation program, and by the end an airborne reliability of 85.7 per cent was achieved. The FJ-4Bs of VA-212 made the first overseas deployment with the Bullpup aboard USS *Lexington* in April 1959.

The FJ-4B was also capable of carrying a buddy refueling package consisting of a hose and drogue that extended from an external fuel tank, allowing the transfer of 3,000 pounds of fuel to another aircraft. The system was used operationally by VA-151 during a cruise aboard USS *Bennington* in June 1958.

The 1958 Taiwan Strait crisis was a conflict that took place between the People's Republic of China (PRC) and the Republic of China (ROC). In this conflict, the PRC shelled the islands of Quemoy and the Matsu Islands along the east coast of mainland China. In response to the shelling incident, Col. Paul J. Fontaine organized "Operation Cannonball" to reinforce the Marine units deployed in Taiwan. In August 1958, twenty-four FJ-4Bs of VMA-212 and VMA-214 became the first single-seat aircraft to cross the Pacific in squadron strength. The FJ-4B's exceptional range coupled with its aerial-refueling ability made the record-breaking flight possible.

By the early 1960s, the FJ-4 and FJ-4B were withdrawn from frontline service. VA-216 completed the last FJ-4B fleet deployment on August 20, 1960, aboard USS *Hancock*, and VMA-214 flew their last Fury from Marine Corps Air Station Kaneohe, Hawaii, to NAS Barbers Point, Hawaii, on January 23, 1962. On October 1, 1962, the FJ-4 and FJ-4B were redesignated F-1E and AF-1E, under the Department of Defense uniform designation system. The Furys continued in reserve and training service at Andrews AFB and Naval Air Stations Gynco, Memphis, Atlanta, Glenview, New Orleans, and Willow Grove until 1964, when they were retired and stored at the Naval Air Facility, Litchfield Park, Arizona.

FJ-4F Fury

On August 12, 1955, only ten months after the FJ-4 maiden flight, initial design work started on NAA project NA-234, a rocket-assisted variant designated the FJ-4F. The second and fourth production Furys (BuNos 139282 and 139284) were modified to receive North American Rocketdyne AR-1 rocket engines mounted above the tailpipes of their standard J65 turbojets. The AR-1 ran on a mixture of hydrogen peroxide and JP-4 jet fuel, producing 6,000 pounds of thrust under throttle control. The FJ-4Fs were flown with removable instrumented nose cones and flush belly tanks. While the rocket engine enhanced performance dramatically by setting unofficial speed (Mach 1.41) and altitude records (71,000 feet),[25] the FJ-4F never went into production, serving primarily as a test bed for the Rocketdyne engine. In 1960, both FJ-4Fs were retired to Litchfield Park.

F-86F and F-86H: The Fury's Cousins

On September 29, 1950, shortly after NAA opened the Columbus Division, an F-86F production line was

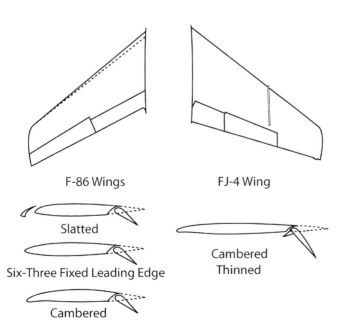

F-86 Wings

FJ-4 Wing

Slatted

Six-Three Fixed Leading Edge

Cambered

Cambered Thinned

The line drawing documents the difference between the F-86 and FJ-series wing. Aerodynamicists utilize wind tunnels for testing and then validate concepts by flight-testing modified aircraft.

constructed at the new plant. Demand for the air superiority fighter exceeded NAA's ability to deliver them on time from Inglewood, so a second source was established in Ohio. The Air Force issued contract AF-18988 on September 6, 1951, for 441 Columbus-built units, but production was slowed by an inexperienced work force. The first aircraft did not fly until May 1952, and the order was incomplete until January 1953. The entire lot was delivered to stateside training units. Meanwhile, the Air Force also issued a requirement for a fighter-bomber version of the F-86F that could carry four underwing stores, but this left no room for external fuel tanks. The combat-radius was barely 50 miles in this configuration. The problem was addressed by adding two inboard pylons for drop tanks, but the limits of the F-86F had been reached.

By the end of the Korean War, the Air Force was convinced that it needed a purpose-built fighter-bomber to replace the modified, overburdened F-86F. Design work on a dedicated fighter-bomber variant started at Inglewood on March 16, 1951; the mockup was completed by July. While retaining its F-86 heritage, the mockup reflected a substantially redesigned airplane. The nose intake was enlarged for the airflow needs of its J73 engine, which produced 8,920 pounds of thrust, or 3,000 pounds more

than the J47 installed in the F-86F. The enlarged inlet required deepening the fuselage, which, in turn, provided the benefit of increased internal fuel capacity. The tail surface area was increased from 35.3 to 47.2 square feet, and the dihedral angle was removed from the horizontal stabilizer. A clamshell canopy and ejection seat were adopted from the F-86D. Four underwing stations were provided for stores or drop tanks. Only the landing gear and wing assembly were retained from the F-86F.

The Air Force designated the new variant F-86H and ordered two prototypes plus a static-test article on November 3, 1952. The prototypes were built at Inglewood, but production was assigned to Columbus. The first prototype, serial number 52-1975, was flown by NAA test pilot Joe Lynch on April 30, 1953. Early test flying was performed with the original slatted wing, but a new 6-3 wing was installed when the F-86H was sent to Edwards AFB for Phase II testing. The 6-3 wing, which featured a leading edge extended by 6 inches at the root and 3 inches at the tip and no slats, improved speed and maneuverability on the F-86F—but not on the F-86H. Test flight reports recommended that the wing should be extended by 12 inches at each tip, but that modification didn't produce the desired result. High-altitude maneuverability was poor,

The F-86 was nearing the end of the line with the F-86H. The more powerful Pratt & Whitney J57 engine would need a new airframe, and that became the F-100. The F-100 was the first US fighter to achieve supersonic speed in level flight.

and behavior in the landing pattern was substantially worse than the slatted wing. Over 130 test flights with various wing configurations were conducted, and ultimately a slatted version of the 6-3 wing with the 12-inch tip extensions was found acceptable.[26]

The first Columbus-built production aircraft flew on September 4, 1953, and deliveries to various test facilities started eight months later. Thirteen aircraft were assigned to Edwards, Eglin, and Wright-Patterson AFBs by the end of June 1954. Deliveries were halted after a series of accidents. The sixth production aircraft, 52-1982, was lost on May 24 at Edwards AFB. When deliveries started again on August 2, another accident occurred almost immediately. Air Force captain Joseph McConnell (a Korean War ace with sixteen MiG-15 kills) was killed in 52-1981 on August 25. It was reported that McConnell's Sabre suffered a complete hydraulic failure, but the accident report concluded that it was a loss of pitch control due to an improperly secured elevator control rod. It was reported that he tried to land the stricken aircraft on the lake bed, using elevator trim, but it became uncontrollable. McConnell's ejection was initiated below 500 feet—too low for parachute deployment.[27] In September 1954, Maj. John Armstrong set a 500-kilometer closed-circuit speed record of 649 mph at the National Air Races in Dayton, Ohio. Another F-86H, flown by Capt. Eugene Sonnenberg, set a 100 km closed-circuit record of 692.8 mph. Unfortunately, Armstrong was killed two days later while trying to beat Sonnenberg's record.

The high-thrust General Electric J73 had developmental problems, which resulted in several F-86H losses. A rash of flameouts occurred because of frozen variable inlet guides. Differential expansion between the blade and the housing allowed the guides to freeze in the open position when power was reduced in the landing pattern, resulting in flameouts. Engine starter failures were also common. One failure during an engine start caused a fire that consumed the entire aircraft. The F-86H was the only production aircraft to use the J73 engine, and the engine was produced in four variants that were not interchangeable. An airframe modification was required before another engine variant could be installed, and limited use of the J73 affected spare-parts availability, making maintenance difficult.

The F-86H, designed as a fighter-bomber, was equipped with LABS (low-altitude bombing system) equipment, which provided tactical nuclear capability. The system, which used a 1,200-pound Mk. 12 nuclear device, was originally developed for the F-86F-35 block at Inglewood. It was installed on all F-86Hs (after the fifth unit) and all FJ-4B Furys built at Columbus. Early F-86Hs were armed with the six .50-caliber guns system used on the F-86F. A four-cannon 20 mm bore system was installed on all subsequent units, starting with serial number 52-2090, the 115th production article.

There were 473 F-86Hs produced at Columbus (two prototypes were built at Inglewood), but the variant was merely a placeholder until the significantly advanced F-100 was introduced. Operational units began receiving the F-86H in November 1954, the first being the 312th Fighter Bomber Wing at Clovis AFB, Clovis, New Mexico. Unfortunately, the unit was staffed with inexperienced pilots who had trained on less demanding F-84Es and F-86Fs. Landing mishaps were quite frequent, since the 6-3 wing, even with wingtip extensions, had difficult low-speed characteristics. The installation of slats on the leading edge of the 6-3 wing solved the problem, but the slats didn't appear until the last ten production aircraft, at which point they were retrofitted to the rest of the fleet. Production was spread among the 312th Fighter Bomber Wing, the 3595th Combat Crew Training Wing, the 479th Fighter Day Wing, the 50th Fighter Bomber Wing, and the 83rd Fighter Day Wing.[28] The F-86H served with these frontline units until 1956 and 1957, when they were transferred to the Air Force Reserve and Air National Guard. In that service they were deployed during the Berlin Wall crisis in 1961 and the USS *Pueblo* crisis in 1968. They served briefly in Vietnam with air national guard units but were withdrawn after significant losses.

While in Vietnam service, it was realized that the F-86H possessed flight characteristics akin to the MiG-17 and -19. In August 1966, the Air Force employed Air National Guard F-86Hs in "Feather Duster II" at Nellis AFB, an operation intended to evaluate contemporaneous fighters (McDonnell F-4 Phantom IIs, Northrup F-5s, North American F-100 Super Sabres, Lockheed F-104 Starfighters, and Republic F-105 Thunderchiefs) against simulated MiG tactics. It became apparent in low-speed dogfights that the F-86H (and therefore the MiG) had a distinct advantage.

By 1969, the Navy had captured an airworthy MiG-19 and flew it against two F-86Hs in operation "Have Drill" at Nellis AFB. It was determined the Sabers had a higher roll rate, but the MiG turned tighter and decelerated faster. In 1970, the Navy assigned approximately twenty F-86Hs to act as aggressor aircraft with VX-4 in training exercises. About the same time, it was realized that several air-to-air weapon systems, such as the AIM-54 Phoenix, AIM-7F Sparrow, and AIM-9L Sidewinder, would benefit from testing in a more realistic air-combat-maneuvering environment.

The availability of aging F-86Hs with their MiG-like flying characteristics made them desirable for the Navy's full-scale aerial-target program. Two examples (53-1294 and 52-2091) were converted into QF-86H drones at the China Lake Naval Weapons Center. The conversion allowed the aircraft to be flown by a live pilot or controlled from the ground in unmanned missions. The program was extremely successful, and twenty-nine additional aircraft were modified between 1972 and 1974. By 1980 most

The F-100 Super Sabre was the first jet fighter that could exceed the sound barrier in level flight. Large numbers were built at Columbus but never saw US Navy shipboard service.

QF-86Hs were expended, with AIM-9L Sidewinders accounting for most losses; however, a few survived. The rigorous testing that became possible under the program is illustrated by a Sidewinder that shot down a QF-86H while the drone executed a hard 8.2 g turn—well above the airframe's 7.3 g limit.

NAA Single-Engine Swept-Wing Fighters, General Characteristics

Model	No. built	First flight	Length	Span	Empty lbs.	Gross	Max. mph
FJ-1	33	1946	34 ft., 5 in.	38 ft., 2 in.	8,843	15,118	547
FJ-2/3	741	1951	37 ft., 7 in.	37 ft., 1.5 in.	11,802	18,790	675
FJ-4	374	1954	36 ft., 4 in.	39 ft., 1 in.	13,210	23,700	680
F-86	9,860	1947	37 ft., 1 in.	39 ft., 1 in.	11,125	18,152	687
F-100	2,294	1953	50 ft.	38 ft., 9 in.	21,000	34,832	924

Reflections on Columbus Fury and Sabre Production

The Inglewood plant fabricated the batch of thirty FJ-1 as demonstrators before Columbus opened. Testing and design remained in the California area even as production for FJ-2, F-86F, and F-86H moved to Ohio. The F-100 Super Sabre came later. Each of these types provided Columbus with experience in large-volume aircraft production. No longer needing assistance from headquarters, by 1954 the new division had evolved into an autonomous airplane facility fully capable of designing, building, testing, and producing the advanced FJ-4 Fury. Within a few years of opening, the Columbus plant was churning out 7 million pounds of airplanes annually, and the number exceeded 10 million in a few years. Between November 1952 and May 1958, Columbus delivered 1,112 Furys to the Navy plus 1,173 Sabres to the Air Force. Total F-86 output (including licensed units by allied nations) was 9,860, a formidable number akin to World War II production metrics.

The US military outspent potential foes as it constantly prepared for war in Europe; however, in two consecutive Asian wars (Korea and Vietnam), the Americans arrived with warplanes ill suited for the task at hand, while the Soviets supplied better and cheaper solutions. The military-industrial complex was failing America. Unfortunately, a reworked F-86 may have been a learning tool but was not the best match for the needs of the US Navy.

T-2 Buckeye

A Navy T-2 Buckeye is posed for a builder's side-view photo, which is part of the documentation package. The posed mechanics help the viewer gauge the aircraft's compact size.

By 1955, production of the FJ-4 Fury was well underway, and the NAA-Columbus preliminary design team was looking for a new project. Concurrently, the Navy was drafting an outline specification, OS-141, for a jet trainer to be used in a wide array of missions: jet transition, formation flight, night flying, instrument training, carrier qualification and limited weapons delivery were the essential ones. In early 1956, the RFP based on OS-141 was issued to several airframe manufactures for a carrier-capable jet trainer with a gross weight of no more than 10,500 pounds, a maximum speed of at least 400 knots at 25,000 feet, a stall speed of no more than 65 knots (with 20 percent fuel remaining), a service ceiling of at least 35,000 feet, and a range of 700 nautical miles. The trainer was to be easy to fly either visually or on instruments and have provisions for limited armament. Reliability and maintainability were primary considerations. According to *Aviation Week* magazine, the North American–Columbus proposal was selected over submissions from eighteen manufacturers.[1]

While the NAA-Columbus winning design made liberal use of proven features from other North American aircraft, this would be the first design exclusively from the Columbus plant; therefore, the Buckeye name was merited. The California dream was fading. The paradigm of wide-open spaces and cheap labor from 1935 was now in the rearview mirror. Too many automobiles filled the once-pristine skies with ugly brown smog. Roadways were constantly jamming. Every void around Los Angeles was being paved over. Taxation and regulation were becoming issues. Middle America may be "flyover country," but it now offered cost savings, thus becoming increasingly attractive for airplane builders.

T-2 Buckeye General Characteristics

Model	No built	First flight	Length	Span	Empty lbs.	Gross	Max mph
T-2	529	1958	38 ft., 3.5 in.	38 ft., 1.5 in.	8,115	13,179	521

Charles Gallant and his Columbus team were granted a large measure of autonomy. Kindelberger trusted Gallant to grow Columbus into a stand-alone operation that conceived, designed, marketed, built, flight-tested, and delivered new and innovative military aircraft. The core competency of high-rate aircraft production at Inglewood entered a slow descent with the loss of the F-107 contract in 1957. That mantra now resided in Columbus; however, other divisions continued to prosper as they diversified into other aerospace niches.

T2J-1 / T-2A Buckeye

The T-2 Buckeye wing was borrowed from the FJ-1 Fury—which itself evolved from the P-51 Mustang. The control system, with the addition of hydraulic boost to handle jet airspeeds, was adapted from the T-28 Trojan. And the Westinghouse J34 turbojet, one of the most reliable engines of the time, was selected as the power plant. This engine had accumulated over two million flight hours since it was developed in 1947, and it had seen combat in Korea powering F2H Banshees and F3D Skyknights.[2] The airframe design consisted of simple, conventional structures that were conventionally fabricated. On the basis of the preference expressed by Training Command instructors, tandem seating with an elevated rear seat was selected as

the cockpit configuration. Excepting a new rocket-propelled ejection seat to permit ground-level ejections (above 75 knots), off-the-shelf components were used whenever possible to reduce testing lead time. Ease of maintenance was facilitated by locating assembly operations within reach at waist height, eliminating the need for ladders and workstands. Full access to the engine was provided through three main doors. A large tail was employed to provide good control and stability at low airspeeds. The horizontal stabilizer was mounted high to minimize buffeting, and 45 percent of the rudder area was located below the horizontal stabilizer for positive spin recovery. The main landing gear was mounted at midspan, providing a wide track to ensure excellent crosswind control on the ground.[3]

Mockup inspection went smoothly and generated an order for six preproduction YT2J-1s on June 29, 1956. The order was increased to 121 production units in December 1956. One year later the first YT2J-1, BuNo 144217, was rolled out of the Columbus plant and prepared for test flight. The T-2 program manager was Richard "Dick" Peticolas, with Ed Kelly as primary project engineer.

First flight was on January 31, 1958, by Dick Wenzell, who encountered some minor landing-gear-door difficulties during the first two flights, but no significant problems. Confidence gained from Wenzell's first flights allowed chief engineering test pilot Jim Pearson to fly the aircraft at a public display on February 10. John Moore handled

The sole invention of the Columbus Division, a trio of Navy T-2 Buckeye trainer aircraft repose outside the factory hangar doors. The name Rockwell became more prominent with the passage of the years.

Ed Gillespie (ca. 1958) flashes a big grin as he prepares to strap into a T-2A Buckeye, then the Navy's newest jet trainer. The name "Buckeye" pays tribute both to Columbus and the state of Ohio.

A T-2C Buckeye (BuNo 157033) is surrounded by deck crew on a busy afternoon aboard USS John F. Kennedy at 4:39 p.m. on May 2, 1998. Adding to the noisy din is a landing Douglas TA-4J (BuNo 153463). US Navy

subsequent test flights at Columbus and characterized the aircraft as a "tough little creature and a blast to fly."[4]

In late February, Moore ferried the YT2J-1 to Palmdale to continue the test flight program in the high desert. While in California, the Navy subjected the trainer to an NPE (Navy preliminary evaluation) and cleared it for further testing at NATC. Three YT2J-1s were delivered to Pax River for evaluation by the various divisions of the Test Center. The testing confirmed that the Navy was getting the trainer it needed. The maximum speed was 428 knots, 28 knots faster than required. Takeoff and landing distances were nearly 1,000 feet shorter than specified. Range was 99 nautical miles greater than expected, and maximum mission endurance was within ninety seconds of the specification. Only the stall speed (of 68 knots) and the service ceiling of 30,000 feet were deficient, but the Navy was satisfied. Ninety additional T2J-1s were ordered in February 1959.

An important milestone was reached in May 1959, when carrier suitability trials were successfully conducted aboard USS Antietam (CVS-36), the first US carrier with an angled deck. However, a stall characteristic study was ordered by BuAer when several incidents of unpredictable stall behavior were reported. Four aircraft (BuNos 146009,

A formation of T-2 trainers are over USS Lexington (CV-16) at sea. Lexington was a World War II Essex-class aircraft carrier built in 1942, overhauled, and later retained for training purposes at NAS Pensacola until 1991.

147431,147432, and 147434) were modified with "stall strips": triangular shaped, 10 inches long, 1 inch wide, and mounted 24 inches from the wing fuselage intersection. The flap shroud was trimmed by 1 inch, and the full-flap deflection was rigged to 33 degrees. Stalls in the clean configuration (flaps and landing gear retracted) were satisfactory and consistent for all four aircraft, but in the dirty configuration (flaps and landing gear extended) the stall resulted in wing roll that varied in rate and controllability among the aircraft. The study concluded that

> the abruptness and severity of roll-off at the inception of the stall are not as severe in comparison with the configuration without the leading-edge spoiler or with the spoiler installed further outboard. However, the differences in roll-off and roll rate at the stall exhibited between airplanes are undesirable.[5]

Careful rigging of the flaps during manufacture was required to minimize the condition.

Spin tests were approached with apprehension after NACA (predecessor to NASA) tests on a 1/20-scale model produced pessimistic results. The tests predicted that different recovery techniques would be required for specific loads and spin types. When the tests were conducted on full-sized aircraft, the results were surprisingly benign. Recoveries were accomplished by retarding the throttle to idle, holding full opposite rudder with the stick held in neutral until the rotation ceased. Aft stick was the final step to recover from a dive. Intentional inverted spins were prohibited to avoid exceeding the airframe's negative "g" limit.[6]

Seeking to build awareness of the new trainer among members of the basic training command, NAA announced a contest to name the T2J-1. The winning name, "Buckeye," was submitted by Ens. Gordon O. Prickett. Deliveries of the Buckeye to the naval air basic-training command started on July 9, 1959. BTG-9 (redesignated VT-4 in 1960) was the first unit to receive the new trainer. Instructor familiarization flights were conducted, and a training syllabus was developed. The first student flights of the Buckeye occurred on November 2, 1959. On September 18, 1962, the Department of Defense Tri-Service designation system became effective, and the T2J-1 became the T-2A. Several notable accomplishments were achieved by the Buckeye during its first full year of operation. On June 2, 1960, 2Lt. J. B. Hammond (USMC) became the first student to carrier-qualify aboard USS *Antietam*. Buckeye became the first jet trainer used for air-to-air gunnery practice in May 1960.

The final T2J-1 (number 217) was delivered in April 1961, with the inventory spread among VT-4, VT-7, VT-9, and VT-19. The Buckeye earned a reputation as an excellent training platform. It was safe and reliable, with superb flying qualities. Furthermore, several reliability records were established by VT-9, which recorded a total of 382 Buckeye flight hours in a single April day in 1968 and a total of 6,510 flight hours in the month of May 1968. VT-9 accumulated a total of 55,567 hours with their Buckeye fleet over a twelve-month period while training 462 students. VT-4 accomplished the most notable achievement by winning the NAA safety award for 70,000 accident-free hours over a three-and-one-half-year period between October 1962 and May 1966.

Like an automobile in constant hard usage, by the late 1960s the T-2A was rapidly showing its age. Several Buckeyes were grounded when wing cracks were discovered in some airframes. One aircraft was lost from a runaway trim control, which resulted in a four-month rework program on all T-2A control systems. Then a series of repeated engine flameouts resulted in a grounding order for the fleet. When the problem was solved and the order was lifted, it was discovered that sixty-eight Buckeyes needed modification of main landing-gear struts. Most T-2As had reached their service life limit by the early 1970s, causing the chief of naval air training to predict that there would be insufficient aircraft to satisfy needed training by 1972.[7] By 1973 the last two T-2As were retired from training duty.

T-2B Buckeye

A new generation of small turbojet engines was developed since the Buckeye program started in 1956, when the Westinghouse J34-WE-48 was the only suitable choice. The J34 had become an antiquated engine that produced 3,400 pounds of thrust, weighed 1,212 pounds, and had poor fuel efficiency. On January 26, 1962, the Navy awarded NAA-Columbus a contract to modify two separate airframes of single-engine Buckeyes into a twin-engine configuration using modern engines. The selected engines were Pratt & Whitney J60-P-6s, which produced 3,000 pounds of thrust and weighed only 468 pounds. Therefore, the twin-engine Buckeye would have 2,600 pounds of additional thrust available with a 276-pound reduction in engine weight. The new Buckeye was originally designated T2J-2 but became the T-2B in 1962 under the Tri-Service designation system. The twin-engine modification was accomplished by simply widening the engine bay and increasing the size of the air intakes. The first T-2B, BuNo 145997, flew on August 30, 1962, only eight months after the contract was issued. Performance improvements were immediately apparent: takeoff gross weight was increased by 1,784 pounds, service ceiling was increased by 4,500 feet, maximum speed was increased by 54 knots, range was increased by 200 nautical miles, and climb time to 25,000 feet was cut in half.

Marking Time ©
North American T-2/T2J Buckeye

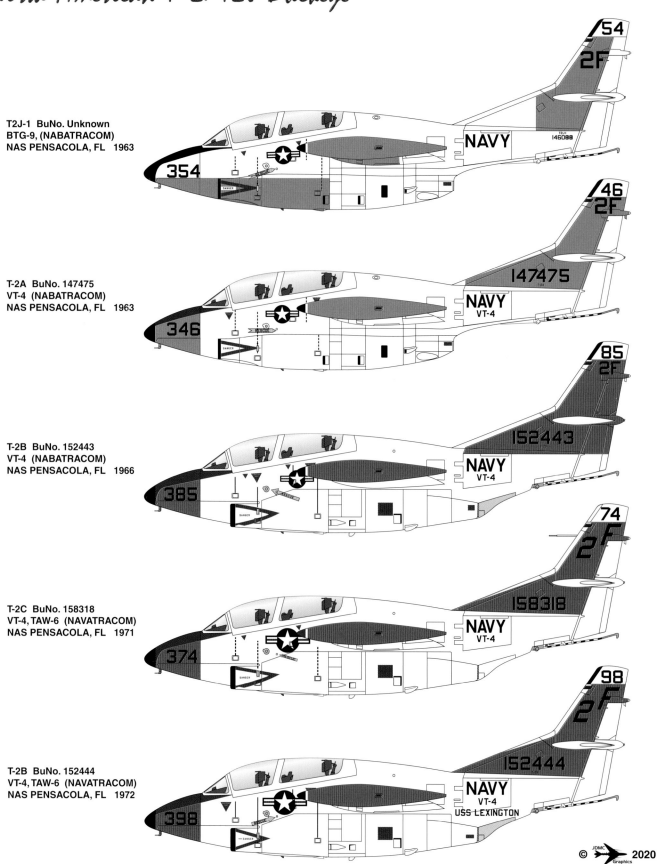

T2J-1 BuNo. Unknown
BTG-9, (NABATRACOM)
NAS PENSACOLA, FL 1963

T-2A BuNo. 147475
VT-4 (NABATRACOM)
NAS PENSACOLA, FL 1963

T-2B BuNo. 152443
VT-4 (NABATRACOM)
NAS PENSACOLA, FL 1966

T-2C BuNo. 158318
VT-4, TAW-6 (NAVATRACOM)
NAS PENSACOLA, FL 1971

T-2B BuNo. 152444
VT-4, TAW-6 (NAVATRACOM)
NAS PENSACOLA, FL 1972

© JDMC Graphics 2020

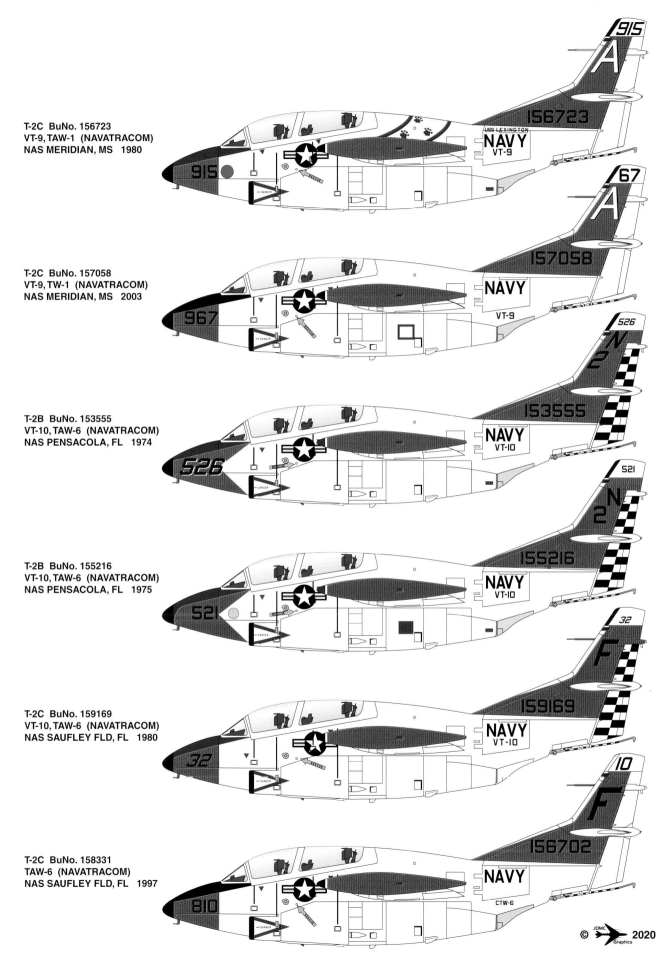

T-2C BuNo. 156723
VT-9, TAW-1 (NAVATRACOM)
NAS MERIDIAN, MS 1980

T-2C BuNo. 157058
VT-9, TW-1 (NAVATRACOM)
NAS MERIDIAN, MS 2003

T-2B BuNo. 153555
VT-10, TAW-6 (NAVATRACOM)
NAS PENSACOLA, FL 1974

T-2B BuNo. 155216
VT-10, TAW-6 (NAVATRACOM)
NAS PENSACOLA, FL 1975

T-2C BuNo. 159169
VT-10, TAW-6 (NAVATRACOM)
NAS SAUFLEY FLD, FL 1980

T-2C BuNo. 158331
TAW-6 (NAVATRACOM)
NAS SAUFLEY FLD, FL 1997

© JDMC Graphics 2020

This view of the cockpit shows the arrangement of the instrumentation. Student and instructor pilots are the primary users of trainer aircraft. Deskbound pilots might also fly them to maintain proficiency and qualify themselves for flight pay.

But the Navy's evaluation of the prototypes was protracted, and it was not until March 3, 1964, that a production order for ten aircraft was awarded. As production ramped up, a second order for thirty-six units was issued in October 1964. The first production T-2B was flown on May 21, 1965, and deliveries to the Naval Air Training Command started on December 5 of that year. Fuel cells, each holding 50 gallons, were installed in the leading edge of each wing from the thirty-fourth production aircraft onward, giving the T-2B the fuel capacity to fly 100 miles offshore, complete carrier qualifications, and return without refueling. Hardpoints under each wing permitted the installation of gun pods, target tow containers, rocket launchers, and bomb racks for weapons training.

VT-4 at NAS Pensacola was the first unit to operate the T-2B. At first, the twin-engine Buckeye was assigned to the more rigorous stages of training, while aging T-2As were still used for routine sorties. Eight months later, VT-7 at NAAS Meridian, Mississippi, received three T-2Bs for testing and evaluation. The squadron also evaluated the Air Force Cessna T-37B under the Department of Defense's interservice commonality policy, but a detailed study concluded that continued T-2 production was more economical. In January 1966, a third order was placed for fifty-four additional T-2Bs, bringing the total to a hundred aircraft. VT-9, also based at NAAS Meridian, received its first T-2B on June 6, 1968 and by December it had twenty-one T-2Bs on hand. By 1970 VT-9's inventory had grown to eighty-one T-2Bs, and by March 1971 the squadron had become the largest jet operator in the Navy, leading to its reorganization into two squadrons, VT-9 and VT-19.

T-2C Buckeye

In 1967 a more cost-effective engine, the General Electric J85-GE-4, became available. The GE engine was developed earlier than the Pratt & Whitney J60 (first run date on May 16, 1958) but was not as readily available, since early production was committed to the Air Force's T-38 Talon program. The J85-GE-4 produced nearly the same thrust as the Pratt & Whitney J60-P-6, yet it weighed 52 pounds less. The Navy issued a contract to NAA-Columbus for the installation of two J85s in a T-2B to assess airframe compatibility. Columbus used the earliest T-2B, 152382, which it had retained under a bailment agreement from the Navy for use as a test and demonstration aircraft. The T-2B was redesignated YT-2C and flew on April 17, 1968. The results were so encouraging that the T-2C was ordered into immediate production, and the last three T-2Bs were built to the T-2C standard. On April 30, 1969, the first T-2C was delivered to VT-9. Test pilot Ed Gillespie described the Buckeye in *Air Enthusiast* magazine:

The T-2C is a solid, safe, simple training airplane, with excellent flying qualities and outstanding visibility, although it appears rather homely from some aspects. However, many of us have the same problem and, as in the case of the Buckeye, manage to get the job done with personality, not appearance.

The T-2C possesses excellent stability and good control characteristics over its wide speed range. Good low[-]speed handling characteristics, certainly desirable for carrier operations, as well as adequate control and handling characteristics in the compressibility speed range, are provided. . . . The Buckeye can be trimmed to zero control forces at all operational speeds: however, in a high Mach number dive, compressibility effects will cause an increase in push forces required to maintain the dive angle . . . forward stick force increases as the aircraft approaches its limit Mach number. This characteristic is considered desirable for a trainer since it makes it almost impossible for the student to exceed limit speeds.

The Buckeye exhibits excellent stall characteristics, with power approach (PA) and landing (L) configuration stalls identical. A rudder shaker on the left pedal in the forward cockpit is the primary warning of impending stalls and is actuated through the angle-of-attack system at a speed of 7–10 knots before the stall, depending on the power setting. . . . Mild rolling tendencies in either direction may occur at the stall. . . . Recovery from the stall is affected immediately by relaxation of the back stick force. High[-] or low[-]speed accelerated stalls display similar characteristics for any configuration.

The T-2 is a safe spin trainer and is being used as such by the US Navy. Erect spins are entered conventionally from normal or accelerated stalls by holding full back stick and full rudder in the desired direction. The resulting spin is non-oscillatory if aileron is held anti-rudder or oscillatory if aileron is held pro-rudder. In any case, a post-stall gyration usually develops through at least two turns. . . . Recovery is conventional with full opposite rudder to the spin direction while maintaining neutral aileron and neutral elevator. When the rotation ceases, the rudder is neutralized, and the dive recovery must be monitored to prevent entry into an accelerated stall.

Inverted spins are more difficult to achieve, but easily recoverable. Pitch oscillations are not as noticeable[,] and recovery in a near vertical attitude results in less than one turn after application of full opposite rudder and neutral stick.

The spin training capability of the Buckeye is a valuable asset in providing familiarity in spin motions and recovery techniques for pilots progressing to higher[-] performance airplanes.

Speed can be controlled easily during approach due to the excellent acceleration/deceleration characteristics in response to small throttle movements. The airplane will float moderately if brought in fast, but the stiff, wide landing is not conducive to "greased" landings. They are the exception, not the rule. . . . The Navy technique with the T-2 is to maintain 15 units of angle-of-attack all the way onto the runway at the same attitude, neither flaring nor diving for the deck. The landing gear is extremely rugged and can be smashed onto the runway at sink speeds up to 20 feet per second with no damage.

The writer admits to being partial to this airplane as the T-2C and T-2D reflect many of the results of his quantitate and qualitative evaluations of the Buckeye from its inception in the mockup stage through all the developmental testing of the T-2A and T-2B.[8]

As production progressed, the T-2C was eventually assigned to nine squadrons: VT-4, -7, -9, -10, -19, -23, -26, -43, and -126. It proved to be reliable, with an average availability of 75 percent, requiring only 7.1 man-hours of maintenance per flight hour, a low ratio for an operational trainer. The T-2C retained the maintenance ease of the T-2A. Servicing was performed at ground level without the need for ladders or workstands, and engine replacements could be accomplished in less than three hours. Like the T-2B, the T-2C featured two underwing hardpoints that allowed installation of a weapons training package with a wide array of ordnance: .50-caliber machine gun pods, antiaircraft 37B-3 bomb racks, Mk. 86 and Mk. 15 practice

This T-2D Buckeye is one of a dozen built for export to Venezuela. Forty Buckeye aircraft designated T-2E were also built for Greece.

bombs, 2.75-inch rocket packages, and Aero 1A or 1B banner target carriers, and Mk. 1 target containers could be carried. Production for the Navy was completed in December 1975 after 231 units. Export orders from Venezuela (twenty-four units) and Greece (forty units) kept the Columbus production line active until 1977.

In addition to training naval aviators destined for fleet service, the T-2C trained naval flight officers, flight surgeons, and foreign air force students. After nearly twenty years as the Navy's sole basic trainer, the Buckeye was scheduled for replacement by the McDonnell Douglas T-45 Goshawk. However, numerous developmental problems delayed the T-45's introduction, and the Buckeye soldiered on. A group of eight students from VT-9 were the last to carrier-qualify with the Buckeye on July 25, 2003, aboard USS *Harry S. Truman* (CVN-75). The final Buckeye carrier landing was made aboard USS *Harry S. Truman* on April 9, 2004. At that time, most T-2s had accumulated well over 11,000 airframe hours—with one example, BuNo 156705, having logged 14,527 hours. Most high-time Buckeyes were flown to Davis-Monthan AFB for disposition (most often storage followed by scrapping), but a few low-time airplanes continued to serve in advanced naval flight officer training at NAS Pensacola and the Naval Test Pilot School at Pax River until 2008. Several others continued flying in utility roles as drone directors or chase aircraft. The final operational flight occurred with a T-2C attached to VX-20 on September 25, 2015. In total, NAA-Columbus built 609 Buckeyes between 1956 and 1977.

T-2 Proposals and Experiments

Both North American and the Navy received ample benefit from the Buckeye. Columbus enjoyed twenty-one years of production and the profits from 609 airplanes, while the Navy obtained a jet that trained more than 11,000 naval aviators over a period of forty-nine years. Yet, the product planners at Columbus proposed numerous variations of the Buckeye during its many years of production, to derive even more benefit from the enduring design.

Near the end of the T2J-1 production run, North American submitted an unsolicited proposal for a simplified, lighter-weight version of the trainer. The Westinghouse J34 that powered the T2J-1 weighed 1,212 pounds and produced 3,400 pounds of thrust. Pratt & Whitney had just introduced an engine that weighed only 468 pounds yet produced 3,000 pounds of thrust (the same engine that would power the T-2B). North American's promotional brochure describes the concept in detail:

> Economy in the pilot training program can be furthered by utilizing the T2J in two configurations—a lightweight T2J for early basic flight instructions, and the current

Attaching tufts to the skin of an airplane is a way to capture and visualize airflow about the airframe. It helps identify and resolve situations of drag or aeronautical inefficiency.

A four-seat Buckeye was contemplated on the basis of yielding a cost-savings advantage by combining training new pilots with weapon systems officers (sometimes called MIB, or "man in back"). Seen here in the plywood mockup stage, it never entered service. Nolan Leatherman

T2J-1 for follow-on basic and subsequent operations.

The lightweight configuration consists of the standard production T2J-1 with certain systems not normally required for early basic flight instruction removed. In the lightweight T2J, a Pratt & Whitney J60-5 (JT12) turbojet replaces the T2J-1's J34-WE-48 engine.

The economy of the lightweight T2J is largely derived from the lower fuel specifics of the J60, plus the subtracting of the weight and cost of the special systems that are removed. Fuel cost savings with the lightweight T2J originate in the capability to exceed in the clean configuration the time-in-the-air of the T2J-1 with tip tanks.

A 1,200-pound weight reduction was projected by an engine substitution and eliminating gear necessary for carrier operations, armament provisions, navigational equipment, and tip tanks. Anticipated performance gains included higher service ceiling, faster rate of climb, lower stall speed, shorter landing distance, and longer flight endurance. Nevertheless, the Navy was uninterested, and none were built.

Another proposal emerged in the spring of 1964 for a "variable-stability advanced trainer" version of the T-2B, intended to simulate the characteristics of high-performance aircraft in the fleet. This modified Buckeye would be used for advanced training under a concept known as "all-through training." It would allow the Navy to use just one aircraft for the entire jet-training syllabus. North American reasoned that less than 18 percent of a fleet pilot's training was flown in an afterburning aircraft capable of supersonic flight. The variable-stability T-2B could provide that same training more efficiently and inexpensively by eliminating the need for familiarizing the student with the systems and procedures of a new airplane, thereby reducing the advanced-training syllabus from 140 hours to 120 hours. The variable-stability aircraft would employ a fully powered control system and increased-thrust engines and provide more agile roll response with increased aileron deflection and spoilers. Any fleet aircraft of that time could be simulated with "plug-in models . . . a small card-shaped package consisting of passive solid-state electronic networks. The simulation capabilities included aircraft response, pilot feel or handling qualities, pitch and trim changes due to operation of gear, flaps, speed brakes, and store loadings."[9] The proposal for a variable-stability T-2B included structural enhancements to permit more-aggressive catapult acceleration and the faster arrestment speeds typical of tactical jets. Like the lightweight T2J, no variable-stability T-2Bs were built.

The "all-through training" concept resurfaced in 1973, when the Columbus Division proposed an "alternate stability kit" for the Buckeye. Once again, the intent was to expand T-2 capability beyond basic training into advanced training. The kit consisted of two pylon-mounted underwing pods that housed auxiliary speed brakes used to simulate the low-speed approach/landing characteristics of swept-wing frontline carrier aircraft. The auxiliary speed brakes were governed by sensors programed to simulate the approach drag, control system sensitivity, stick force, stall behavior, and throttle response of the A-4, F-4, A-7, F-14, S-3, and F-18. The first T-2C, 152382, on bailment to NAA-Columbus, was modified with the "kit" and evaluated by three Columbus and two Navy test pilots. It was found to perform well, but the system was not ordered into production.

The single-engine lightweight proposal was revisited during T-2C production in 1969. This time the objective was to extend the T-2's role to the earliest stage of basic training with a single General Electric J85. It was unofficially called the T-2D (the T-2D designation was later used for a block of Buckeyes exported to Venezuela in 1972). It was offered as a land-based trainer with no carrier capability and was expected to weigh 1,400 pounds less than the T-2C, with diminished but adequate performance for its role. It was intended to replace the aging, propeller-driven T-28 Trojan used in the early stages of basic flight training. Once again, none were ordered.[10]

In the spring of 1970, NAA-Columbus was awarded a research-and-development contract to design, build, and test a supercritical airfoil based on a concept that had been developed at NASA by noted aerodynamicist, Dr. Richard T. Whitcomb. The supercritical airfoil avoided transonic drag rise, allowing an aircraft to operate more efficiently at transonic speeds. The T-2C was selected for the program because its wing arrangement permitted engineers to alter the airfoil without changing the fuselage, wing structure, or systems. The thicker supercritical airfoil, which is flattened on its upper surface and has a concave curve on its undersurface, was superimposed over the standard T-2 airfoil with balsa wood and fiberglass, increasing the wing thickness from 12 to 17 percent. The supercritical airfoil contour was designed at the Columbus Division by William E. Palmer, and the test aircraft was flown extensively, allowing a direct comparison with standard production aircraft.

Another T-2C was modified to test a fiber optic flight control system in 1983. Pilot Ed Gillespie flew 3.6 hours over three flights, using a digital fly-by-light system, which operated flawlessly. Because of its high immunity to electromagnetic interference, Lloyd Kohnhorst, the project engineer, described the fiber optic system as a highly desirable addition to the "Advanced Flight Control Actuation System" (AFCAS). The system was jointly developed by the Naval Air Development Center and the Columbus Division.

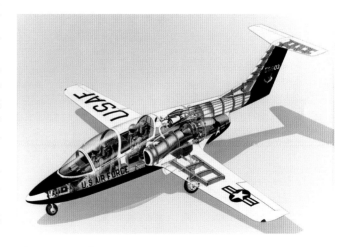

This cutaway illustration demonstrates hypothetical events. The Air Force did not purchase the Buckeye. Nor did a fan-powered version with a single engine (as shown here) ever emerge.

A late 1960 Pentagon study found the expense of Navy flight training to be much greater than Air Force cost. This caused the chief of naval air training to seek cost savings. NAA-Columbus submitted a proposal to combine pilot and naval flight officer (NFO) training into one aircraft. It was named the four-place multimission trainer, and a T-2C was modified with an enlarged cockpit that could train pilots and naval flight officers simultaneously, thus providing a realistic environment for both. The proposed airframe retained most its T-2C components but received a widened cockpit and fuel bay area. A detailed mockup of the multimission trainer was built. After further consideration, the Navy declined procurement.

Finally, in 1978, the Navy introduced a comprehensive "expanded training system" (the awkward acronym was VTXTS) to replace its aging T-2C and TA-4J trainers with one airplane type. The program required the winning contractor to provide not only the aircraft but also a complete and comprehensive training program consisting of cockpit procedures trainers, flight simulators, manuals, lectures, computer-assisted instruction, and a training management system. The Navy sought a turnkey system that would produce a competent pilot at an affordable cost. After three years of study, a RFP was released to industry in March 1981. North American (now Rockwell International) submitted a bid on the basis of its successful T-2C named T-2X. Rockwell emphasized the fact that the T-2X provided the lowest-risk submission among the competing bids, since all key performance and equipment factors were known and fully developed. Further, the use of existing assets with minimal development lead times promised an initial operational capability (IOC) by early 1986. The Navy rejected Rockwell's T-2X bid and instead embraced McDonnell Douglas's T-45 proposal, which was based on the well-proven British Aerospace Hawk. Unfortunately, the conversion of the shore-based Hawk to a carrier-capable T-45 proved far more time consuming and expensive than anticipated. The first T-45A was not delivered to the Navy's training command until the end of 1992, and further developmental issues prevented its use until early 1994—eight years beyond the projected date for the T-2X.[11]

Vigilante

Resplendent in factory-fresh paint, the Vigilante has been carefully posed for an enduring publicity photograph. The type first flew in 1958 and was retired in 1979.

The crowning achievement of the Columbus Division was an airplane named Vigilante. Conceived as a supersonic attack bomber, its primary mission evolved into reconnaissance. Caught in the middle of political turbulence in Washington, DC, interservice bickering, role uncertainty, and shifting designations, it is easier to simply call it by its consistent moniker, "Vigilante," an edgy name implying a self-appointed enforcer of justice. The preponderance of factory documentation is filed under NA-247, and the huge volume is on par with the other massive NAA projects.

North American General-Purpose Attack Weapon: NAGPAW[1]

The first usage of the atomic bomb (fission) came in August 1945. The more powerful thermonuclear hydrogen bomb (fusion) arrived on November 1, 1952. The centerpiece of the Navy's strategy in the aftermath of World War II was nuclear deterrence through using carrier-based heavy-attack aircraft. From the late 1940s to the early 1960s, only three aircraft types served in this role. Two of them, the AJ Savage, and the A3J-1 Vigilante, were NAA products. Better bombs merit better bombers. The Savage, conceived in 1946, was the world's first aircraft designed specifically for atomic-weapon delivery but was troubled because it was rushed into service. Insufficient testing left much of its development to be done in the fleet. Furthermore, its performance was marginal for the demands of the nuclear mission. In 1949 Douglas was awarded a contract to replace the Savage with the A3D Skywarrior, a swept-wing, twin-engine jet intended to improve the Navy's nuclear-strike capability. The Douglas's design promised dramatic performance improvement, but its development was seriously delayed by the problem-plagued Westinghouse J40 engine. Operational deliveries did not commence until 1956. By then, improved Soviet defenses threatened to make the subsonic Skywarrior obsolete.

In November 1953, a small group of managers and engineers at NAA-Columbus met to explore emerging technologies that could optimize nuclear delivery from

Multiple fire trucks have gathered, and that is indicative of a first flight. The compartment behind the pilot has side windows. The two red triangles warn firefighters of ejection seats, which can pose a lethal hazard to potential rescuers.

sea. The group consisted of chief engineer George Gehrkens, head of preliminary design Frank Compton, manager of the aerodynamics group Mac Blair, production specialist Reggie Clark, avionics specialist Wilbur Mitchell, and program manager John Fosness. The group was emboldened by the results of a secret test flown by an AJ Savage that launched from Spain and flew at low altitude to Paris and back without being detected by French radar. The test confirmed that the Soviet radar-guided surface-to-air missile defense could be defeated by low-level delivery, but several vexing problems had to be solved. First, low-altitude penetration to avoid radar detection complicated long-range navigation and target acquisition. Second, escaping the nuclear blast required supersonic dash speed. Finally, high-speed weapon release from a conventional bomb bay was difficult—as NAA experienced with its first jet bomber, the B-45 Tornado.

Eventually, solutions emerged. The high-speed delivery problem could be overcome by rearward ejection of the weapon from a linear bomb bay. High-speed escape could be accomplished with an auxiliary rocket motor to enhance acceleration and top speed. An inertial navigation system developed for the Navajo intercontinental ballistic missile was selected for precise long-distance navigation and target acquisition. By January 1954, the internal name "North American General-Purpose Attack Weapon" (NAGPAW—another dubious acronym) was assigned to

the project, and the team prepared an unsolicited proposal. In its original form, NAGPAW was defined as a small, single-place, high-subsonic-speed, twin-engine jet augmented by rocket propulsion. It was intended to deliver both nuclear and conventional weapons at low altitude, with high-altitude delivery being a secondary consideration.

The Navy Bureau of Aeronautics (BuAer) initially welcomed the proposal with enthusiasm, but after a year of study, two revisions were demanded. Hidden within the military are well-meaning but imaginative people who create "scope creep." If asked to invent a mouse, a specification for an elephant would result. Scope creep (sometimes called "gold plating") prevailed, and the goal of small, fast, and agile was sacrificed. The aircraft had to be capable of a zero-wind launch with full weapons load when the carrier was at anchor (or incapacitated), and high-altitude weapon delivery at Mach 2 speed was also demanded. Extremely different solutions were necessary to satisfy these mutually exclusive requirements with a single design.

The zero-wind launch meant increasing the wing area to lower the wing loading, but Mach 2 performance could be achieved only with a wing of limited size. Furthermore, low-altitude, high-speed penetration required a small wing to endure turbulence encountered at sea level. Compton's preliminary design group struggled to reconcile these competing requirements. A variable-geometry (swing-wing) design was considered, but the Navy was unwilling to try that after the Grumman XF10F swing-wing program was canceled less than a year earlier. By January 1955, the Navy recognized the impossibility of their requirements and accepted a compromise. High-altitude Mach 2 performance was now considered primary; low-altitude penetration became secondary. This resulted in a total restructure of the NAGPAW design.

The wing configuration was revised to accommodate better high- and low-speed operation. The overall airframe grew bigger, and a second crew member was added to handle the increased cockpit workload. "Small and fast" was giving way to "big and fast." The wing area grew, but the thickness ratio (airfoil height to chord width) was reduced. Full-span "blown" flaps (high-energy air from the engine compressor ducted over the flaps) were employed to augment lift for the zero-wind launch requirement (which was only "almost" achieved). Now, on paper at least, NAGPAW promised Mach 0.95 at sea level and Mach 2 at 40,000 feet—the broadest performance envelope of any large aircraft at that time. On July 18, 1955, the

Vigilante General Characteristics

Model	No. built	First flight	Length	Span	Empty lbs.	Gross	Max. speed
AJ-3 / RA-5	167	1958	76 ft., 6 in.	53 ft.	32,783	63,085	Mach 2

Marking Time©
North American A3J/A-5 Vigilante

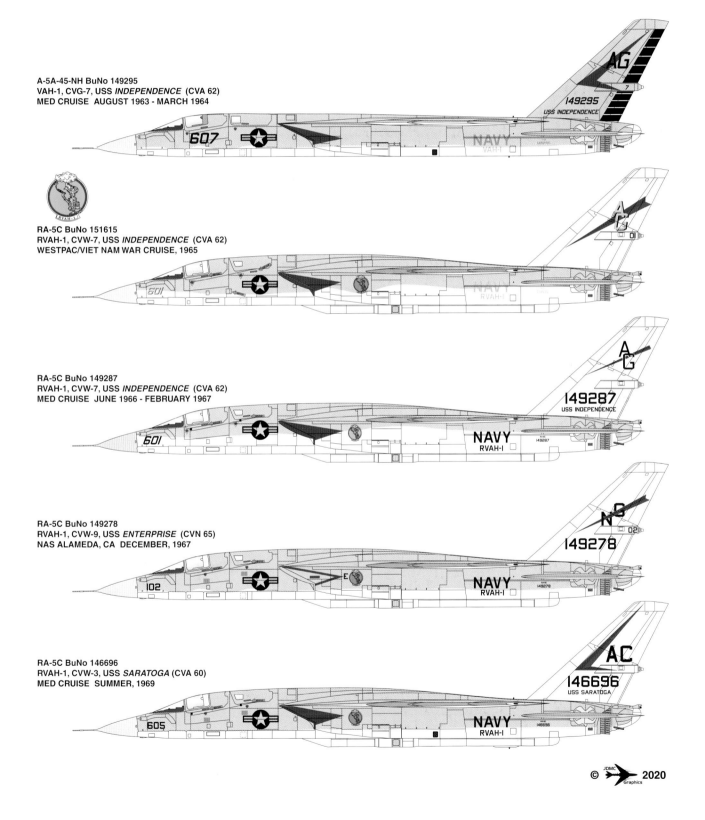

A-5A-45-NH BuNo 149295
VAH-1, CVG-7, USS *INDEPENDENCE* (CVA 62)
MED CRUISE AUGUST 1963 - MARCH 1964

RA-5C BuNo 151615
RVAH-1, CVW-7, USS *INDEPENDENCE* (CVA 62)
WESTPAC/VIET NAM WAR CRUISE, 1965

RA-5C BuNo 149287
RVAH-1, CVW-7, USS *INDEPENDENCE* (CVA 62)
MED CRUISE JUNE 1966 - FEBRUARY 1967

RA-5C BuNo 149278
RVAH-1, CVW-9, USS *ENTERPRISE* (CVN 65)
NAS ALAMEDA, CA DECEMBER, 1967

RA-5C BuNo 146696
RVAH-1, CVW-3, USS *SARATOGA* (CVA 60)
MED CRUISE SUMMER, 1969

© JDMC Graphics 2020

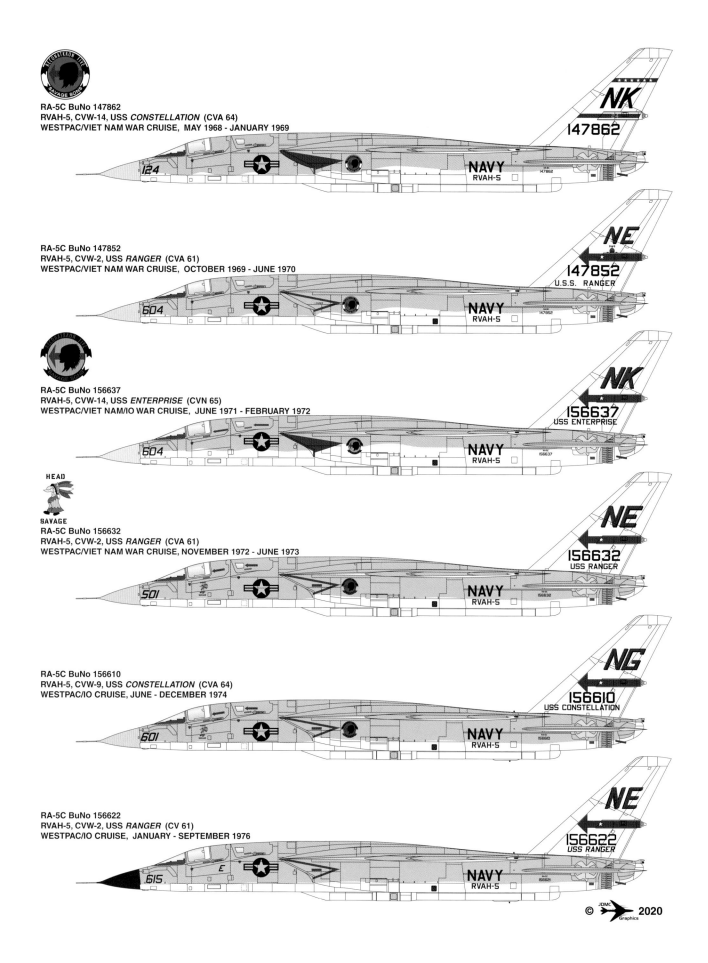

RA-5C BuNo 147862
RVAH-5, CVW-14, USS *CONSTELLATION* (CVA 64)
WESTPAC/VIET NAM WAR CRUISE, MAY 1968 - JANUARY 1969

RA-5C BuNo 147852
RVAH-5, CVW-2, USS *RANGER* (CVA 61)
WESTPAC/VIET NAM WAR CRUISE, OCTOBER 1969 - JUNE 1970

RA-5C BuNo 156637
RVAH-5, CVW-14, USS *ENTERPRISE* (CVN 65)
WESTPAC/VIET NAM/IO WAR CRUISE, JUNE 1971 - FEBRUARY 1972

RA-5C BuNo 156632
RVAH-5, CVW-2, USS *RANGER* (CVA 61)
WESTPAC/VIET NAM WAR CRUISE, NOVEMBER 1972 - JUNE 1973

RA-5C BuNo 156610
RVAH-5, CVW-9, USS *CONSTELLATION* (CVA 64)
WESTPAC/IO CRUISE, JUNE - DECEMBER 1974

RA-5C BuNo 156622
RVAH-5, CVW-2, USS *RANGER* (CV 61)
WESTPAC/IO CRUISE, JANUARY - SEPTEMBER 1976

© JDMC 2020 Graphics

A wind tunnel model of the Vigilante undergoes testing. Wind tunnel models are heavier than most people expect. They are built very precisely and are normally retained for future validations.

Navy issued a contract to proceed with design studies, engineering tests, and mockup for the NAGPAW proposal. Extensive wind tunnel testing was done to verify the performance, stability and control, air loads, aeroelastic effects, inlet duct characteristics, spin characteristics, weapon release, flutter analysis, and exhaust efflux patterns.

By March 1956, the preliminary wind tunnel testing was complete, and a formal mockup review was conducted that resulted in approval of the design, with several changes. The vertical tail configuration was changed from a twin-fin design to a tall single surface that folded flat at midspan for carrier storage. The rear cockpit transparency was reduced, leaving only small windows for the radar operator, the air inlet shape was changed, and the linear bomb-bay tail cone was changed from a clamshell design to an expendable fairing that was jettisoned for weapon release. The rocket booster was deleted, since the hydrogen peroxide necessary to operate the rocket presented a severe handling risk aboard ship, and the twin J79 afterburning turbojets were deemed sufficient to meet the mission profile.

An unexpected benefit of the design was its stealth qualities. Chief engineer George Gehrkens recalls that the airframe's radar signature was tested on a range built at the Port Columbus Airport, using a copper wire mesh model. Radar signals were impinged on the model from all angles, and it was found to have very low reflectivity. Signal reflections were concentrated at the wingtips, such that the airframe would produce a flash during a flyby but no large response typical of an aircraft of that size.[2]

The Precursors: Small, Fast, and Agile

The initial intention was to size Vigilante on the basis of the NAA legacy of small, fast, and agile—as had been done with the iconic P-51D Mustang of World War II fame. Airplanes designs tend to gain size, weight, and clutter faster than a hoarder at an estate sale. Despite wartime challenges, NAA delivered the premier escort fighter because it was kept simple, small, fast, and agile. North American scored a second home run when the mantra of world's best fighter was handed to the F-86 Sabre because of dogfights in the skies over Korea. The Sabre was also small, fast, and agile and the only design in the United Nations arsenal capable of dogfighting the nimble MiG-15. The Navy joined the bantam-weight movement when it embraced the FJ Fury as its own.

People such as Dutch Kindelberger and Lee Atwood fully expected the F-100 Super Sabre to be followed by the fourth iteration of a relatively small, fast, and agile NAA fighter jet. It was the Mach 2 dogfighter designated F-107A. Three prototypes of "the airplane without a name" were fabricated at the Inglewood factory in 1956 and trucked to Edwards AFB for a "winner take all" flyoff against the Republic F-105 Thunderchief. As the flyoff approached, NAA executives began to realize they were already the underdog. The generals running the Air Force wanted a bomber, and the F-105 had a bomb bay.

As expected, the F-105 was pronounced the winner and ordered into production—a decision still debated by a cadre of aviation buffs. Some of them dubbed the F-107

The F-107A was a sophisticated airplane intended to replace the F-100 and leave behind some of its chronic issues. Instead, a flyoff with the Republic F-105 Thunderchief was lost, and no more were built. The Vigilante was the beneficiary of advanced technology first invented for the F-107A.

as the "best airplane <u>never</u> built." The two surviving airframes found homes in museums. But it was the advanced technology hidden within that was far more valuable. The war in Vietnam arrived when the F-105 was still a newcomer in the Air Force inventory. With afterburner, it was fast like the F-107—but with smaller and shorter wings (technical term, "less aspect ratio"), the Thunderchief was neither agile—nor small. Why is this story relevant? With the flyoff lost and nothing else in the California pipeline, elements of the very advanced technology made its way into the Vigilante.

Cooperation prevailed within NAA during the 1950s. Both engineering and manufacturing were shared between sites. Engineers at Columbus were collaborating on secret projects, including the XB-70 and F-108. These two Mach 3 speedsters shared engines and other advanced methods. F-108 was canceled at the mockup phase on September 23, 1959, thus liberating fresh ideas and more engineering talent for the Vigilante. Separately, north of the US border, a promising interceptor was in development. Five flying prototypes were built before the Avro Canada CF-105 Arrow project was surprisingly and abruptly canceled by Prime Minister John Diefenbaker on February 20, 1959. The reason for the cancellation? Some think budgetary, while others still wonder. In any case, yet another iteration of innovations arrived at Columbus infused within the cadre of freshly unemployed Canadian aerospace engineers.

Creating a new airplane as technologically advanced as the Vigilante required a talented engineering staff and capable leadership to guide them. Chief engineer George Gehrkens was gathering such a team. John Fosness was overall Vigilante project manager. Assisting John was Bob Carroll, with responsibility for aircraft and systems, and Ed Barfield as program manager for reconnaissance systems. Furthermore, aircraft carriers or shore stations hosting RA-5C would need a separate facility called "integrated operational intelligence center" (or IOIC). I. R. "Bud" Dudley was program manager and supported by Dewey Starks for inventing and then installing the IOICs on selected aircraft carriers (or elsewhere) as needed.

As discussed in chapter 2, better electronics were evolving quickly. The traditional airborne large-format cameras using conventional photographic film were being augmented and then superseded by new technology whereby digital data was also captured. Computers of that era were then utilized to store and analyze the collected intelligence data. Eventually, the size of the equipment would continue to shrink, and the need for film would disappear.

A Vigilante is prepared for the 21-feet-per-second drop test, mandatory for aircraft destined for service aboard aircraft carriers. All new aircraft designs are subjected to many forms of abuse before certification.

Vigilante benefited from evolving technology intended for three separate (but canceled) projects. First was the F-107, and second was the NAA F-108 Rapier, a design intended to cruse at Mach 3. It was aborted by the Pentagon in September 1959. Third, a contingent of Canadian engineers arrived in Columbus after the Avro CF-105 Arrow was defunded.

A3J-1/A-5A Vigilante

A contract between the Navy and NAA was issued on July 18, 1955. It covered design studies and a manufacturing mockup for the YA3J-1 (designator NA-233). On June 29, 1956, a letter of intent was issued allowing NAA to proceed with two flying prototypes and one static-test article. The Navy designation was YA3J-1, and North American assigned project number NA-247 to the program. By 1957 the design was nearly finalized, but a contentious debate over the Navy's nuclear role, which had its origins in the late 1940s (see "Revolt of the Admirals" in chapter 2), resurfaced during congressional budget hearings. The assistant secretary of the Navy for air operations, Garrison Norton, argued against the Vigilante, but he was countered by the proponents, who argued that the aircraft was also necessary for low-level conventional weapon delivery. Congress finally appropriated the funds for A3J-1 production in the fiscal 1959 budget, and the Navy issued a contract for fifty-two examples on November 16, 1959. All groups at Columbus were excited to be in the middle of a project of national priority. The various overhead functions geared up for this undertaking.

Flanked by an honor guard, Dutch Kindelberger demonstrates his formidable lifelong speaking skills to the crowd gathered at Columbus. To his rear are plant manager Charles "Chuck" Gallant and Adm. Arleigh Burke. Kindelberger delivered motivational speeches over nationwide radio during World War II.

Prototype construction was started in August 1957, and the first article, BuNo 145157, was rolled out of the Columbus plant on May 16, 1958. At the rollout ceremony, the CNO, Adm. Arleigh A. Burke, and NAA president J. H. "Dutch" Kindelberger revealed an elegant airplane 70 feet in length and nearly 20 feet high—enormous by carrier standards. The pilot and navigator cockpits were arranged in tandem in a slender forward fuselage that blended into a wide rectangular afterbody that contained twin YJ79-GE-2 engines mounted on either side of the bomb tunnel. A thin swept wing with 769 square feet of area extended from the top of the fuselage, and large, all-moving slab tail surfaces extended from the rear of airframe. Immediately after the rollout ceremony, the airframe was disassembled for instrumentation installation in preparation for test flight. When reassembled, chief test pilot Dick Wenzell began three months of systems checks and taxi tests at the Port Columbus Airport.[3]

Wenzell was preparing to fly an airplane that bristled with advanced features, some totally futuristic, others simply novel. The flight controls, adapted from the F-107A, were operated by the first "fly-by-wire" system ever developed for a production aircraft. Control commands were transmitted by electronic signals to hydraulic-ram-controlled surface actuators with no mechanical link (the electronic system was supplemented by mechanical reversion in the event of a failure). Rudder control, however, was completely mechanical. Ailerons were eliminated on the Vigilante wing to avoid diminished effectiveness at high speeds, a problem experienced with several aircraft of the time with thin swept wings. Instead, the Vigilante

Left to right: Plant manager Gallant, Adm. Burke, unidentified, Lee Atwood, and Dutch Kindelberger. By this point, Columbus was an autonomous business unit and major contributor to the profits of NAA.

generated roll forces with a series of spoilers and deflectors at midspan, well forward of the trailing edge. Pitch control was provided by large, all-moving, horizontal stabilizers (called stabilators), which could also be deflected in small independent amounts for roll trim. Directional control was achieved by an all-moving vertical stabilizer, with its deflection governed by airspeed and flap setting. A boundary layer control system provided enhanced lift, using high-velocity air from the engine compressors ducted to the upper surface of the flaps. The "blown" air came in automatically at 7 degrees of flap deflection, increasing in mass flow up to the maximum of 50 degrees.

The twin J79 engines received air from large, rectangular inlets that incorporated variable geometry to provide an efficient airflow to the engines. The Vigilante was among the first to employ a sensor system to detect shock wave buildup and automatically position internal ramps to maintain high-pressure recovery and low compressor face distortion.

Egress Systems

The parachute was invented during the days of observation balloons and well before aircraft. Senior officers on both sides forbade the wearing of parachutes during World War I, on the basis of the false premise that aviators would bail out rather than fight. World War II found seat-style parachutes fabricated of nylon in wide usage. Thousands of lives were saved. Generally, ejection seats arrived in combat aircraft after World War II and have progressively become more sophisticated. The Nazis left behind medical data regarding human tolerance for rapid acceleration, and those data influenced ejection seat design.

Back-style parachutes became common as survival kits were placed in the seat pan. The canopy is 28 feet in diameter and fabricated of ripstop nylon. Ejection seats are fast-acting devices with multiple interconnected steps that play out within a second or two. Initiators are secured with pins attached to "Remove Before Flight" streamers when on the ground. The person in the seat most often initiates their own ejection. Multiple initiators are common—at some combination of the hand rest triggers, a handle between the legs, or pulling down a screen from above to protect the face. Typically, the canopy is first blown clear. Retractors might restrain the hands, feet, and helmet to prevent injury or amputation of extremities. A ballistic charge sends the seat up the rails. Sometimes a rocket pack ignites to provide more altitude. Phasing the thrust reduces the chance of spinal injuries. Improvements came in incremental steps. Seat belts and other straps fall away as a "kicker" separates the human from the ejection seat. The goal is for automatic operation in case the aviator is unconscious or otherwise incapacitated.

Ejection seats were a postwar innovation that saved the lives of countless pilots. North American Aviation built and tested their own ejection seats. Rocket sleds traveling on specialized segments of railroad track were utilized.

A3J ESCAPE PROGRAM
SLED RUN NO. 9
7-30-58

A military emergency parachute canopy is 28 feet in diameter and fabricated of ripstop nylon. Every user hopes for an idyllic landing in peaceful surroundings—but that is not always possible during wartime.

NAA designed and built their own ejection seats at both Inglewood and Columbus. Different model numbers were manufactured, including the LS-1 for the T-2 trainer, and LW-3B for the OV-10. NAA seats were standard equipment on their aircraft—unless the customer specified otherwise. The Navy ordered Martin-Baker (British built) seats installed in some FJ Fury aircraft.

Windblast tears into and rips human flesh when a person is ejecting at speeds greater than Mach 1; therefore, aircraft designers dabbled with escape capsules of various styles in aircraft, including the Convair B-58 Hustler, General Dynamics F-111, and XB-70A. None proved to be totally satisfactory. The first three B-1A Lancer bombers had big, cumbersome escape capsules. Doomed by too many time-sensitive and expensive pyrotechnics, the capsules were quickly abandoned in favor of traditional individual ejection seats—ACES-II (advanced crew escape system) from Weber Aircraft.

Vigilante featured ejection seats designed and built by North American. The prototypes and early models used the HS-1 seat, which was capable of escape either at supersonic speeds or as low as 100 knots. Later Vigilantes used the improved HS-1A seat, which was capable of "zero-zero" egress (zero altitude and zero airspeed—in essence, an aircraft parked on the ground).

Progress on Vigilante Continues

The YA3J-1 was as advanced structurally as it was aerodynamically. Many of the components were made from materials or processed in new ways never previously used in airframe construction. Wing and tailplane skins were machine-milled into large sheets from slabs of a new aluminum-lithium alloy (Alcoa 2020-T6) that offered superior strength and elasticity and reduced density. The engine bays were constructed of titanium, with inner surfaces coated in gold film to reflect heat. The landing-gear legs were made from an advanced steel alloy called TRUX, and the load-bearing fuselage frames were machined from H-11 hot-work tool steel. Aluminum honeycomb was used in secondary structures. The windscreen was formed from a multilaminate of tempered glass and silicone and was claimed by the supplier, Libby-Owens-Ford, to be the largest one-piece curved, laminated aircraft transparency ever made (this was replaced in production with a stretch-formed acrylic windscreen).

The avionics systems were, by far, the Vigilante's most advanced (and troublesome) features. While not installed in the prototypes, the production aircraft had the following innovations: the first airborne digital computer for bombardier/navigational (bomb/nav) computations; the first bomb/nav system with inertial autonavigator coupled to radar, and television sight for checkpoint acquisition; the first production head-up display; the first fully integrated auto pilot and air data system for bomb/nav release solution; and the first multimode Ku-band monopulse radar with terrain avoidance features.

For some nebulous reason, breaking the sound barrier on the first flight was a military priority in that era. The Air Force offered cash bonuses to contractors who did so. To this day, Edwards AFB is one of the few places where the crack of a sonic boom can regularly be heard. People who have flown supersonic report nothing special. There is no snap, bump, bang, or thunderclap when exceeding Mach 1—just smooth and quiet; however, the crushing g-forces resulting from sharp turns remain memorable.

When Wenzell flew the YA3J on August 31, 1958, no significant problems were initially encountered, and he fully intended to take the aircraft supersonic; however, a radio failure then intervened, so that objective was scrubbed. His top speed was Mach 0.92 at 35,000 feet. The postflight report concluded with two issues as most significant: a moderate flap-horizontal stabilizer buffet, and roll control difficulties at approach speed with 40 degrees of flap. Ten other malfunctions were noted in the report, but none were considered critical. Contractor test flights continued into October. It had completed eleven flights totaling nine

Both images are part of a single sequence by the same Columbus plant photographer. First, pilot William "Bill" Ingram is preparing to take the Vigilante aloft. Next, he takes off and then performs a low-level flyby.

hours and forty minutes and reached an altitude of 40,000 feet and a speed of Mach 1.4. At that point, the test program was paused for the installation of a bomb-bay fuel system.

The second prototype, BuNo 145158, joined the flight test program in November 1958 for use in aeroelasticity and control system tests. After exceeding Mach 2 on several occasions and performing full deflection rolls at Mach 1.7, the aircraft suffered a fire in its nosewheel well on June 3, 1959, during its forty-ninth flight. Leaking hydraulic fluid was ignited by a test instrumentation battery, causing a loss of control and forcing test pilot Zeke Hopkins to eject. The aircraft impacted vertically, burying its nose nearly 40 feet in the ground.[4]

By early1960, fourteen initial production aircraft[5] joined the first prototype at NATC Pax River for service acceptance trials. These aircraft were spread among the various test divisions (armament, electronic, service, and flight test) for evaluation. Production A3J-1s differed little from the prototype YA3J-1s. None were equipped with complete avionics systems, and some were powered by uprated J79-GE-8 engines (each providing 850 pounds of additional thrust), but the most notable change was elimination of the enormous belly speed brake, which, according to Wenzell, caused a sharp crack that could be felt and heard when opened and caused trim change and airframe buffet. In lieu of the belly panel, production aircraft used the wing spoilers and deflectors as speed brakes. These provided the additional benefit of a more immediate response during missed landings, described as "wave-offs" or "bolters" (when the arresting wires were missed).

The service acceptance trials were conducted for nearly three years. Test flying commenced on February 29, 1960, and ended on December 31, 1962. Except for carrier suitability tests and nuclear-weapons delivery trials, most of the testing was conducted at NAS Pax River, Maryland. Extensive aircraft carrier testing was conducted aboard five ships: *Saratoga, Forrestal, Midway, Ranger,* and *Enterprise.* Initial testing went well for an airplane of such complexity, but several serious deficiencies were discovered. Capt. George Klett, the Navy bureau of aeronautics representative (BAR) assigned to the NAA-Columbus plant, recalls the drop tests:

> One problem that arose early in development was the failure of the longeron attachment fitting, also known as the "barrel nut" located just aft of the B/N [bombardier/navigator] cockpit. This fitting provided structural continuity between the forward and after sections of the fuselage, beginning just aft of the engine intakes. The first failure occurred during a drop test at about 17 feet per second while attempting to meet the specification of 21 feet per second. The forward section of the plane sheared off as if someone had hit it with a guillotine. I was present at the drop test when the next failure occurred at about 19 feet per second, and saw the tail resting on the safety support straps provided under the empennage, while the nose was sitting on the floor. The program was in serious trouble. . . . An improved barrel nut was developed to ensure that the upper longeron met its specification requirements. The resulting airframe service change was to be installed as soon as possible.[6]

Another area of great concern was the novel flight control system, which was initially pronounced unsatisfactory by the flight test division at Pax River. Both the lateral (roll) and longitudinal (pitch) controls suffered from "dead band." Test pilot remarks included "The stick feels like it is attached to rubber bands instead of flight controls" and "I can move the stick a considerable distance in all directions without affecting the airplane." The cause was a lag in the control surface hydraulic actuators. Test pilots found that they could move the stick to its limit instantly, but the control surface could take as long as 1.28 seconds before reaching its limit. Furthermore, small stick movements produced little roll response, since the spoiler-deflectors, which barely opened when the stick was nearly centered, deployed in the wing's slow-moving boundary layer air with little roll effect. Ultimately, the control system deficiencies were corrected after considerable engineering effort.

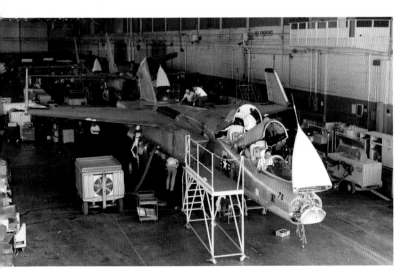

The assembly line concept was borrowed from the automobile industry during World War II. Each unit is numbered. That number helps workers maintain configuration control by ensuring that the needed parts find their way onto every unit. Each airplane is called a ship, and a bundle of like parts (for instance, tires, wheels, or brakes) is called a "ship set."

Jacqueline Cochran Achieves Mach 2

The place, date, and circumstances of Jacqueline "Jackie" Cochran's birth and early childhood are clouded in mystery to this day—because that was the way she wanted it. Cochrane (1906–1980) was born dirt poor but rose to great wealth—first with self-generated wealth earned in cosmetics and then by marriage to corporate titan Floyd Odlum, one of the wealthiest persons in the US. She also developed a passion for fast airplanes as a highly accomplished pilot during the heyday of air racing in the 1930s. Service during World War II as founder and leading WASP (Women Air Service Pilot) further cemented her place in aviation history.

Cochran was determined to be the first American woman to break the sound barrier, but the US Air Force would not allow females into the cockpit. So, Jackie worked a deal with the Royal Canadian Air Force to borrow a CF-86 Sabre 3, while her friend, Chuck Yeager (1923–2020), provided the coaching. On May 19, 1953, they both went aloft in separate planes. Yeager led her in a climb to 45,000 feet. Thereupon, with both airplanes in full afterburner, they pushed over toward the desert below. As predictably happens when an F-86 under maximum power performs a straight-down vertical dive—at about 18,000 feet, Mach 1.05 will be achieved. The pullout and landings were safe for each of them, thus yielding for Cochran yet another entry in the record book.

By June 1960, the Vigilante had achieved several impressive performance milestones, and the Navy was eager for publicity. The NAA public-relations department was authorized to invite noted aviatrix Jackie Cochran to ride in the rear cockpit of a Vigilante as it exceeded Mach 2. Test pilot John Moore recalls the event:

We checked Jackie out in the rear seat of the A3J-1 Vigi. There were no flight controls in that cockpit, but she really did not care on this mission. She just wanted to achieve Mach 2. With the wisdom of a woman who held many aviation records, she carefully reviewed and digested cockpit matters related to safety—the ejection system, radios, and the like. But she was impatient and wanted to get on with it.

The day was clear and warm, which caused me some concern. At 35,000 feet the temperature norm is minus 65 degrees[,] but on this day the weatherman gave us a minus 56 degree reading, which would be marginal for attaining Mach 2. Our performance guys said it might be close, but I should make that speed okay with my precious cargo in the back seat. So off we went. Our FAA[-]assigned supersonic corridor stretched from Knoxville, Tennessee[,] to Columbus, Ohio[,] with the provision that we be subsonic over both cities.

About Mach 1.6 our acceleration rate became noticeably slower as the "Vigi" engines struggled with the warmer air. At Mach 1.9 we were accelerating very slowly, and I was running out of fuel and supersonic corridor at the same time. But I knew exactly what to do. I pushed the intercom button and said with pride, "Jackie, here we are at Mach 2." There was a moment's silence, then she replied, "Buster, you may be at Mach 2 in the front cockpit, but I am only at Mach 1.96 in this cockpit."

Rats! I had forgotten that she a Mach meter on the instrument panel in her cockpit. . . . She elected to stay another day to try again with more optimum temperatures projected along with a faster pilot. So, our boss, Jim Pearce, saved the day by taking his elegant passenger to Mach 2.01 in both cockpits of the Vigilante at the same time.[7]

Jackie Cochran, the maven of speed, was familiar in the highest circles of celebrity, industry, and government. With the assistance of Chuck Yeager, she was first woman to achieve Mach 1, on May 18, 1953. By 1962, she was training to take a Lockheed F-104G to 1,303.24 mph. Alamy T81PFK

Six months after the record-setting Jackie Cochran flight, the Navy decided to challenge the world altitude record. A Russian pilot, Vladimir Smirnov, had reached a record altitude of 69,000 feet over Bykovo Aerodrome on July 13, 1959, with a specially prepared experimental aircraft. The flight test division at NATC possessed data suggesting that the Vigilante could exceed the record by a comfortable margin. The A3J-1 program project manager, Cmdr. Leroy Heath, and fellow project officer Lt. Larry Monroe were selected to fly a record attempt. The official rules required that the aircraft carry a payload of 1,000 kilograms (2,204.62 pounds) during the official flight, so linear bomb-bay fuel cells were filled with enough fuel to meet the stipulation. Heath and Monroe developed a profile maximizing the altitude reached at the end of a zoom climb. They determined that a 3 g pull-up into a steep climb, followed by a zero g pushover as airspeed decayed, was the best maneuver to maximize altitude. The risk of entering a fully developed spin was a big concern, since NAA engineers considered that condition unrecoverable. During practice flights at Pax River, Heath and Monroe achieved an altitude of 80,000 feet from a 35-degree climb entered at Mach 1.8, but the Vigilante tumbled out of control in the thin air at that altitude. At the onset of the tumble, Heath had the presence of mind to center the flight controls, reduce engine power, and simply ride the aircraft to a lower altitude, where control effectiveness returned in the thicker air. In the cool early-morning air of December 13, 1960, at Palmdale, California, Heath reached the pull-up point at 53,000 feet and a speed of Mach 2.11. The Vigilante zoomed beyond 91,000 feet before nosing over, flipping onto its back, and entering a series of half rolls. At 42,000 feet, control response returned, and Heath was able to restart the engines and land normally. Officially the Vigilante reached an altitude of 91,450.8 feet (27,874.2 meters).

Not all Vigilante publicity was favorable. Capt. R. A. "Bob" Elder, now director of flight test at NATC, earned fame for his pioneering achievements in jet carrier operations with the FJ-1 Fury. Elder ferried one of the first production A3J-1s from the Columbus plant to Pax River in May 1959. The Vigilante had never been displayed in public before, and Elder received approval to stop at Andrews AFB, where he was authorized to display the new aircraft statically at the annual air show. Elder recalls:

Now static display may be better than nothing, but not much! In fact, the thought of that sleek bird roosting on the ramp while the show went on was depressing to me. So much so that I decided to test the water with DCNO (Air) Vice Admiral Robert B. Pirie. . . . I placed the phone call to his quarters the evening before the show, along about cocktail hour. Approval was granted, with some constraints.

Unfortunately, my performance the next day neither lasted very long, nor did much to credit my confidence, or the Admiral's decision. Every aircraft manufacturer seems to have an Achilles heel, and with North American Aviation it was wheel well doors or panels. Shedding one or more seemed to be a necessity in the developmental test history of a number of their airplanes. I acquired that test point shortly after takeoff, a rather sporty chandelle reentry to a burner pass down the runway on the deck—all out—streaming parts down the runway and along the flight path! Not all of them, however[,] as the right main wheel well door buried itself about three feet deep into the leading edge of the stabilator, none of which did anything to improve the aerodynamics or control qualities of the airplane, or my morale.

Following a somewhat gimpy trip from Andrews 50 or so miles south to Patuxent, I made an uneventful landing and filled out the not[-]so[-]uneventful reports.[8]

Conventional armament trials started at NATC in February 1961, and numerous problems with the bomb avionics were revealed in short order. The bombing computer and related components were persistently unreliable, but a concerted effort by the Navy, NAA, and all affected subcontractors resolved most of the deficiencies. Additional testing in June 1961 determined that level flight deliveries from 20,000 feet at Mach 0.9 were accurate, but loft and over-the-shoulder deliveries from a 500-foot run-in at Mach 0.9 were unsatisfactory.

Nuclear-weapons trials were conducted at the Naval Weapons Evaluation Facility (NWEF), Kirtland AFB, Albuquerque, New Mexico. The trials, which started on May 5, 1962, and concluded on December 28, 1962, consisted of 136 flights totaling 183.1 flight hours. Numerous weapon types were delivered from the linear bomb bay as well as conventional underwing pylons. Low-level loft and over-the-shoulder drops, as well as high-altitude deliveries from 61,000 feet at Mach 1.8, were accomplished. In all, thirty-eight full-scale nuclear-store deliveries were made, but persistent problems with bomb-delivery electronics coupled with mechanical difficulties in the ejection system and postejection stability of the store train made the linear bomb bay unreliable. The acceptance trials report concludes, "Numerous deficiencies are reported in the special weapons trials which directly affect the ability of the aircraft to safely and reliably carry out the nuclear strike mission."[9] While the Vigilante proved to be an excellent bomb platform when releasing ordnance from underwing pylons, the linear bomb bay, a fundamental feature of the aircraft, proved hopelessly troublesome and was never used in fleet service.[10]

Fleet deliveries of the A3J-1 started on June 16, 1961, when four factory-fresh Vigilantes were delivered to VAH-3, the training squadron for Heavy Attack Wing One at

NAS Sanford, Florida. The squadron had been commissioned in 1951 with the primary mission of long-range, all-weather delivery of nuclear and conventional weapons. The Vigilante fleet indoctrination program (FIP) was probably the most complex ever run, and the Navy insisted on "contractor support," a new concept that required the manufacturer to provide technical training, spare parts, and maintenance assistance throughout the indoctrination program. While this level of contractor support was common in test and development phases, it had never been required at the fleet level. In compliance, NAA sent thirty-five technical representatives to NAS Sanford to introduce pilots, bombardier/navigators, and ground support personnel to the new airplane.

A virtual campus of classrooms complete with simulators and system mockups was established to train Vigilante squadrons for fleet operations. The initial FIP class consisted of 170 sailors from VAH-3, VAH-7, and the overhaul-and-repair facility at NAS Jacksonville, where major maintenance would be performed. Flight crews trained in weapons system trainers built by Link, inventor of the famous Link Trainer that taught instrument flight to thousands of pilots during World War II. These weapons system trainers, specifically designed for the Vigilante, simulated all phases of an attack mission. Takeoff, weapon delivery, landing, and even emergencies could be replicated. After numerous hours in the system trainers, actual flight training was conducted in two-seat F9F-8T Cougars for pilots, while bombardier/navigators trained in R4D Skytrains and A3D-2T Skywarriors. Familiarization flights in the A3Js were scheduled later in the syllabus to provide experience in aerobatics, night flight, and weapon delivery techniques. When an aircrew was fully qualified in the A3J, they were in competition against other aircrews to further polish their bombing and navigation skills. The competition culminated in a weeklong annual "Bombing Derby" that pitted the top four Vigilante crews against each other.

The first operational unit to receive the A3J-1 was VAH-7, with their new aircraft arriving at NAS Sanford on January 25, 1962. The squadron aircrews had been trained under the fleet indoctrination program in the summer of 1961, using VAH-3 airplanes. Six months later, VAH-7 deployed with twelve new Vigilantes on the first operational cruise of USS *Enterprise* (CVN-65) to participate in a NATO exercise. The deployment was terminated after only two months at sea because of the Cuban Missile Crisis. *Enterprise* returned to Florida on October 11 to participate in the quarantine of Cuba. From February to September 1963, VAH-7 participated in a second *Enterprise* cruise, without incident. Upon return to port at Norfolk, VAH-7 was awarded the CNO safety award for the year.

On February 8, 1964, VAH-7 departed aboard *Enterprise* for its last deployment with Vigilantes. Rather than returning on July 29, when relieved by USS *Forrestal*, *Enterprise* joined "Operation Sea Orbit," a 30,565-mile round-the-world cruise to display the Navy's ability to conduct prolonged operations on a global basis. "Operation Sea Orbit" ended on October 3, 1964, when *Enterprise* arrived at Norfolk, nine months after it had departed.

The Tri-Service aircraft designation system was introduced on September 18, 1962, and the A3J-1 was redesignated the A-5A. VAH-1 started its transition to the Vigilante in August 1962, using VAH-3 aircraft. Its first Vigilante was delivered to the squadron on January 22, 1963. By August 6, the squadron had received a full complement of a dozen aircraft and deployed aboard USS *Independence* (CV-62). Several unique mishaps occurred with the Vigilantes during the seven-month cruise. A tailhook failure resulted in the first barrier engagement of an A-5A. Damage was not severe, but shipboard repairs lasted for several months. An in-flight engine failure forced a Vigilante to divert to a civilian airport near Nice, France. The replacement engine had to be barged ashore and installed by Navy personnel, who much enjoyed temporary shore duty on the French Riviera. Later in the cruise, during night operations, a recovering F-4 Phantom II struck the ramp. The crew was able to eject before the aircraft went over the port side, but an A-5A in the landing cycle was lost when its nose gear collapsed, and it slid off the angled deck, thus trapping the crew.

A highlight of the *Independence* cruise was the successful launch of nine Vigilantes for a long-range strike exercise. All aircraft completed their assigned missions and recovered, with only three reported minor discrepancies. USS *Independence* returned to Norfolk on March 4, 1964. In all, the A-5A was deployed on four cruises: three by VAH-7 aboard *Enterprise* and one by VAH-1 on *Independence*. Of the fifty-nine A-5As built, five were lost during test and development, two were lost to the fleet during onshore field operations, and three were lost at sea.[11] The overall assessment of the A-5A's performance at sea was not favorable. Capt. James D. "Jig Dog" Ramage, skipper of *Independence* during the Vigilante's last cruise, remembered it as the most demanding of all aircraft for his pilots. Further, it was the least available because of complexity and lack of spare parts. The end of the *Independence* cruise also marked the end of the A-5A in aircraft carrier service. The complex, maintenance-intense A-5A, with an unreliable internal bomb bay, was removed from the heavy-attack inventory and relegated to a training role.[12] Yet, in a strange twist of fate, several events converged to give the Vigilante a new lease on life.

A3J-2/A-5B, the Second-Generation Vigilante

In mid-1961 the Navy agreed to relax the arduous zero-wind launch requirement that forced North American to alter the original NAGPAW design. Now, with the assistance of wind across the bow, the gross takeoff weight was therefore increased by 60 percent, and the mission profile could be expanded. An improved Vigilante, initially designated A3J-2, was proposed by North American. It promised greater range, increased ordnance load, improved high-altitude performance, and better landing characteristics. The fuselage was redesigned to improve volumetric efficiency with a hump-shaped fairing (sometimes referred to as the "top cap" modification) that ran from the aft cockpit to the trailing edge of the wing. It provided space for 500 gallons of additional fuel. Lift was increased by expanding the wing flap area and redirecting boundary layer airflow over the entire wing rather than just the flaps. Ordnance capacity was doubled with the installation of two additional underwing pylons, making the new Vigilante a more capable attack aircraft.

But enthusiasm for the Navy's nuclear-attack mission was waning. The CNO, Adm. Arleigh Burke, had been studying the possibility of submarine-launched ballistic missiles since January 1958. The first submerged launch of a Polaris missile was successfully demonstrated on July 20, 1960. The Air Force's Strategic Air Command (SAC) owned the B-52 manned bombers and underground Minuteman Missiles, but Polaris bestowed upon the Navy its own leg of the nuclear triad; however, the simmering fifteen-year debate regarding the surface Navy's strategic nuclear-weapons role was reignited. An acrimonious accord was finally reached by the JCS, and the Navy's carrier-based strategic nuclear mission was rescinded. Hoping to salvage a conventional attack role for the Vigilante, North American presented the A3J-2 to Congress as a low-level, supersonic attack aircraft capable of delivering large conventional weapon loads. At the same time, a reconnaissance version with a long ventral fairing that could carry sensors, cameras, and side-looking radar also was proposed.

Initially, Congress agreed to the attack proposal, allowing the Navy to modify the existing Vigilante contract to build the last eighteen aircraft as A3J-2s. The first, BuNo 149300, flew on April 29, 1962, and showed substantial promise. Nevertheless, only two A3J-2s (BuNos 149300 and 149302) were delivered before the Department of Defense considered terminating funds for the entire program. SecDef Robert McNamara (1916–2009), while still new on the job, was determined to eradicate wasteful defense spending. He was aware that Vigilante funding was projected to escalate from $177.9 million in fiscal year 1962 to more than $200 million in fiscal 1963; unit costs would exceed $16.5 million by 1964.

The Vigilante was a perfect target for termination because of its expense and disappointment as a strategic bomber. However, a study by the Darrow tactical-reconnaissance board to eliminate intelligence-gathering overlap concluded that the Vigilante would make a "superior reconnaissance platform" and that its information-gathering capability could not be duplicated by "any other device in the Navy inventory." This endorsement saved the Vigilante program from termination. Of the eighteen Vigilantes intended as A-5Bs (the post-September 1962 designation for A3J-2s), four (149301, 149303, 149304, and 149305) were completed and delivered as YA-5Cs, an interim trainer version. The remaining twelve aircraft were completed as A-5Bs and held at the Columbus plant, pending a decision on their use.

A3J-3/RA-5C, the Ultimate Vigilante

Aerial photography was deemed vital to war fighting from the earliest days of US naval aviation. Counted among the first combat flights flown by naval aircraft during the Vera Cruz Insurrection in 1914 were photographic and observation missions.[13] By the 1950s, photographic reconnaissance played a decisive role in Korea. Photo-equipped F2H Banshees and F9F Panthers provided nearly 95 percent of all intelligence available to the naval task forces. Between 1957 and 1959, the CNO, Adm. Arleigh Burke, defined the Navy's requirements for an advanced multisensor tactical-intelligence system. By the early 1960s the importance of tactical reconnaissance became indisputable when supersonic RF-8A Crusaders from VFP-62 and VMCJ-2 repeatedly flew low-level missions over Cuba, capturing some 160,000 images. This intelligence was so central to the successful outcome of the Cuban Missile Crisis (October 1962) that President Kennedy personally awarded the Navy unit commendation to VFP-62. Prior to that crisis, the Vigilante's future was uncertain, but the endorsement from the Darrow study and the growing awareness of the need for a dedicated tactical-reconnaissance capability in the fleet gave the Vigilante renewed life. Initially designated A3J-3, the "recon" Vigilante was redesignated RA-5C in September 1962 under the McNamara Tri-Service aircraft designation system.

Production of two prototypes was approved early in 1962, but before the prototypes flew, the ventral canoe that carried most of the reconnaissance equipment was aerodynamically tested on an A3J-1 (BuNo 146695). The canoe had no detrimental effect on speed, range, or handling qualities. Since their airframes were nearly identical, the

A3J-2 prototype, BuNo 149300, also served as the A3J-3 prototype. It flew for the first time in the reconnaissance configuration on June 30, 1962, and was joined in the test program by BuNo 146699, an A3J-1 that been upgraded to the A3J-3 standard. The reconnaissance equipment consisted of frame cameras, panoramic cameras, side-looking radar (SLAR), passive electronic-countermeasures equipment (PECM—a "passive" device listens but does not emit energy), and infrared sensors. A digital data system installed on board the aircraft displayed the date, time, altitude, and geographic coordinates of each image. The linear bomb bay was now used to carry passive electronic-countermeasures equipment and additional fuel cells.

Thus, the RA-5C became the first integrated multisensor reconnaissance system. It had approximately one hundred flush-mounted antennas, with only a single conventional antenna protruding from the aft fuselage. These sensors fed data for recording electronic radiations on special code matrix film.

Vigilante Flight Test Recollections of Ed Gillespie

The Vigilante could use this entire spectrum of equipment in one supersonic pass to fulfill its mission. To demonstrate the new Vigilante's range and speed, chief test pilot Ed Gillespie flew a fast dash from Columbus, Ohio, to NAS Sanford, Florida (near Orlando), on a high-Mach, high-altitude test. He maintained Mach 1.5 to 1.8 between 35,000 and 50,000 feet, landing at Sanford only fifty-eight minutes after brake release, in what could be characterized as a maximum-range "super cruise" flight. He departed Columbus with 22,000 pounds of fuel and landed with 2,400 pounds. Shortly thereafter, both prototypes were assigned to the Naval Ordnance Test Station (NOTS) at China Lake for electronic and reconnaissance testing. Ed continued:

> When I was practicing for carrier suitability, I was making landings at Port Columbus with the Vigilante. I touched down gently but I knew right away something was wrong. The magnesium casting on the left main gear failed. When I left the runway, I blew the canopy because I thought I was going to nose over. The airplane skidded across a runway intersection into the dirt doing 130 knots. I didn't have any control and was headed for a B-25 that was waiting to cross the runway. The copilot saw me coming right for him. He jammed the throttles and moved quickly out of the way. I went right through where he was sitting. It was a wild ride.
>
> One time during a low[-]altitude weapon drop when the Vigilante was still a bomber, I was at Tonopah, Nevada, which is now what they call Area 51. I talked to a guy on

the ground in a block house. I told him I would be supersonic and very close to him. He said, "Don't worry about it. We work with projects like this all the time." I came in at 500 feet doing 1.3 Mach. I called them to see if everything went all right. He shouted, "Damn, don't ever do that again!" He didn't realize an airplane that size could make such a difference. I really knocked the [crap] out of that place. The plaster came off the walls and ceiling. The windows were broken, and they were the real thick ones.

> I filed my flight plan back to Albuquerque and I had 8,000 pounds of fuel—plenty to get me there. On climb out I noticed I'm down to 7,000 pounds and I hadn't gone that far. I wondered, do I believe the gauge or don't I? I had just kicked out a big heavy weapon and which really thumped the airplane good. I checked the gauge closely and I could almost watch it go down. I decided to believe the gauge, so I declared a "Mayday" and headed for the close-by China Lake at Inyokern. Now I'm down to 3,000 pounds. When I touched down, I knew I was light. I had less than 1,000 pounds. I taxied in and real happy to be aboard. I couldn't believe it. The civilian crash crew would not come close to the airplane. They thought it might blow up. What the hell is a crash crew for? I climbed out of the cockpit and hung by my fingers. I dropped to the ground and into a puddle—no, a lake—of fuel that was cascading out of the bomb bay. Like a damn fool, I took off my glove and crawled up into the bomb bay to try and stop the leak. All I did was get some JP-5 fuel burns. I was mad at the crash crew for not properly responding, but I was also mad because the main three-inch fuel line had been "Murphy'd" [Murphy's law—factory error] and installed wrong. When the weapon was released, it ripped open the fuel line.[14]

Vigilante Goes to War

A Navy contract for production of RA-5Cs was issued in late September 1962. Eighteen would be upgraded from the interim A-5Bs and YA-5Cs, forty-three would be new-build aircraft, and forty-three would be converted from existing A-5As. Deliveries began on June 27, 1963, when training squadron VAH-3 at Sanford, Florida (later redesignated RVAH-3 in recognition of its reconnaissance role), received its first RA-5C. In preparation for delivery to operational units, carrier suitability trials were conducted aboard USS *Saratoga* (CV-60) in December 1963. BuNo 150823, the first of the new-build RA-5Cs, was used for the trials. Once carrier-certified, RA-5C deliveries started for nine operational squadrons: RVAH-1, 5, 6, 7, 9, 11, 12, 13, and 14. The first to receive the new Vigilante was RVAH-5 on March 1, 1964. After two months of workups at NAS Sanford, RVAH-5 deployed aboard USS *Ranger* (CV-61) on May 8 for a western Pacific cruise.

On August 2, while *Ranger* was conducting training exercises off the coast of Hawaii, there were allegations (now controversial, still debated by some, but basically lost to the fog of war) that USS *Maddox* and *Turner Joy* were attacked by North Vietnamese gunboats in the Gulf of Tonkin. The United States launched retaliation strikes on August 5, and *Ranger* departed for Southeast Asia. Untested in combat, RVAH-5's Vigilantes were assigned to fly reconnaissance sorties over the relatively safe territory of South Vietnam. These early missions provided photoreconnaissance to develop attack routes for strike aircraft, but in early 1965, as the US bombing intensified, the airspace north of the seventeenth parallel was open for operations by RVAH-5 Vigilantes.

Since the RA-5C was unarmed, each sortie received an F-4 Phantom II escort. RVAH-5's deployment aboard *Ranger* ended prematurely on April 13, 1965, when a fire in the ship's engine room forced a retreat for repairs to Subic Bay in the Philippines. On May 10, *Independence* (CV-62) set course for Vietnam with the Vigilantes of RVAH-1, which were tasked with mapping the entire area of North Vietnam. It had been apparent from the outset of the war that existing maps of Vietnam were notoriously inaccurate. It was common to find errors of 4 miles or more, causing operational confusion both for air strikes and ground operations. Within two weeks, RVAH-1 mapped the entire country, which built familiarity and confidence

Employees of the sales and marketing department drool at the opportunity for new customers. An artist has been commissioned to paint Vigilante with Air Force markings and place it in the sky with an AWACS (Airborne Warning and Control System), which dates the painting to ca. 1970.

in the RA-5C and confirmed its value as an essential element of naval air warfare.[15]

While the RF-8 Crusader provided light photoreconnaissance in a smaller, more nimble aircraft, nothing could provide the quality, diversity, and volume of information gathered by the Vigilante. "That thing was like a big sponge" was one pilot's description of the Vigilante. "We had a six-inch forward camera, side-looking cameras[, and] side-looking radar. We had infrared and we had what was called a PECM [passive electronic-countermeasures equipment] package that just picked up anything that was being transmitted."[16] As previously described, the Vigilante had the unique capability of feeding its reconnaissance data into the IOICs (integrated operational intelligence centers) placed aboard large deck carriers and shore stations. The IOIC could process, analyze, print, store, and disseminate readouts of the data within minutes of landing. This allowed continuous updates of targeting and orders of battle information. Every wartime mission puts aircrews at risk, but gathering bomb damage assessments (BDAs) was the most dangerous.

The enemy came to expect a reconnaissance pass shortly after a strike, and Vigilante crews expected to be greeted with intense ground fire. With speed as their only defense on these low-altitude passes—it was inevitable that the number of aircraft losses would mount. Over the course of the war, twenty-three Vigilantes were lost, eighteen from enemy fire and another five from ramp strikes and other operational causes. One carrier alone, USS *Kitty Hawk* (CV-63), accounted for six of the losses. As fewer aircraft were available to accomplish the mission workload, maintenance demands on surviving aircraft burgeoned. By 1967 it became necessary to replenish the dwindling fleet. In a rare move, the assembly line at Columbus was reopened and forty-six new Vigilantes were procured in three blocks—twelve in fiscal year (FY) 1968, twenty-four in FY69, and ten in FY70. A public-relations brochure refers to these final Vigilantes as "the 1969-model RA-5C," which incorporated several design improvements: J79-GE-10 engines, each capable of 1,400 pounds of additional thrust, replaced the earlier J79-GE-8; larger air intakes, heavier afterburner petals, and longer tailpipes were required for the uprated engines; and wing root fairings (known as LEXs or "leading edge extensions") were installed, improving lateral control and allowing a higher angle of attack for reduced landing speed.

In December 1969, funds were diverted to F-14 development, which forced cancellation of the final block of ten RA-5Cs. North American (now NAR) had already acquired material for all forty-six Vigilantes, to avoid cost overruns and ensure availability of unique long-lead-time assemblies (wing skins, for example, milled from an exotic lithium aluminum alloy, were difficult to obtain). The contractual and financial problems facing both the government and contractor were resolved by an agreement worked out between John Fossnes, president of the Columbus Division,

An enterprising paint salesman convinced safety officials that bright-orange markings (conspicuity paint) would minimize midair collisions. The color was ubiquitous ca. 1960.

and Capt. Thomas Kilcline, NAVAIR program manager. Material either on hand (or on order) for the canceled Vigilantes would be stored as spares for future years. Landing-gear components, reconnaissance equipment, wing sections, and empennage assemblies were placed in a bonded warehouse to be used in the repair of battle-damaged aircraft. This turned out to be fiscally responsible and helped return several Vigilantes to service expeditiously.[17]

The Vigilante's career in Vietnam spanned the entire period of US involvement from the Gulf of Tonkin response in August 1964 to the ceasefire in 1973. Vigilante squadrons completed thirty-one combat zone deployments: RVAH-5 and RVAH-6 each deployed five times to the war zone; RVAH-1, RVAH-7, RVAH-11, and RVAH-13 logged four deployments; RVAH-12 logged three deployments; and RVAH-9 logged two. Two Vigilante squadrons were not assigned to Vietnam: RVAH-3, the training squadron, was never operationally deployed, and RVAH-14 operated with the 6th Fleet in the Mediterranean. RVAH-14 became the first Vigilante squadron to be disestablished, on May 1, 1974. The last squadron to stand down was RVAH-7, on September 29, 1979, which, coincidently was the first operational squadron to receive an A3J-1 in August 1962. The last RA-5C in the active inventory was BuNo 156608—which was retired on November 20, 1979.

Vigilante in Retrospect

The F-4 Phantom II emerged from the St. Louis plant of McDonnell Aircraft Company in 1958. Over five thousand were built—sometimes at a pace of three per workday. With the same engines and sized similarly to the Vigilante, the F-4 came in multiple versions and performed an amazing mix of missions, ranging from bomber to air superiority, reconnaissance, close air support, and more. The Vigilante was faster because it was unencumbered by external racks, fuel tanks, and munitions. Some argue the Phantom was not the best at any single mission; however, all agree it was versatile. The Marines, Air Force, and many allied nations also came to rely on the Phantom, and that dominance relegated Vigilante to a supporting role and limited production.

The Vigilante, in further retrospect, was a bitter disappointment as a strategic nuclear bomber but became the world's benchmark for tactical reconnaissance aircraft and served in that role for more than sixteen years. It clearly represented the most advanced warplane of its era, with an impressive list of firsts:

- a supersonic high-/low-altitude carrier aircraft
- fly-by-wire on a production aircraft

- deflector/spoiler controls (no ailerons)
- variable-geometry horizontal ramp inlet (engine cowl)
- subsonic and supersonic escape system
- very high-pressure hydraulic system
- integrated inertial navigating bombing controls
- digital navigation and bombing computer
- heads-up display on a production aircraft
- integrated terrain avoidance system
- integrated multisensor reconnaissance system

In total, 156 Vigilantes were delivered, 140 of which were built as RA-5Cs or rebuilt to that standard from earlier A-5As. The Vigilante program was noteworthy for its short development cycle. The "go-ahead" for A3J-1 development was in June 1956, the prototype flew in August 1958, and operational squadron service was achieved by June 1960—four years from paper to operation. RA-5C development required even less time: the contract was issued in December 1960, the prototype flew in June

1962, and operational deployment was achieved in July 1964—one month later, the RA-5C was in combat over Vietnam. Current military aircraft programs such as V-22, F-22, and F-35 have taken more than two decades to develop. NAR executive Roger L. Wood (1933–2019) attributes the Vigilante's rapid development to a unique procurement practice:

Weapon System Management was a key factor in all of this because North American's freedom to manage interface controls and fully optimize the airborne and shipboard systems permitted a level of system integration not possible under prior "GFE" [government furnished equipment] policies. In fact, the RA-5C was the only system ever carried fully to service use under the weapon system management approach[,] and DOD needs to give serious consideration to returning to this powerful practical management tool.[18]

A McDonnell F-4 Phantom II flies in formation with a Vigilante as they go "feet dry" (flying over land). The radio call when departing land for ocean is "Feet wet." These radio calls provide aviators with situational awareness in case of bailout and were most prescient on missions over Vietnam.

OV-10 Bronco

The OV-10 Bronco was created to fill a void that became evident during the Vietnam War. A jungle war of insurgency demanded aircraft that flew low and slow. Older airplanes, including the North American T-28 trainer and Douglas A-1E Skyraider, filled the void pending availability of the Bronco.

In 1958, NAA-Columbus became a pioneer in the development of counterinsurgency (COIN) aircraft when the French government expressed a need for light strike/reconnaissance aircraft to be used in their Algerian campaign. The French planned to convert North American T-28A trainers into light fighters by installing a larger engine, reinforcing the wings, armor-plating the cockpits, and adding ordnance systems. These converted T-28As were redesignated T-28S Fennecs ("Desert Fox") by the French air force. Although the Algerian conflict was resolved in late 1961, the Fennecs served long enough to demonstrate their operational effectiveness and became popular with flight crews and maintainers.

By 1961 the US Air Force also needed COIN fighters for Southeast Asia, and the Fennec served as a template. As covered in chapter 4, 313 retired T-28As were removed from storage and remanufactured to a new T-28D standard by NAA-Columbus. Under license, Fairchild Republic produced an additional seventy-two. Larger engines, airframe enhancements, provisions for ordnance, armor plating, and self-sealing fuel tanks were added. The T-28D initially showed promise; however, within two years, hard

A scale model of the OV-10 Bronco takes its turn in the wind tunnel. The close-air-support (CAS) mission demands a sturdy airframe and redundant flight controls that can survive an encounter with small-arms fire.

usage and the heat and humidity of Vietnam, combined with aging airframes, yielded a series of structural failures. To replace the deteriorating T-28D fleet, NAA-Columbus proposed the YAT-28E—a more dramatic T-28A upgrade powered by a Lycoming turboprop engine. Three prototypes were built and tested, but the Air Force declined to order production. Something more than reworking an aging trainer was needed.

Origins of the Bronco

Also in the late 1950s, two Marine pilots with extensive experience in close air support, Maj. W. H. Beckett, and Lt. Col. K. P. Rice, found themselves stationed in Southern California. Rice had a master's degree in aeronautical engineering from MIT, a bachelor's degree in electronics from Cornell University, and a reputation for innovation at China Lake's experiential Squadron 5 (VX-5). Rice demonstrated a knack for designing multiple carriage bomb racks. They were installed on many US strike aircraft and even "borrowed" by the Russian air force. Beckett and Rice frequently discussed the optimal characteristics of a hypothetical close-air-support aircraft, and by 1960 an idealized airplane emerged. They dubbed the airplane L²VMA (light, light marine attack aircraft), which focused on low-speed performance and maneuverability that had been lost with jets. It would have the dive performance of a Junkers Ju 87 Stuka, the maneuverability of a North American T-6/SNJ Texan, and the durability of a Vought F4U Corsair.

But integrating the airplane with ground troops was foremost. In Beckett's words, "The airplane would have to live with the troops." Short takeoffs and landings from

Many Army soldiers in Vietnam were draftees. They called themselves "grunts," and most preferred dockside duty over toting a rifle while patrolling a jungle trail. Cocooning protects the airframe, wiring, and engines from exposure to salt water.

dirt roads and jungle clearings were essential. This limited the wingspan to 20 feet and the landing-gear width to 6.5 feet. The aircraft used the same ammunition as the ground troops for ease of reloading and logistics. A small bomb bay was incorporated for internal storage of ordnance. It was powered by two lightweight turboprop engines in a twin-boom configuration and a center cockpit pod. Retractable floats were proposed to permit water-based operations. "The design we came up with was not 'normal,'" recalls Beckett, "but it could hopefully do tactically useful jobs that nothing else could do."[1]

Rice had contacts at Douglas, Ryan, and Convair. Each analyzed the L^{2}VMA design and found it "interesting and feasible," but none were willing to develop it with corporate funds. Dr. Bill McLean, technical director at China Lake and creator of the Sidewinder missile, became interested in funding a prototype. With no manufacturer support, Beckett and Rice were faced with the prospect of building a twin turboprop "military" prototype in Rice's garage. Fortunately, Rice had home-building experience dating back to a Goodyear racer he built in 1949. However, as the airframe came together and was nearly ready for engine installation, Adm. Schoech of BuWeps issued a cease-and-desist order when he became convinced that the project was unfeasible and a waste of money.

Undeterred, Beckett and Rice redoubled efforts to get an official program started. Using all their industry contacts, they briefed anyone who would listen. Col. Marion Carl (the noted fighter ace and test pilot) at Marine Corps headquarters took an interest and had Rice assigned to the recently formed Department of Defense counterinsurgency aircraft program. At that time, interest in COIN aircraft was growing. The military assistance program was interested in procuring counterinsurgency aircraft for allied forces, the Army was interested in replacing their OV-1 Mohawk, the Marine Corps was interested in close-air-support aircraft, and the Air Force was interested in forward air control aircraft. Dr. Harold Brown, the Pentagon's director of research and engineering (and later secretary of defense under the Carter administration), sent a letter to the undersecretaries of the Army, Air Force, and Navy outlining a "light armed reconnaissance aircraft" (LARA) for counterinsurgency operations. This was of great interest to SecDef Robert McNamara, since it conformed to his philosophy of commonality in weapons acquisition. McNamara became so supportive of the "one-size-fits-all" approach that he formed a triservice committee of Army, Navy, Air Force, and Pentagon officials to draft a joint requirement for an aircraft that would meet the needs of each service, with only minor modifications.

The committee arrived at a requirement known as LARA (light armed reconnaissance aircraft), which resembled the L^{2}VMA but was larger, more complex, and more expensive. Structurally, LARA was required to withstand fighter flight loads (8 g positive and 3 g negative), land on rough fields with a 1,200-pound payload, provisioned for two AIM-9 Sidewinder missiles, and fly close-air-support missions with 2,400 pounds of ordnance, and enough fuel for an hour of loiter time. In addition, it was expected to fly 3.5-hour reconnaissance missions on internal fuel, airdrop 2,000 pounds of cargo or six paratroopers, operate from aircraft carriers with no catapult

The protective coating must be removed. Airplanes vulnerable to a single small-arms round need not apply for work at the Vietnam War. Low, slow, and rugged are the watchwords in a jungle war of insurgency.

The OV-10 assembly line at Columbus. The Bronco (like its older sibling the Mustang) is considered a success, and some people rue its passing. Close air support is a vital mission to ground troops that some in the Air Force prefer to ignore.

Marking Time ©
North American OV-10 Bronco

Part 1: USAF Service

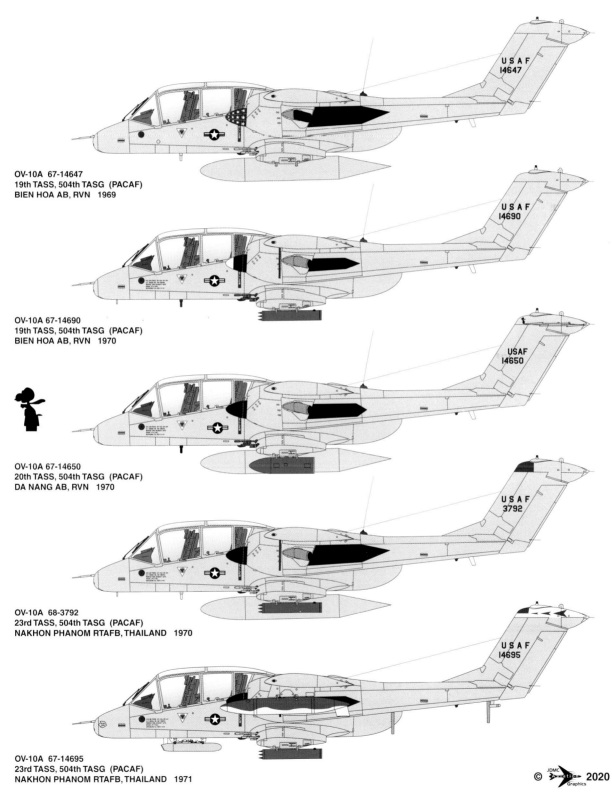

USAF 14647

OV-10A 67-14647
19th TASS, 504th TASG (PACAF)
BIEN HOA AB, RVN 1969

USAF 14690

OV-10A 67-14690
19th TASS, 504th TASG (PACAF)
BIEN HOA AB, RVN 1970

USAF 14650

OV-10A 67-14650
20th TASS, 504th TASG (PACAF)
DA NANG AB, RVN 1970

USAF 3792

OV-10A 68-3792
23rd TASS, 504th TASG (PACAF)
NAKHON PHANOM RTAFB, THAILAND 1970

USAF 14695

OV-10A 67-14695
23rd TASS, 504th TASG (PACAF)
NAKHON PHANOM RTAFB, THAILAND 1971

Part 2: USMC Service

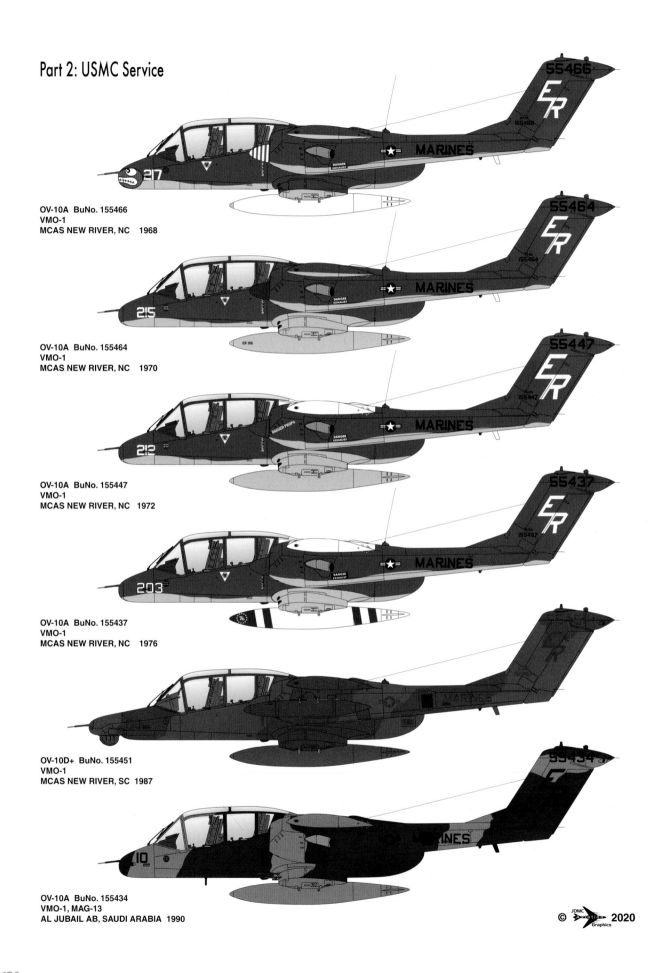

OV-10A BuNo. 155466
VMO-1
MCAS NEW RIVER, NC 1968

OV-10A BuNo. 155464
VMO-1
MCAS NEW RIVER, NC 1970

OV-10A BuNo. 155447
VMO-1
MCAS NEW RIVER, NC 1972

OV-10A BuNo. 155437
VMO-1
MCAS NEW RIVER, NC 1976

OV-10D+ BuNo. 155451
VMO-1
MCAS NEW RIVER, SC 1987

OV-10A BuNo. 155434
VMO-1, MAG-13
AL JUBAIL AB, SAUDI ARABIA 1990

JDMC Aviation Graphics © 2020

The cover of a brochure making the case for an L²VMA aircraft. The OV-10 ultimately met the need.

or arrestment gear, have a top speed of 350 mph, and take off within 800 feet.

The Navy managed the LARA program, and on October 28, 1963, the Navy's Bureau of Weapons (BuWeps) issued an RFP. Nine companies responded by March 1964: Beechcraft, Convair, Douglas, Goodyear, Helio, Hiller, Lockheed, Martin, and North American. In Rice's view, Ryan not only was first to express interest but also proposed the most interesting design; however, they declined to submit a formal proposal. Convair, on the other hand, was so interested in the program that work commenced on a flying prototype (utilizing only company funds) two months after the RFP was released.

The Convair Model 48 Charger

In 1961, two years before the RFP, Convair's preliminary design group started working on layouts for limited-warfare and counterinsurgency aircraft. Convair was well ahead of the other manufacturers when the request arrived. Jim Fink, who would become program manager, convinced Convair president Joe Famme to build a flying prototype with corporate funds. The prototype was built in nine months and rolled out on September 29, 1964. It flew on November 25, with chief test pilot John W. Knebe at the controls. Convair's model 48 was faithful to Rice and Beckett's original L²VMA concept, with a short wingspan (27.5 feet) and light weight (4,450 pounds of dry weight—that is, without fuel, crew, or weapons). The Convair named model 48 "Charger" and powered it with twin Pratt & Whitney (Canada) YT74-CP-8 engines, originally rated at 550 shaft horsepower and later increased to 750. Initial flights were made with both engines rotating in the same direction, but they were later modified to rotate in opposite directions (the Charger's propellers rotated outboard, unlike the Bronco's, which rotated inboard). An impressive array of armament totaling 2,510 pounds could be carried on five external pylon stations and two internal store stations for close-air-support missions. Fuel capacity for ferry missions was 5,269 pounds.

The Charger's configuration consisted of a tandem two-place cockpit contained in a fuselage pod. The engines were mounted in twin booms that were positioned under a constant-chord wing. The horizontal stabilizer was mounted between vertical stabilizers at the end of each boom. The Charger's wing was almost entirely immersed in the propeller slipstream, allowing Convair to employ

The Convair model 48 was first rolled out to an adoring throng before being posed with an impressive array of inert weapons. Convair withdrew from the competition after their prototype crashed. Image courtesy of Aldrich

a deflected-slipstream thrust-vectoring system. The system was so effective in augmenting lift that Charger could take off with a ground roll of only 225 feet. In fact, applying takeoff power while extending full flaps when the aircraft was restrained would cause the airplane to levitate, making it behave "somewhere between a plane and a helicopter," according to Convair test pilot Howie Auten.[2]

Early test flights revealed lateral control problems caused by the short wingspan. Aerodynamicist Stan Piskan devised new wingtips to replace the original square tips, which added 2 feet, 7 inches to the span. From head on, the revised wingtips canted 45 degrees upward, not only correcting the lateral control issue but also reducing a severe drag penalty and increasing the top speed by 40 knots.

On October 7, 1965, the Charger joined the preliminary joint service evaluation, where it was flown by Capt. Jim Read, USMC; Capt. Joe Storface, USAF; Capt. Don Wray, USA; and Lt. Cmdr. Dave Harden, USN, for a total of eighteen flights. On October 19, Harden crashed the aircraft during an aborted single-engine landing; he ejected and survived, but the aircraft was destroyed. Harden was cited with eleven counts of pilot error.[3] In the aftermath of the crash, Convair withdrew from the competition.

On October 15, 1964, nearly a year before Convair withdrew from the program, North American was selected winner of the LARA competition on the basis of computer studies and the triservice committee's evaluation. BuWeps issued a contract for nine articles—seven of them to be flying prototypes (BuNos 152879–152885) and two static-test airframes. Designated YOV-10A and named Bronco, the prototypes were intended to demonstrate the design's capabilities and identify changes necessary before production. First flight was expected by September 1965, but North American was able to compress the schedule, and on July 7 the first ship (BuNo 152879) was rolled out of Building 7 hangar to a crowd of eight thousand enthusiastic observers. The ceremony was hosted by NAA-Columbus president Will Yahn, with corporate chairman Lee Atwood in attendance. Capt. J. L. Coleman, Navy bureau of weapons project officer for the OV-10A, presided over the unveiling, and the keynote speaker was assistant secretary of the Navy Robert Morse, who commended North American on being nearly two months ahead of schedule on the "radically new and different aircraft.[4] Nine days later, test pilot Ed Gillespie took off from Port Columbus Airport for an uneventful maiden flight. In less than a year, all seven YOV-10As were completed and active in the test program.

The YOV-10A was a simple airplane by mid-1960 standards. The flight control system relied on mechanical principles (which had been essentially ignored by military aircraft builders since 1950 in favor of high-speed electro-servos). The airframe consisted of a conventionally constructed semimonocoque aluminum pod and boom

configuration (akin to Convair's model 48 Charger). The weapons were mounted on two sponsons that sprouted from the bottom of the fuselage and looked like small wings. The actual wing was constant chord (the root and tip were the same width) mounted high and aft of the two-place cockpit. The first six aircraft were powered by twin Garrett AiResearch YT76-G-6/8 engines, producing 660 shaft horsepower and spinning Hamilton Standard three-bladed, constant-speed, full-feathering, reverse-pitch propellers. The seventh prototype (BuNo 152885) was powered by twin Pratt & Whitney (Canada) YT74 turboprops, rated at 650 shaft horsepower. Even though the YOV-10A had grown beyond Beckett and Rice's original concept of a 20-foot wingspan, NAA limited the wing to 30.3 feet, which still permitted operation from unimproved roads. Chief engineer Emerson W. Smith characterized the early flight prototype as "an advanced wind tunnel model that flies."[5] Smith's team designed the aircraft for a wide speed envelope. It was expected to fly at speeds below 60 mph, to meet its short-takeoff-and-landing (STOL) requirement, yet accelerate to a maximum sea level speed of 305 mph (with a redline speed of Mach 0.75) at altitude. Its maximum sea level speed was later determined to be 288 mph.

Despite its simple configuration and conventional structure, the YOV-10A had some novel features. Lateral control was provided by a combination of ailerons and spoilers. The spoilers, pie-shaped quarter circles, extended into the airstream from lateral slots located in front of the ailerons. Similar pie-shaped sections located in the upper and lower skins of the inboard wing sections were used as dive brakes. The engines were geared to rotate toward the centerline of the aircraft, which canceled engine torque and raised the opposite wingtip in the event of an engine failure. The high-lift flaps consisted of four identical double-slotted sections with an underwing "gipper door" that opened to form a ram air scoop to feed air to the flap slots. Full deflection of 45 degrees on landing provided maximum lift without excessive drag, according to chief engineer Smith: "We can be assured of getting back into the same field we take off from if we lose an engine."

One of the unique features of the aircraft was the landing gear, designed by Maurice E. King for extremely rough field operations from jungle clearings, primitive roads, and damaged runways. Both the nose and main gear used a trailing-arm design with two-stage air-oil telescoping shock absorbers and large, low-pressure tires. To verify the durability of King's landing gear, the Navy devised a series of unique tests that were conducted from two 500-foot sections of undulating runway that became known as the "washboard" runways. The first section had obstacles 6 inches high, spaced 200 inches apart; the second had obstacles 12 inches high, spaced 600 inches apart. Columbus test pilots Archie Lane and Ed Gillespie taxied prototype ship number 4 over these irregular surfaces at increasing speeds to determine the limits not only of aircraft but also pilot. In preliminary tests, an automobile was barely controllable at 12 mph over the obstacles, so operating a YOV-10A at speeds over 90 knots caused substantial apprehension.

After ten runs at increasing speeds, Lane had difficulty reading the instruments at 47 knots and could barely keep the aircraft aligned with the runway. On the fourteenth run, at 57 knots, he reached his physiological limit—only gross control movements were possible. The aircraft, however, was perfectly capable of handling the short-frequency undulations. The long-cycle undulations over 12-inch obstacles proved less difficult. During the third taxi test, the aircraft stabilized and the landing gear insulated the cockpit from the destructive vibrations by entering a plane over the obstacles. Ultimately, the aircraft reached a speed of 90 knots and was able to execute a smooth takeoff. The tests demonstrated that the airplane was capable of extremely rough field operation, limited only by human factors. Lane's conclusion appeared in an AIAA technical paper:

Excessive physiological stresses were experienced by the pilot during landing roll-out and takeoff through the six-inch[-]high continuous undulations spaced 200 inches apart. Such will be the case whenever the airplane couples with the terrain to produce continuous vibrational frequencies near the natural frequencies of the human body, about 3–6 cycles per second.[5]

Structural demonstrations, which started in 1966, revealed a serious problem that was not solved for over four years. NAR guaranteed that the Bronco could withstand a 430-knot dive, well above its normal operating speed, but achieving that speed required a vertical dive from high altitude under full power—a particularly perilous maneuver. The buildup to 430 knots started with numerous dives at gradually increasing speeds to monitor the Bronco's behavior. It became increasingly apparent that the airframe was too flexible, and that the onset of destructive flutter was likely. After numerous airframe revisions, evidence of flutter remained, which caused growing apprehension among the test pilots. In late April 1968, after one particularly troubling dive, test pilot Don McCracken complained to chief test pilot Dick Wenzell that the antiflutter solutions were not effective. Wenzell, who had a deep reverence for Columbus engineering, removed McCracken from the program and flew the next test himself. Archie Lane observed that flight as chase pilot in a T-2B Buckeye and recalls that the Bronco's horizontal stabilizer buckled at 435 knots, followed by disintegration of the airframe. Wenzell managed to eject successfully at 1,400 feet but departed the aircraft horizontally while in a 35-degree dive, which resulted in severe injuries. Structural

demonstrations were halted while NAR conducted a major flutter evaluation that lasted until late 1970. Broncos already in service were restricted to a 360-knot maximum dive speed, still well above the normal operating parameters. In a 1969 memo, chief engineer George Gehrkens wrote the following:

It has now been determined that this problem evolves from a dynamic coupling of the elevator tab / control system with the airplane tail and booms. The necessary changes to eliminate this problem will be under test shortly[,] and it is expected that the plans for final demonstration of the airplane will be negotiated with the Navy. Technical experts of both the Air Force and Navy have recently reviewed this information with us and concurred.

The dive speed limitation imposed during this period has had absolutely no affect [sic] on the utilization of the aircraft[,] as the limitations are well beyond any operational requirement. The contract speed requirement was intended to provide structural demonstration that the airplane could not be damaged by the pilot under the most extreme possible conditions and was not required for operational use.[6]

Thicker horizontal tail skins and modifications to the elevator control system provided sufficient flutter margins to allow Archie Lane to demonstrate 435 knots on December 30, 1970, comfortably exceeding the contract guarantee.[7]

Meanwhile the military started a preliminary evaluation of the YOV-10A in March 1966, when Marine, Navy, Air Force, and Army pilots flew the fifth prototype (BuNo 152883) to determine the aircraft's suitability for the needs

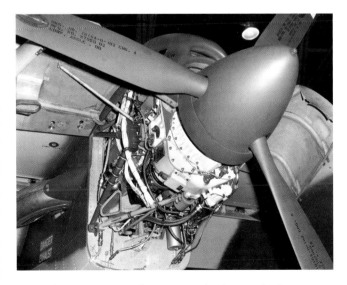

The turboprop engine of an OV-10. The OV-10 also has ejection seats; however, immediate egress might be a bad idea when "take-no-prisoner" enemy troops are lurking below. One hopes that the engine is rugged and will endure long enough to get the aircrew to safety.

Builder's front-view portrait on an OV-10. The OV-10 Bronco Association is a Fort Worth–based advocacy group devoted to preserving the history of this novel airplane.

of each service. Thirty-seven deficiencies requiring mandatory correction were reported. A second evaluation, conducted at Columbus on July 5–9, 1966, revealed that a significant redesign was required to make the Bronco acceptable for service use. Cockpit noise was considered excessive—capable of inducing physical and mental fatigue along with permanent ear damage. Ventilation was inadequate, allowing cockpit temperatures to exceed 125 degrees at low altitude. Operations in high ambient temperatures caused the engine exhaust gas temperature (EGT) to exceed its limits, resulting in degraded performance. Weapon release from the sponsons was not reliable. And the aircraft was laterally unstable at high airspeeds.

At the same time, the need for forward air control aircraft in Southeast Asia was acute. Combat reports from the field supported the need for significant changes in the Bronco. These included more communications equipment, self-sealing fuel tanks, cockpit armor, and the ability to operate in a high-heat-and-humidity environment. The increased weight from these changes made the need for more power essential. The redesign delayed the operational debut of the OV-10A by more than two years. The new airframe featured a 40-foot wing (replacing the original 30.3-foot wing), relocation of the engine nacelle booms 6 inches outward (moving the propeller tips away from

Marine version of the OV-10 in flight. Military advocates believe the OV-10 Bronco should an active component of the US arsenal because too many big and expensive warplanes were worn out by overusage in such places as Iraq and Afghanistan. The Bronco is better sized for wars of insurgency.

the cockpit, resulting in acceptable noise levels), and canting the sponsons downward to ensure better ordnance release. The Garrett AiResearch T76-G6/8 engines were replaced with more-powerful T76-G10/12 engines, rated at 715 shaft horsepower. Dorsal fillets were added to the base of each fin to improve structural stiffness, and the original squared-off wingtips were replaced with curved Hoerner tips. The first production-standard Bronco flew on August 6, 1967, and showed substantial promise. Service acceptance trials of the improved Bronco commenced eight months later—March 29, 1968, and concluded October 31, 1968. Four early-production OV-10As were utilized for a total of 397.9 hours over 234 flights. The test aircraft met all contract guarantees, excepting only maximum sea level airspeed (1.5 knots, or 0.6 percent deficient) and ferry range (4 nautical miles, or 0.3 percent deficient). The Navy Board of Inspection and Survey (BIS) recommended operational deployment.

The Columbus plant program manager for OV-10 was Tom Clancy (no, not the famous novelist). Production orders for the OV-10A consisted of 157 Air Force and 114 Marine Corps aircraft, and the balance were exported to multiple nations. Reuben Best assumed the program manager position for OV-10D, with Don Alexander as project engineer.

The Navy declined to order any Broncos even though they managed the program. Nevertheless, from 1969 until 1972 the Navy borrowed eighteen Broncos from the Marine Corps and operated them in a specialized light-attack role. The Army had participated in early planning and flight evaluation of the Bronco but ordered none. By the time the Bronco went into production, the Army was precluded from fixed-wing combat aircraft operations by a 1967 agreement with the Air Force. Some Broncos found new homes after retirement from military service.

Marine Corps Service

The Marines and Air Force received their first Broncos (BuNo 155390 for the Marine Corps and 66-13552 for the Air Force) on February 23, 1968. The Marine Corps established a training syllabus for the new aircraft with VMO-5 at Camp Pendleton, California, in March 1968. The first squadron to operate the OV-10A in combat was VMO-2, which shipped six Broncos to the Philippines aboard an aircraft carrier in June 1968. Upon arrival, VMO-2 pilots flew their Broncos to Marble Mountain, an airstrip in Vietnam near Da Nang. On July 6, just two hours after arriving at Marble Mountain, they flew a reconnaissance sortie in support of Marines near the demilitarized zone. During the next six months, VMO-2 Broncos accumulated five hundred combat hours in 250 sorties. They were joined by VMO-1 and, later, VMO-6. Marine squadrons were normally equipped with a complement of eighteen Broncos operating from Da Nang, Chu Lai, Marble Mountain, Phu Bai, Quang Tri, and smaller airstrips. Virtually every type of mission within the Bronco's capability was flown by the Marines: forward air control, radio relay, artillery spotting, helicopter escort, visual reconnaissance, convoy escort, and attack.

The Marines found their OV-10As to be effective in daylight operations but of limited use at night. In 1970, NAR and Ling Temco Vought (LTV) combined to propose a night observation gunship system (NOGS) that would give the Bronco night interdiction capability. To evaluate the proposal, Naval Weapons Center (NWC) China Lake, California, had equipped two OV-10As (BuNos 155395 and 155396) with a nose-mounted ball turret that housed forward-looking infrared (FLIR) and laser designators. A 20 mm gun turret was mounted under the rear fuselage, and the sponsons were removed from the fuselage sides.

OV-10 Bronco General Characteristics

No. built	First flight	Crew	Length	Span	Empty lbs.	Gross	Max. mph
360	1965	2	44 ft.	40 ft.	7,190	14,444	290

These modified Broncos, designated YOV-10Ds, were initially evaluated at China Lake, then sent to Navy Light Attack Squadron Four (VAL-4) at Binh Thuy, where more than two hundred operational missions were flown between June 5 and August 13, 1971. This YOV-10 activity was supported by NAR Columbus.

The Broncos proved to be an effective night interdiction solution during this trial. On two occasions they were instrumental in preventing beleaguered outposts from being overrun. But the YOV-10D was considered underpowered, so T76-G-420/421 engines, each providing 325 additional shaft horsepower, were specified for production. The FLIR sensor system avionics was mounted in the cargo bay, making paradrop missions impossible. While the 20 mm gun turret proved quite lethal, program budget limits eliminated it from production, and the sponson-mounted machine guns were restored. By now the US was reducing its commitment in Southeast Asia, and funding for the NOGS program was dwindling. In 1978, funds were approved to convert only eighteen Broncos to the OV-10D standard. The first eight production OV-10Ds went to VMO-1, at Marine Corps Air Station New River, North Carolina, in February 1980. VMO-21, at Camp Pendleton, California, received nine shortly thereafter. One aircraft was retained by NAR for defensive-countermeasures testing.

A service life extension program (SLEP) was scheduled in 1985 to extend the Bronco's useful life beyond the year 2000. At the same time, the factory (now Rockwell International) proposed a further upgrade, which was referred to as the OV-10D+ (D plus) standard. The upgrade consisted of structural reinforcement, a new FLIR system, improved wiring and plumbing, new avionics, improved communications, and a reconfigured (modernized) cockpit. Funding to convert fourteen OV-10Ds and twenty-three OV-10As was approved, and the work was assigned to the naval air rework facility (NARF) at MCAS Cherry Point, North Carolina.

The first major military operation after the frustrating quagmire of Vietnam was the Gulf War of 1991. With military power fully unbridled, this was an opportunity for the US military to redeem its reputation.

Serious questions were raised about the effectiveness of the OV-10 in the desert warfare environment. The OV-10 was intended for low, slow, and up-close combat in a jungle environment. The USAF thought that the OV-10 was too vulnerable for war in the sandbox. Nobody was quite sure what might happen—but the Marines sent VMO-1 and VMO-2 to bases in Saudi Arabia. A six-plane detachment from VMO-2 arrived in September 1990 after a monthlong sojourn from California's Camp Pendleton. The remainder of the squadron followed—arriving in

place by January 18. Joining with AV-8 Harriers, these were the most-forward-based fixed-wing aircraft of any service in the war.

OV-10s crews performed many of the same missions that were refined during Vietnam—controlling airstrikes, guiding naval artillery, and relaying reports from Navy SEALS and other commando units. A typical combat load included an AIM-9 Sidewinder for defense against enemy fighters, various marking rockets, flares, and the standard M60C machine guns.

The standard defensive against a missile attack was to maneuver so that the missile stayed visible in the top center of the canopy while pulling the throttles back to idle. Flares or chaff (or both) could be released. The goal is to shield the exhaust of the engines from the view of the missile, causing it to lose tracking. Despite a defensive strategy, two Broncos were lost during the Gulf War.[9]

It can be concluded the OV-10D+ was one of the Marine Corps' most valuable airborne assets during the Gulf War (Operation Desert Storm), but in the drawdown after Desert Storm, the Marine Corps faced significant reductions in force. To reach their manpower goals, three Bronco squadrons (VMO-1, VMO-2, and VMO-4) were deactivated between May 1993 and June 1994. The aircraft were distributed to several quasi-governmental agencies, including the California Department of Forestry and the Federal Bureau of Alcohol, Tobacco, and Firearms. Other Broncos were placed in storage at Davis-Monthan AFB, Arizona.

A swarm of Rockwell OV-10 Bronco and Cessna O-2 Skymaster light observation aircraft arrived at Thailand's U-Tapao Airfield in 1973. Roadways became taxiways as a parade of airplanes were marshaled nose to tail onto unpaved lots for storage. The canopy rail is inscribed "Lt. Abbott." The frustrating war in Vietnam was winding down. John Fredrickson photo

OV-10 Bronco in Air Force Service

Initially, the Air Force was ambivalent toward the Bronco. They were more interested in acquiring larger, faster, better-armed "Super COIN" aircraft. They deemed the Bronco good only for forward-air-control missions, but they preferred fast aircraft such as the F-100F and F-4C in that role. In the early stages of the Vietnam War, the Air Force used converted T-28 trainers to fly light-attack and observation missions, but the harsh jungle environment and limited ordnance capacity forced the Air Force to look for a replacement, and the Bronco seemed like a good candidate. The Air Force received its first Bronco in February 1968 and started training pilots under a six-week syllabus at Hurlburt Field, Florida. Eventually twenty-four Broncos were assigned to the training program, where former A-1 Skyraider pilots with forward-air-control experience served as instructors.

The first six operational USAF Broncos were airlifted to Bien Hoa aboard Douglas C-133 Cargomasters on July 31, 1968. They were uncrated, assembled, and made airworthy for their pilots and subjected to ninety-day evaluation known as "Combat Bronco." The evaluation consisted of forward air control and visual reconnaissance missions in unarmed Broncos flown by the 19th TASS (Tactical Air Support Squadron). Three months later, the 23rd TASS began OV-10A operations into North Vietnam from Nakhon Phenom (NKP) Air Base, Thailand, a far more hostile environment. The 20th TASS was also equipped with Broncos. Each squadron operated from forward locations, placing their aircraft near combat areas.

Armed with 2.75 mm white phosphorus marking rockets or two M60 machine guns firing two thousand rounds of 7.62 mm ammunition, a typical Air Force Bronco combat mission lasted up to five hours with a 230-gallon drop tank mounted on the centerline. Most OV-10A sorties were "in country" daylight missions flown with a single pilot, while night missions were conducted "out of country" (Laos, Cambodia) with a second crew member, but these missions were hampered by light reflections caused by the Bronco's canopy design.

In 1970, Ling Temco Vought's Electro-systems Division modified fifteen Broncos to improve their night and precision strike capabilities. These modified aircraft carried sensors in an under-fuselage external pod that enhanced navigation and target acquisition and were known as "Pave Nail" Broncos. The system included a stabilized night periscope sight, a combination laser rangefinder and target illuminator, a LORAN navigation receiver, and a Lear Siegler LORAN coordinator. Pave Nail Broncos were used by the 23rd TASS in the latter days of Vietnam conflict, proving particularly useful for search and rescue of downed pilots and providing target illumination for early laser-guided bombs. In 1974, the surviving Pave Nail Broncos were retrofitted back into standard OV-10A configuration.

The progressive US withdrawal from Vietnam in 1972 reduced the number of Broncos in theater. Following the ceasefire signing on January 27, 1973, the 20th TASS ended Bronco operations on March 27, but the 23rd TASS continued to operate Broncos over Cambodia until August 15, 1973, while remaining in Thailand until 1975. Several Air Force units in Europe, Korea, and Panama were equipped with Broncos that had been withdrawn from Vietnam. The last Air Force units to operate OV-10As were the 20th and 21st TASS of the 507th Air Control Wing at Shaw AFB, South Carolina, which relinquished their Broncos in the late summer of 1991.

OV-10 Bronco in Navy Service

The Navy managed the Bronco program but declined to order any production. They rethought this decision when it became apparent that their river patrols along the Mekong delta required faster, better-armed aircraft than the UH-1E Huey helicopters that they were using. Marine Corps and Air Force success with Broncos in the light-attack role convinced the Navy that it was the ideal replacement. On January 3, 1969, the Navy borrowed eighteen Marine Broncos, formulated a training program, and established Light Attack Squadron 4 (VAL-4, the "Black Ponies") to operate the type.

Air Replacement Group Squadron VS-41 at NAS North Island was tasked with conducting a fifteen-week Bronco training course that emphasized gunnery, ordnance delivery, riverine warfare operations, air-to-ground coordination, and forward-air-control techniques. The "Black Ponies" arrived in Vietnam in March 1969 and started combat

The OV-10 program was a joint services endeavor managed by the Navy; however, the Navy never procured the Bronco. This Marine Corps version is chocked and posed for photograph with open canopy.

operations from Binh Thuy and Vung Tau in April. The Navy was the only branch of the Pentagon to use Broncos exclusively as attack aircraft, providing close air support for "brown water" river and coastal operations. They also attacked Viet Cong supply routes and provided fire support for the SEALs. The aircraft were typically armed with Mk. 32 Zuni rockets on wing stations, a 7.62 mm minigun or Mk. 4 20 mm cannon pod, and 2.75-inch air-to-ground rockets. The "Black Ponies" participated in the initial May 1970 Cambodian incursion strikes, followed by strikes against sanctuaries in the U-Minh forest. In 1972, VAL-4 was withdrawn and disbanded. Their Broncos were returned to the Marine Corps.

OV-10 Bronco in Foreign Service

From the outset, North American expected the Bronco program to generate foreign orders. In 1968, the factory sent Ed Gillespie in a new OV-10A on a demonstration tour of nine Latin American countries. The aircraft flew 127 demonstrations and covered more than 20,000 miles. In 1969, Gillespie flew a second demonstration tour in Europe, which generated the first foreign orders. In May 1969, Germany ordered eighteen units, which received the designation OV-10B. The Germans intended to use

twelve Broncos as target tugs, which required more power to overcome drag from the target banner. Columbus proposed mounting a J85-GE-4 turbojet in a pod above the wing and replacing the rear cargo door with a glass enclosure to give the target winch operator a clear view of the target. These jet Broncos, designated OV-10B(Z)s, were 100 mph faster, had triple the rate of climb, and needed half the takeoff run of a standard Bronco. According to Archie Lane, the jet Bronco was such a delight to fly that chief test pilot Dick Wentzell reserved most test flights for himself.

The Royal Thai Air Force ordered sixteen Broncos in November 1969, which were delivered at Don Muang airport (Bangkok, Thailand) in July 1971. The order was increased by sixteen more in May 1972, which were delivered in June 1973. Thai Broncos were designated OV-10Cs and differed from US OV-10As with the elimination of Sidewinder missile capability. Thailand retired its last surviving Broncos on March 31, 2004.

In December 1971, the Venezuelan air force ordered sixteen OV-10s, which were designated OV-10Es. They differed from US OV-10As in their avionics suite. The first Venezuelan Bronco was completed in January 1973 and delivered in March. In 1991, the sixteen OV-10Es were supplemented by eighteen refurbished former USAF OV-10As. At least six Broncos were operational with the

The Germans purchased some of their Broncos to tow target sleeves. A dozen were modified with more thrust by installing a jet engine overhead.

The Bureau of Land Management (BLM) claimed this OV-10 Bronco and applied fresh paint. It was seen parked next to an F/A-18 at the Reno Airport in September 1996. Aldrich photo

Venezuelan air force as late as mid-2006. But strained relations between the US and Chavez governments made continued Bronco use unlikely after that.

The last sixteen new-built Broncos were ordered by Indonesia (twelve in February 1975 and four additional units in April). These Broncos received the OV-10F designation and were delivered in September 1976. They represented the sixth variant to come off the production line and served until July 2005.

Columbia, Morocco, and the Philippines acquired refurbished OV-10As from the US in the 1980s and 1990s, bringing the number of foreign operators to seven. These were not new-build aircraft and thus retained the original OV-10A designation.

OV-10 Bronco in Civilian Service

Some Broncos were diverted into civilian roles on their return from Vietnam. NASA employed several for experimental purposes, while governmental agencies such as the Bureau of Alcohol, Tobacco, and Firearms (ATF); the California Department of Forestry (CDF); and the Bureau of Land Management (BLM) acquired demilitarized versions for use in specialized duties.

The third prototype YOV-10A, BuNo 152881, was turned over to NASA in 1972 for slow-speed-flight experimentation. The wing (an early short-span wing) was modified with large trailing-edge Fowler flaps with a hydraulically spun cylinder at the leading edge of the flaps. The rotating cylinder created a boundary layer control effect, which augmented lift. With this system the Bronco's STOL (short takeoff and landing) characteristics were enhanced—the aircraft was capable of flying under full control at speeds as low as 54 mph. The first production OV-10A, BuNo 155390, was transferred to NASA's Lewis Research Center (now renamed the John H. Glenn Research Center) in 1983, where it was used for noise abatement experiments. There is some irony in the fact that the OV-10A was used for noise reduction studies, since evaluations concluded that the YOV-10A produced dangerously high cockpit noise levels.

In 1994, NASA-Lewis acquired two OV-10Ds, BuNos 155436 and 155406, which were used in the Voice Recognition / Speak to the Aircraft Program. This allowed pilots to command functions by voice, using a two-hundred-word vocabulary, while wearing an oxygen mask and microphone during high-g maneuvering, despite propeller noise. These OV-10Ds were also used in Air Force advanced cockpit projects. In 1993, NASA-Langley received one former Air Force Bronco, 67-14687, for use in the CERES (Clouds and Earth Radiant Energy System) study. The CERES mission was intended to determine the role that clouds and the earth's surface play in the flow of heat energy through the atmosphere. The Langley Bronco was also used in wake vortex studies.

In military service the OV-10A was considered underpowered when carrying ordnance loads in high-temperature environments, but without weapons the Bronco's agility and superb visibility made it ideal for guiding aerial-firefighting tankers. In 1992, the Bureau of Land Management obtained four former Air Force and two former Marine OV-10As to lead heavy "water bombers" through smoke and haze. In addition, the United States Forest Service acquired seventeen former Marine OV-10As that were operated by the State of California for fire spotting and suppression.

The communications and night-surveillance equipment installed on OV-10Ds made that version a perfect platform for the Bureau of Alcohol, Tobacco, and Firearms. In July 1995, twenty-two former Marine OV-10Ds were transferred to the ATF. The suite of surveillance equipment was retained, but the aircraft were demilitarized in all other respects (sponsons were removed and the ejection seats were deactivated). Some of these OV-10Ds were equipped with liquid herbicide spray gear to eliminate "cash crops" in Central and South America. These aircraft were modified by DynCorp at Patrick AFB, Florida, and operated under the State Department's air wing.

Reflections on the OV-10 Bronco

The Bronco proved far more versatile than originally imagined. It performed a wide array of missions for the US military for twenty-five years, while it continues to serve civilian agencies well into the twenty-first century. The Columbus Division built a total of 360 Broncos between 1963 and 1977—157 for the Air Force, 114 for the Marines, eighteen for Germany, thirty-two for Thailand, sixteen for Venezuela, sixteen for Indonesia, and seven preproduction YOV-10As for test and evaluation. The Bronco's durability, adaptability, and cost-effectiveness have sparked interest in reopening the production line. Boeing, which now owns the assets of Rockwell International, considered the possibility in 2010. Mark Pierce led Boeing's business development effort under the OV-10(X) program. "In theaters where the air defense threat has been peeled back," explains Pierce, "this would be a perfect platform to do convoy support or light-attack / armed reconnaissance at a fraction of what the [services] have been doing with F/A-18s, F-16s, F-15s, and A-10s."[10]

It is ironic, notes Archie Lane, that after the prolonged rough-terrain tests, the Bronco never operated from such extreme conditions. On occasion the Marines would conduct training exercises from unimproved surfaces, but actual missions were, for the most part, flown from smooth runways.[11]

Rockwell's X-Planes: XFV-12A and X-31

The experimental Rockwell XFV-12 was a Navy project (ca. 1977) intended to achieve both a vertical takeoff and supersonic flight. The goal of the failed project was defending aircraft carriers by operating from small but distant picket ships.

The last RA-5C Vigilante rolled off the production line in August 1970. Aircraft production had been declining over the past decade. Only limited orders then remained for the T-2 Buckeye, leaving the OV-10 Bronco stuck with an unfair share of the Columbus Division's overhead expense.

At age forty-nine, Adm. Elmo Zumwalt (1920–2000) was the youngest CNO ever appointed and was considered a "free thinker" who wished to simultaneously modernize Navy weaponry while "humanizing" military life for the younger sailors by elimination of "Mickey Mouse" personnel practices. His fleet messages were sometimes called Z-grams. Zumwalt brought several new initiatives with him. At that time, there were escalating concerns about Soviet Backfire bombers, with the ability to destroy conventional carriers by using cruise missiles fired from up to 300 miles away. Zumwalt's most technically challenging initiative was the sea control ship (SCS) concept, which relied upon a fleet of small ships with neither catapults nor arresting gear. These ships, equipped with short-range supersonic V/STOL (vertical/short takeoff and landing) aircraft, were to perform picket duty ahead of the large aircraft carriers. The Soviet threat was considered urgent enough that David Packard, deputy SecDef, launched a program to prototype a V/STOL airplane that could operate from a sea control ship.

When a hobbyist crafts parts from separate kits into a single creation, it is called a "kit bash." As we see here, two Navy warplanes were cannibalized and then scrapped to fabricate the single XFV-12. The air intakes were transplanted from a McDonnell F-4 Phantom, and the cockpit was from a Douglas A-4 Skyhawk.

Because of the urgency, an expedited procurement process was implemented in November 1971. The usual RFP that initiates the process was replaced by a less formal "letter of interest" outlining the SCS concept and soliciting ideas for advanced-technology VTOL prototypes. Minimum cost and rapid delivery of two prototype aircraft were paramount considerations. Proposals of not more than twenty pages were requested within forty-five days. Of the eleven fighter-attack VTOL proposals received, the McDonnell AV-16, the Convair model 200, and the NAR-Columbus Division FV-12 were selected for formal presentation to the chief of naval development, RAdm. Thomas Davies, on January 19, 1972. The NAR-Columbus design, which promised Mach 2.0 speed and a novel method of achieving vertical lift, known as the "thrust-augmented wing" (TAW), impressed Davies the most. The next day Davies enthusiastically endorsed the NAR-Columbus XFV-12A to Dr. Robert A. Frosch, assistant secretary of the Navy, who approved it almost immediately.

Controversy arose when the evaluation division of NAVAIR expressed reservations about the unproven technology. Nevertheless, the "high risk–high payoff" proposal prevailed,

The XFV-12 was an example of "ready–fire–aim" because the airframe was rushed into fabrication before a proper design was established. The modern (2006–present) Lockheed F-35B Lightning uses a shaft-driven fan plus a swiveling jet pipe to achieve vertical lift.

and the Navy awarded a contract for two XFV-12A prototypes on October 18, 1972. If a chemist wrote down the formula for XFV-12, it might appear as such:

Douglas A-4 cockpit + McDonnell F-4 center wing & inlets + P & W F401 engine + Magic ingredient + Flight + controls = XFV-12A

The thrust augmentation principle ("magic ingredient") at the core of NAR Columbus's proposal was based on emerging technology from NASA and (separately) from the Air Force aeronautical research laboratory at Wright-Patterson AFB. Noted physicist Hans von Ohain, who developed the first German turbojet engine, proposed the theory of producing vertical lift for VTOL flight by using carefully directed jet engine exhaust to accelerate large volumes of air. Unlike the Harrier, which relies on brute engine thrust alone to provide vertical lift, thrust augmentation disperses the engine's exhaust through a network of ducts and releases it through an array of "ejectors" in the aircraft's lifting surfaces. The high-velocity exhaust flow draws a secondary flow of external air through appropriately designed passages under a principle known the "Coandă effect." The air flow volume is as much as eight times larger than the exhaust volume, and the combined flows produce a lifting force 55 percent greater than the engine thrust alone. The "Coandă effect" was the "magic ingredient" that offered promise in the laboratory but failed to deliver thereafter.

Enthusiasm for thrust augmentation at NAR-Columbus was boundless. It was almost as if perpetual motion or the preverbal "free lunch" had been discovered. Columbus engineers announced that the XVF-12A would require an engine only two-thirds the size of a direct-lift jet, saving weight and reducing fuel requirements. Downwash from the thrust augmentation would be cooler, more diffuse,

Front view of XFV-12 bearing fresh paint. Separately, the British developed Harrier Jump Jet used brute force thrust to achieve vertical lift. It demonstrated military utility during the Falklands War of 1982.

and of a lower velocity than a direct-lift jet. This would minimize damage to the landing surface and underside of the airframe, while ground personnel could work proximate to an active aircraft.

The control system consisted of large wing and canard panels, known as "augmenter flaps," rotated into various configurations to provide the necessary control force. The system provided weight savings, enhanced stability, improved transition to forward flight, and excellent agility. When the augmenter flaps were placed in a nearly vertical position for takeoff, engine exhaust was totally diverted through the ducts and ejectors, providing maximum lift. In transition to forward flight, the flaps would rotate aft, allowing the exhaust and airflow to move rearward. In forward flight, with the flaps closed, the lifting surfaces acted as conventional wings and stabilizers. Modulating the exhaust flow—collectively for vertical acceleration or hover or independently for roll, pitch, and yaw—provided a full range of three-axis control.

Varying the lift between the canard and wing produced pitch control, varying the lift between the right and left wing produced roll control, and yaw was achieved by deflecting the wing augmenter flaps in opposite directions. By blending lift and control into one system, the weight and complexity of a separate reaction control system, required in other VTOL aircraft, was eliminated. Exceptionally short takeoff and transition to forward flight performance was expected from "circulation lift" generated by the accelerated airflow over the wings and canards, which was predicted to exceed the lift generated from forward motion alone. Columbus Division president John

The XFV-12 was an unstable creation that never flew independently from its tether. Its performance metrics were design goals that were never achieved.

Fosness stated in an *Aviation Week & Space Technology* feature article the following:

> We were convinced after making exhaustive studies, that there had to be a better way to integrate propulsion, instead of designing an airframe[,] then figuring out how to go 'V' (vertical) . . . the lightest aircraft for the mission would combine many principles to offer a meshed lift-propulsion-control system. We feel we have developed the first truly different approach to that technology in 15 years.[1]

To maximize maneuverability, Columbus designers chose a canard configuration for the airframe. The wing was mounted high on the rear fuselage, and the canard (horizontal stabilizer) was mounted low under the air inlets. The exhaust ducting and ejector network ran the full span of the wings and canards, providing a stable "four post" lift distribution around the aircraft's center of gravity. Since the XFV-12A prototypes were proof-of-concept technology, demonstrators intended to verify the thrust augmentation concept; use of "off-the-shelf" airframe components were maximized to save time and expense.

In a full-sized version of "kit bashing," the forward fuselage, cockpit, escape system, and landing gear were adopted from a McDonnell Douglas A-4 Skyhawk. The inlets, wing box, and fuel cell came from a McDonnell Douglas F-4 Phantom. Approximately 35 percent of the XVF-12A airframe by weight consisted of components from other aircraft. A Pratt & Whitney F401-PW-400 advanced-technology turbofan engine (which had been developed for the Grumman F-14B Tomcat) was selected for power. Rated at 14,070 pounds of thrust, it was expected to provide 21,800 pounds of augmented lift. The ducting and ejector network were formed from thin-gauge titanium running the full span of the wing and canard. The contract specified that two prototypes were to be built and flight-tested in three years under a cost-plus fixed fee estimated to be $46.9 million. Funding was to be provided at the conclusion of design review in three months and at the demonstration of a 1.55 thrust augmentation ratio in eleven months. This tight time schedule coupled with new technology made the program quite ambitious.

Columbus engineers found that it was possible to achieve augmentation ratios over 2.0 in the laboratory, but it required geometry that could not be replicated in the aircraft. Nevertheless, by January 1973 Rockwell completed a full-scale mockup, using actual A-4 and F-4 subassemblies. Large-scale models of the wing and canard (one-fifth full size) were constructed to obtain data on the actual augmentation ratio that could be expected. The wing model achieved a ratio of 1.4, which was encouraging. That led to the construction of full-sized wing and canard sections for testing on a "whirl rig." However, progress was slow, and a three-month extension for the augmentation ratio demonstration was granted:

Wing and canard augmenters were tested in a unique facility, nicknamed the "whirl rig," which consists of a boom more than 100 feet long which is free to rotate. Jet efflux is ducted out the boom to the test augmenter[,] which may then be "flown" remotely by the whirl rig operator. The test rig can be instrumented to measure performance and aerodynamic flow variables. Concurrent with V/STOL system development, wind tunnel and free[-]flight testing of various scale models was conducted to define the aircraft characteristics in the powered lift mode, transition mode[,] and the conventional flight mode.[2]

In late 1974, Rockwell's whirl rig testing of the full-scale sections produced an augmentation ratio of 1.49 for the wing and 1.29 for the canard, but the engineers came to realize that these measurements were not entirely valid. The data were being corrupted by certain ground effect distortions known as "suck down" (an attraction like a vacuum cleaner) and "fountain effects" (pushed away like compressed air). About this time, it was becoming apparent that the use of off-the-shelf airframe components was hindering the augmenter design due to volume and position limitations. The augmenter ducts had to fit into thin swept wings, where much of the volume was occupied by F-4 Phantom wing box and fuel cell structure. As a result, the augmenters in the actual aircraft differed from the whirl rig augmenters that produced encouraging results. This also resulted in changes to ejector nozzle shapes and locations, which were not considered critical at first but proved vital in retrospect.

Construction of the first prototype was expected to go smoothly and quickly due to the extensive use of off-the-shelf components, but numerous problems emerged. Fabrication of the duct system proved difficult because the thin-gauge titanium was resistant to accurate drilling and welding. Parts had to be redesigned, leading to weight increases and assembly delays. The first XFV-12A was finally completed and prepared for ground testing in May 1977. Static-vertical-thrust testing was started in July, but numerous structural problems in the augmenter ducting caused further delays. The formal rollout ceremony was held on August 26, with Columbus Division president John P. Fosness, Ohio governor James A. Rhodes, Navy secretary W. Graham Clayton Jr., and keynote speaker VAdm. Forrest Petersen in attendance. By this time, the program had slipped by nearly two years because of technological and funding problems. The aircraft's weight had grown from Rockwell's original estimate of 13,800 to 15,596 pounds.

Testing started in earnest after the rollout ceremony, but vertical-thrust measurements continued to be disappointing. The measurements were suspect because of the same transient ground effects that had corrupted the whirl rig tests in 1974, so it was decided to conclude the

both static and dynamic vertical tests were planned in a huge framework left over from Apollos space capsule testing. "The facility permits static testing at any attitude and altitude in or out of ground effect, safe evaluation of large control movements, a good-sized hover test envelope and, of course, pilot familiarization training. The tether system is based on a Navy variable speed shipboard underway replenishment winch."

The hoist had a hook, shock absorber, and position sensor that drove the winch during dynamic operation. Horizontal restraint cables were placed around the tether at the 100-foot height to prevent crashing into the gantry structure. In static tests the aircraft was tethered at the top and bottom with load cells, to measure all forces and moments generated as the controls were exercised. In dynamic tests the lower tethers would be removed, and the aircraft was capable of maneuvering.[3]

Static tests began in early 1978, and initial performance results were disappointing. Careful augmentation measurements yielded ratios no better than 1.19 for the wing and 1.06 for the canard—considerably below the anticipated 1.55. A single dynamic test "flight" was attempted using the upper support cable to help with the deficient lift. By this time, it was apparent that the augmenter system was hypersensitive to small geometric details. The encouraging results obtained with the scale wing and full-sized whirl rig proved unobtainable in the actual aircraft because of space and position limitations.

Tests were halted at Langley while the left wing and left canard, along and other components, were returned to Columbus. A diagnostic investigation involving forty-seven runs on the whirl test rig replicated the disappointing Langley results. In January 1979, a program was initiated to improve the augmentation ratio. By mid-May 1981, after replacing the original swept/tapered augmenters with newly designed rectangular augmenters, Columbus was able to claim a much-improved ratio of 1.64. Two new airframes, the XFV-12B and C, were proposed to demonstrate the augmenter improvements. These airplanes would employ fly-by-wire controls, a new high-pressure hydraulic system, and composite structure to reduce airframe weight.[4]

But Navy interest in the proposal ebbed after program costs escalated rapidly from the original estimate of $46.9 million in 1972 to nearly $97 million in 1978. Work on the second XFV-12A was stopped as a cost reduction measure, and program management went through considerable turmoil. Both the Navy program manager and the civilian on-site engineer were replaced, and then renewed debate erupted over sea-based V/STOL aircraft when Adm. Elmo Zumwalt retired. While limited funding was provided for additional augmenter experiments and development, by 1981 the XFV-12A program ended as it began—in controversy.[5]

The XFV-12A is seen suspended in the same framework built for Apollo space capsule testing at the NASA Langley Research Center. It arrived from Columbus aboard a Super Guppy.

ground tests and move on to tethered flight tests. The original concept was to test the aircraft suspended from a sophisticated crane mounted on a specially built flatbed railroad car. The railroad car and crane would be used to simulate VTOL flight with transition to forward flight as well as STOL flight by accelerating along a stretch of track. This concept proved impractical and was abandoned in favor of using the NASA Lunar Landing gantry at Langley, Virginia. Proposals were considered to fly the XFV-12A in conventional horizontal flight at Columbus before ferrying the aircraft to Langley for vertical-flight tests, but these proposals were rejected since vertical-flight ability was considered paramount. Furthermore, there was concern about damaging the aircraft during conventional flight.

In November 1977, the XFV-12A was disassembled and placed aboard an Aero Spacelines Super Guppy for delivery to the NASA Langley Research Facility, where

Reflections on the XFV-12A

North American Aviation is noted for producing two of the most transformative experimental aircraft in aviation history—the XB-70 Valkyrie and the X-15. Both airplanes were products of the Los Angeles Division, designed in the late 1950s and flown for most of the 1960s. The XFV-12A was the first experimental aircraft program from the Columbus Division but, sadly, shared none of the success of the California X-planes.

XFV-12A was the victim of the "ready, fire, aim" phenomenon. The airplane was built before the technical requirements were properly and logically assembled, because of Zumwalt's overeagerness. Hal Andrews, technical director of research and technology at NAVAIR, cited two reasons for the failure. First, Mach 2 V/STOL performance was an overreach. The Navy should have developed a subsonic aircraft with thrust-augmented wing first and then applied the lessons learned to a higher-performance aircraft only when the technology was better understood. Second, the airframe configuration was fixed too early in the process. The technical realities of installing thrust augmentation in an airframe restricted by thin wings and minimal fuselage volume were distorted by favorable laboratory results, which created a false sense of confidence.[6]

in 1974, and a flyoff was forthcoming between archrivals Boeing (with their YC-14) and the Douglas YC-15. Both medium transports utilized vertical lift to enhance short-field operations. The YC-15 won, and its design later evolved into the larger C-17 Globemaster III. The Lockheed C-130J soldiers on nearly a half century later.

In September 1975, a proposal for a VTOL transport was presented to the Marine Corps. Designated NA-382, the proposal consisted of modifying Lockheed C-130s with a new thrust-augmented wing and four GE F101 turbofan engines. This would permit vertical takeoff and landing performance with an aircraft capable of carrying a 15,000-pound payload (as compared to 42,000 pounds for a conventional C-130H). But the NA-382 proposal was never funded.[8] Like the XFV-12A, it became an innovative idea relegated to the "dustbin of history."

As was vividly demonstrated during the Falklands War of 1982 by the British Harrier, vertical takeoff allows container ships to also become aircraft carriers. The Harrier was eventually superseded by the VTOL version of the F-35. There is no evidence the XFV-12A ever flew untethered; however, its strange appearance and intended ability to move from dead stop to supersonic would surely have generated UFO reports. The retired airframe was disassembled and put into storage in Sandusky, Ohio.

Rockwell X-planes General Characteristics

Model	No. built	First flight	Length	Span	Empty lbs.	Gross	Max. mph
XFV-12A	1	1977	43 ft., 11 in.	28 ft., 6 in.	13,800	19,500	1,591
X-31	2	10/11/1990	43 ft., 4 in.	23 ft., 10 in.	11,409	32,187	900

Furthermore, political developments caused frequent funding deferrals, with resultant personnel layoffs that hindered all aspects of the program. As *Aviation Week & Space Technology* noted:

Manpower peaks and valleys on the XFV-12A project at the Columbus plant reflects [*sic*] the difficulty the program has had maintaining consistent work. The wide swings in work on the program are the result of budget slowdowns from Congress, Navy internal problems in getting approved money to the contractor as well as over-optimistic management projections by Rockwell International as work progressed on the aircraft.[7]

All of this was particularly troubling, given the enthusiasm for thrust augmentation at Columbus. Separately and far away on the West Coast, the Air Force was shopping for a Lockheed C-130 Hercules replacement. Contracts were let

X-31 Enhanced Fighter Maneuverability (EFM)

Without any links to the XFV-12 effort, a new and separate pure research-and-development (R&D) project began a decade after XFV-12. Rockwell contracted to build two fresh prototypes without anticipation of a production contract. The benefit of X-planes is keeping a builder on the leading edge of technology, engineers challenged, and the workforce engaged with novel endeavors. Important breakthroughs resulting from pure research and development are possible. Further, the company that masters new technology has a leg up on the competition for subsequent award of production contracts.

The first airplane was BuNo 164584 and the second was BuNo 164585. Like the previous XFV-12, components

Unlike the XFV-12A, which failed to achieve its overambitious goal of vertical takeoff followed by supersonic flight, the X-31 fully accomplished its mission, which was to demonstrate unprecedented maneuverability by using a relatively conventional airframe. The key ingredient, three paddles aft of the engine, is clearly visible.

were borrowed from other airplanes—and the list is long. The forebody and cockpit came from an F/A-18 Hornet. Landing gear, fuel pump, rudder pedals, and leading-edge flap drives were donated by a Lockheed F-16 Fighting Falcon. A GE F404 engine producing 16,000 pounds of thrust (in afterburner) was selected. And so it went. Fabrication and initial flight were based at Air Force Plant 42 in Palmdale, California.

As B-1B production was winding up, Rockwell joined with Defense Advanced Research Projects Agency (DARPA) and Messerschmitt-Bölkow-Blohm (MBB) of West Germany to develop a combat aircraft capable of extreme agility. Jim Dennison was the lead engineer. Germany, a nation of limited geography, sought to master air war within confined spaces. The project was initially named "enhanced fighter maneuverability" (EFM) but was later designated the X-31A by the Department of Defense. The aircraft employed advanced features such as thrust vectoring. The lightweight structure included large amounts of graphite/epoxy, enabling a nimble airplane with a high level of maneuverability.

The thrust-vectoring system of the X-31 consisted of three paddles at the rear of the fuselage that could direct the jet engine's thrust. The system provided precise control

at high angles of attack (AOA) where conventional aircraft would lose aerodynamic control. During the 581 flights of the EFM program, the X-31 flew well beyond the aerodynamic limits of any conventional aircraft by demonstrating controlled flight at 70 degrees AOA, a controlled roll at

The X-31 was an enduring X-plane program that was started at Columbus and remained ongoing beyond the Boeing acquisition of Rockwell aerospace programs on December 6, 1996. The German partnership imparted stability.

Onboard computer hardware and software improvements were mission critical and fundamental to the success of the X-31 program. Flight testing continued a NATC Pax River after testing at Edwards Air Force Base was complete.

around 70 degrees AOA, and a rapid minimum-radius, 180-degree turn using a poststall maneuver, dubbed the "Herbst maneuver" after Wolfgang Herbst, a German proponent of using poststall flight in air-to-air combat.

On January 19, 1995, the X-31 took off on its final scheduled test flight. There was a maintenance error. Somebody forgot to plug in the pitot tube electrical heat. Near the end of a forty-three-minute mission, ice formed

inside one of the X-31's pitot tubes, and incorrect airspeed data were sent to the flight control's computers. The aircraft oscillated uncontrollably and pitched. Pilot Karl-Heinz Lang ejected safely before the plane crashed near the northern edge of Edwards AFB. The remaining X-31 went on to fly twenty-one demonstration flights at the 1995 Paris Air Show, where its performance wowed the crowds. Following the EFM program's conclusion in June 1995, this aircraft was transferred to the US Navy Test Pilot School at NAS Pax River in Maryland, where new tests were undertaken.

In May 2000, the X-31 demonstrated landing speeds of only 142 mph at 24 degrees AOA, as compared to the normal landing speeds of 201 mph at 12 degrees AOA, and landed in about 1,700 feet rather than the more typical 8,000 feet.

In its final flight on April 29, 2003, the X-31 performed the last in a series of fully automated ESTOL landings on an actual runway, approaching at a high 24-degree AOA (twice the normal 12-degree AOA) at only 134 mph, more than 30 percent slower than the normal 201 mph landing speed. The program ended in May 2003, and later that year, the X-31 team—past and present—received the von Karman award from the International Council of the Aeronautical Sciences. The remaining X-31 aircraft is on display in Munich's Deutsches Museum.[9]

Two X-31 aircraft were built. One of them crashed on January 19, 1995, because of a maintenance error. The electrical deicing connection of the pitot tube (for airspeed measurements) was left disconnected. Erratic flight controls forced the pilot to safely eject before the airplane crashed on the northern portion of Edwards AFB.

Building a Better Bomber

Like the Grumman F-14 or the General Dynamics F-111, the B-1 Lancer is a swing-wing aircraft. The wings are extended for landings and takeoffs. They can also be extended when the mission dictates loitering over a battlefield to precision deliver variable ordnance on demand. Air Force. USAF photo

In the wake of hard usage during the Vietnam War, officials within the Air Force and elsewhere were concerned that the nation's remaining fleet of Boeing B-52 heavy bombers was structurally geriatric, technically obsolete, and in dire need of replacement.

A fleet of strategic bombers in the modern age forces the opponent to mount a defense. That defense typically demands radar coverage and the means to destroy trespassers. The choices often include an expensive mix of interceptor aircraft, surface-to-air missiles, or ground-based antiaircraft artillery. Resources expended on defense are unavailable for offensive weaponry. The problem compounds exponentially when the land mass is the size of Russia or China.

Other attempts to fully retire the B-52 failed. The list includes the supersonic Convair B-58 Hustler, the North American triple-sonic XB-70A Valkyrie, the General Dynamics FB-111 Aardvark, the Rockwell B-1B Lancer, and the Northrup B-2 Spirit. In the tradition of the B-2, the Northrop B-21 Raider remains in gestation and is next in line. Like the B-2 Spirit, it is expected to be another stealthy flying wing (sometimes called a "batwing"). The final Stratofortress departed the Boeing Wichita plant in October 1962, yet the enduring B-52H soldiers on with a front-line mission.

Sampler of Postwar Bombers

Introduced	Builder	Model	Range (miles)	Wing	No. built
1951	Boeing	B-47 Stratojet	4,000	Swept	2,032
1955	Boeing	B-52 Stratofortress	8,800	Flexible	744
1960	Convair	B-58 Hustler	4,400	Delta	116
1985	Rockwell	B-1 Lancer	5,900	Swing	104
1997	Northrop	B-2 Spirit	6,900	Batwing	21

Many attempts have been made to displace the tenacious Boeing B-52H Stratofortress as America's premier strategic bomber. So far, none has completely succeeded. The number of B-52s built (all models) was 744, and fewer than 10 percent remain active. Boeing Wichita photo, ca. 1961

B-1 Lancer Genesis

Although the B-1B floundered until 1982, it was originally conceived in 1964 as part of the AMSA (advanced manned strategic aircraft) program. Top brass in the Air Force and Pentagon embraced the concept, but SecDef Robert McNamara favored ballistic missiles and insisted that a new manned system was unnecessary. Despite the rejection of their B-70 bomber at the hands of McNamara in the 1960s, a burning desire remained within the NAA core team to build a bomber combining the dash speed of the Convair B-58 Hustler with the range and payload of the B-52. Only limited funding was released for the initial AMSA studies, and considerable uncertainty surrounded the entire program.

Richard Nixon won the 1968 election and appointed former congressman Melvin R. Laird as SecDef. Laird directed acceleration of AMSA design studies, and in April 1969 the secretary of the Air Force, Robert C. Seamans Jr., formally conferred the designation B-1 on the proposed airplane. The Air Force released an RFP to industry in November 1969. It was assumed that downsizing the war in Vietnam combined with base closures would free up the budget needed to procure a fleet of new strategic bombers.

Responses from Boeing, General Dynamics, and North American Rockwell (NAR) were received by the deadline of January 1970. On June 5, Air Force secretary Seamans announced that NAR was selected to manufacture the B-1 Lancer. A cost-plus-incentive-fee development contract (F33657-70-C-0800) was issued for five test aircraft and two structural-test airframes. Intended as prototypes to demonstrate the most-unusual (for a bomber) twin features of swing wings and afterburners, the innovations yielded an impressive dash speed of Mach 2.2 at high altitude. From the outset the B-1 Lancer was expected to be a production program, which would result in as many as 240 operational bombers, but wavering financial support from Congress made the ultimate size of the production run uncertain.

The political plan of battle to shoot down a proposed new strategic bomber in Congress goes as follows: First, complain bitterly that the quantity is excessive, then cut the number of units to be built. Total cost equals (recurring production costs) plus (nonrecurring engineering, development, tooling, and testing). Second, strangle interim funding. Third, divide total cost by units and then loudly proclaim that the unit price is outrageous and the entire program is unaffordable. This is how the entire Northrop B-2 Spirit ended, with an entire fleet consisting of twenty airplanes (after one of them crashed).

By late summer 1970, Congress capped B-1 funding levels for several fiscal years, which led to the elimination of two test aircraft and one static-test airframe, prolonging the entire development program. This delayed the date of the first flight by one month, the date of the production decision by six months, and the date of the initial operational capability (IOC) by two years.

USAF Intercontinental Heavy Bombers, General Characteristics

Model	No. built	First flight	Length	Span	Empty lbs.	Gross	Max. mph
B-1A	4	1974	152 ft., 2 in.	137 ft.	190,000	395,000	1,390
B-1B	100	1984	146 ft.	137 ft.	190,000	477,000	900
B-52	744	1952	159 ft., 4 in.	185 ft.	185,000	488,000	650
B-2	21	1989	69 ft.	172 ft.	158,000	376,000	628

Assembly of the first prototype (74-0158) was started on March 15, 1972. The Columbus Division was assigned to manufacture several structural elements of the aft fuselage. An Air Force review of the program was initially encouraging; however, the merger with Rockwell Standard became a distraction, which created problems and slowed progress. John L. McLucas, the new SecDef, reported to Congress that construction of the first B-1 had fallen behind schedule, and the start of the second aircraft was postponed.

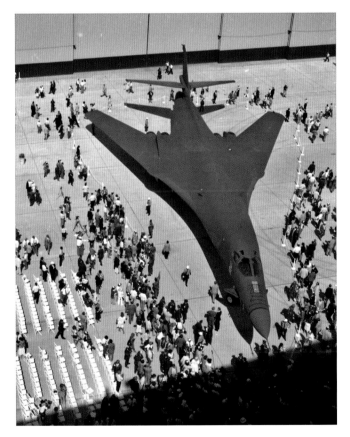

The first B-1B rollout was celebrated at Air Force Plant 42, Palmdale, California, on September 4, 1984. First flight was October 18, 1984. It remains the last warplane in active US military service bearing the proud legacy of North American Aviation.

When the first-flight date slipped another two months, the production decision was delayed by ten more months. Even Senator Barry Goldwater (R-AZ), a long-term supporter of the B-1 program, expressed outrage. Budget estimates for the development costs escalated at an alarming rate. In response, the secretary of the Air Force commissioned a National Science Foundation study that concluded that consideration should be given to terminating the program if any further funding reductions were imposed.

Finally, on October 26, 1974, the first B-1A was rolled out at Palmdale, and it was flown on December 23, six months after the scheduled date. By mid-1976 the second (74-0159) and third (74-0160) prototypes were flying, and by December 1976 the Air Force ordered production of the first three operational aircraft. But Richard Nixon had resigned the presidency two years earlier, and the nation was still dealing with severe recession and raging inflation that followed the 1973 OPEC oil embargo.

The periodic interplay between politics and strategic weapon systems arose after the election of 1976. President Gerald R. Ford, deemed by most to be a "good man," was swept out of the White House by a dovish peanut farmer from Georgia. Like the B-70 before it, the B-1 Lancer program was canceled when the opposite party gained power, as President Jimmy Carter pronounced at a press conference on June 30, 1977:

> My decision is that we should not continue with deployment of the B-1, and I am directing that we discontinue plans for production of this weapon system; however, the existing testing and development program now underway on the B-1 should continue—to provide us with the needed technology base in the unlikely event that more-cost-effective alternative systems should run into difficulty. Continued efforts at the research and development stage will give us better answers about the cost and effectiveness of the bomber and the support systems, including electronic countermeasures techniques.

Why did Carter cancel production of the Lancer? As president, he was on the short list of people privy to a new and top-secret technology—stealth. A stealth airplane is invisible to radar. A small attack warplane from the Lockheed Skunkworks designated F-117 Nighthawk was destined to covertly enter the Air Force inventory starting in 1983. As graceful as an airborne brick, with tiny wings seemingly added only as an afterthought, its lethality was demonstrated in the Gulf War of 1991.

A fourth B-1A (76-0174) entered assembly on August 25, 1975—nearly two years before the Carter announcement. It joined the B-1A flight test program on February 14, 1979. Despite the production cancellation, flight testing continued using the third and fourth prototypes. Historian Dennis Jenkins noted:

Never had so much work been performed on a "cancelled" program. By April 30, 1981, when the fourth aircraft flew the last flight of the B-1A test program, the aircraft had made 70 flights and accumulated 378 hours. Since

The Boeing Company provided both offensive and defensive avionics for the B-1 program. Abraham Goo was the Boeing executive responsible for military business at the subcontractor who wore these badges at important B-1 program milestones.

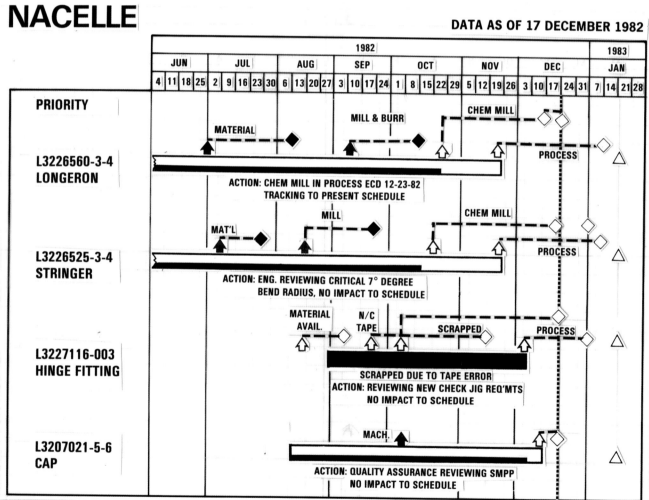

All aircraft manufacturing relies on schedules, and these schedules are created by industrial engineers. The B-1B nacelles were updated from the B-1A design to reduce radar reflection; however, top speed decreased from Mach 2.2 to Mach 1.2 (or roughly 700 mph).

the maiden flight of the first B-1A on December 23, 1974, the four B-1As had logged 1895.2 hours in 247 flights. The YF101 engines had accumulated total of just under 7,600 flight hours.[1]

Hoping to revive the program, Rockwell studied several derivatives of the B-1A in 1979 that would reduce cost and expand mission capability. The resulting concept was a "core" airframe that could be used to build a family of four aircraft. The core would have 85 percent commonality with the B-1A and use many of the subsystems that were already developed, but it could be configured during manufacture to launch strategic weapons, act as a rapid-response "near-term" penetrator, and serve as a conventional bomber or as a refueling tanker. Rockwell argued that this concept would take advantage of the state-of-the-art technology and nuclear hardness of the original B-1A and

benefit from the $5.9 billion already invested in the program. Rockwell's proposal suggested elimination of the variable-geometry wing and limitation of aircraft to subsonic speeds, which would reduce cost, weight, complexity, and subsonic drag. At that time, the Air Force was conducting a "bomber penetration evaluation" (BPE), which recommended that the revised bomber, now designated the B-1B, be selected as the next strategic bomber.

President Ronald W. Reagan promised to rebuild America's military. Resurrecting the Rockwell B-1 Lancer was key to that political commitment; therefore, President Reagan announced on October 2, 1981, that the Air Force would acquire one hundred B-1B Lancers. Rockwell, as prime contractor, was awarded a formal contract. The first four prototypes (already built) kept their white paint and became B-1A. Two were actively flight-tested, while the remaining pair was mothballed.

The sheet metal cowling and nacelles surrounding conventional jet engines are tubular (round); however, supersonic speeds (as in Vigilante and Lancer) demand ramps to condition the air. Hence, the B-1B nacelle has a boxy appearance.

Columbus was assigned responsibility for building three major subassemblies composing about 30 percent of the B-1B airframe. Seasoned factory manager Paul McCormick was given overall B-1 manufacturing responsibility. Starting with the nacelles, engineers reworked the design to reduce the radar cross section for the entire airplane by 90 percent when "variable" ramps were replaced with simpler "S-vanes" and radar-absorbing material. Consequently, in an unprecedented move, the top speed was also reduced from Mach 2.2 to Mach 1.2. For the first time in history, about 700 mph of top speed was sacrificed in the interest of increasing stealth. Don Mullen oversaw nacelle manufacturing. With spy satellites lurking overhead, they were initially wrapped in fabric whenever outdoors.

Again, the overhead functions geared up to meet the challenge. The group of industrial photographers (three or four in number) who worked out of the film-processing lab in Building 6 came forward to request a new and better camera—a Hasselblad. The request was granted. The previously prescribed NAA protocol for numbering of photographs dated back to 1940. It was abandoned and replaced with a new and somewhat chaotic numbering scheme. Some of the markings remain visible on images elsewhere in this book.

Like a dinner sausage, but in reverse, the fuselage of a large airplane starts as sections, which are later joined together. The B-1 Lancer was sliced into a half-dozen major sections. Columbus was assigned fabrication responsibility for two of them. The "wing carry-through" section was under W. Johnson, while the "forward intermediate fuselage" (or FIF) was handled by Jim Milligan. The "carry-through" section was unique. Other large airplanes have long, sturdy spars that pass through the fuselage. B-1 was a manufacturing challenge because of large hinge fittings (with a toilet-seat-sized hole on each side) for attachment of the movable wings via huge hinge pins. With an intended airframe life of thirty years, this unprecedented moving mechanism was mission critical. Failure meant the wings would either fall off or jam.

The "pass-through" was fabricated of titanium—a metal with the attributes of lightness, strength, great expense, and a serious challenge even for the most-skilled machinists. Sophisticated new machines were needed to perform the work rapidly and precisely, as demanded by exacting contract specifications. The largest machine tool order in US history required 4,000 cubic yards of fresh concrete to reinforce the factory floor. Fifteen behemoth Cincinnati Milacron five-axis profilers were installed in Building 6.[2] On disposal, these high-tech machines later triggered a legal dispute of international proportions.

The Columbus plant was a government asset leased rent free to Rockwell, which was responsible for all operational costs. Navy's forty-year ownership of the plant was officially transferred to the Air Force in May 1982, when Lt. Col. Robert J. Pratt replaced Navy captain W. C. Stilwell as the plant representative officer. The historic Columbus airplane factory was now Air Force Plant 85—with no further Air Force plants designated thereafter. By the 1980s, the original 1941 Curtiss factory had been incrementally augmented and expanded with more modern structure. The substantial Air Force investment in infrastructure and equipment transformed the entire Columbus complex.

New Managers Arrive

Chester R. "Chet" Johnson (1927–2015) first burnished his budding mechanical aptitude as a service station attendant in small-town Arkansas before taking a job at Boeing Wichita. The date was February 1951, and the frantic rush to build a fleet of swept-wing, six-engine B-47 bombers was underway. Johnson had a God-given gift for planning and executing aircraft manufacturing. By 1972 Chet was named director of manufacturing at the 747 Division in faraway Everett, Washington. He also had a stint working with VERTOL helicopters in Philadelphia. By 1978, Chet Johnson was back in Wichita.

Apparently, somebody in the Air Force chain of command must have had qualms about existing Columbus managers fabricating major sections of their newest bomber. Executive recruiters were dispatched on a talent hunt and bagged themselves a trophy. Chet Johnson joined Rockwell in 1981 as general manager of the Columbus Division. His entourage included other like-minded people from

The two underslung nacelles held the four General Electric jet engines. The nacelles were covered with fabric, then put into shipping containers. The containers were then loaded aboard railroad cars for transport and delivery to Palmdale, California.

B-1 Lancers

B-1A-1

B-1B

B-1B

B-1B

B-1B

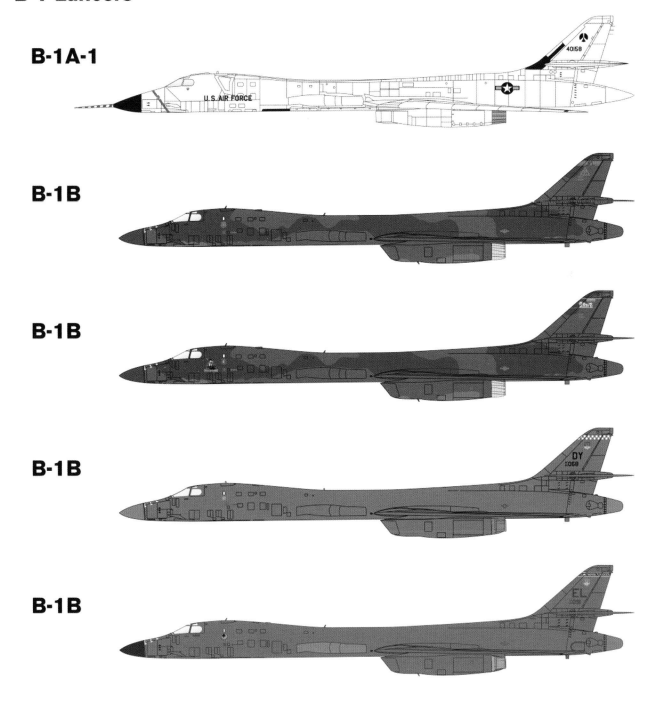

Final assembly of the Rockwell B-1 Lancer was accomplished at Palmdale, California (Plant 42). Most Lancers found operational homes at long-established air force bases in the middle of America—Dyess (Texas), Ellsworth (South Dakota), Grand Forks (North Dakota), and McConnell (Kansas).

SUBCONTRACTS

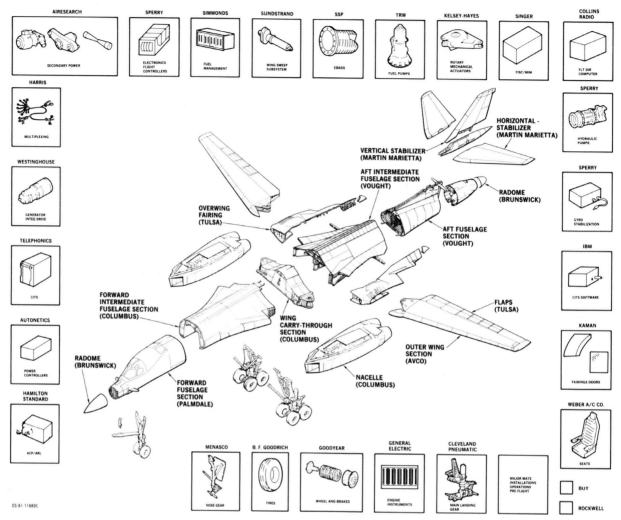

DS-84-11100

This schematic (exploded view) helps everybody understand the source for subassemblies, along with their location in the finished product.

Boeing. Entrenched Columbus managers looked askance as the newcomers assumed the top positions. Their tenure was five years and included manufacturing subsequent space shuttle subassemblies.

Despite cultural challenges associated with the new arrivals, both Rockwell and the Air Force were committed to make delivery dates and cost objectives. Employment, which had dwindled to three hundred before B-1B contract signing, mushroomed to an apex of 7,200 employees, necessary to supply Palmdale with four ship sets per month (peak employment at Columbus was 18,000 in 1953, during the Korean War).

Fabrication of every modern large airplane is divvied up among dozens of suppliers. Rockwell Palmdale built the cockpit and forward fuselage. Weapons bay doors, overwing fairings, and wing flaps came from Rockwell

Tulsa. Aft intermediate and aft fuselage assemblies were ordered from Vought. Horizontal and vertical stabilizers were subcontracted to Martin-Marietta, and radomes were assigned to Brunswick. A myriad of supply chain vendors and their thousands of workers all shared in the windfall.

The first major B-1B subassembly, a forward intermediate fuselage (FIF), was shipped to Palmdale, California, on July 11, 1983, ahead of schedule and under cost. The Air Force awarded Columbus high marks for its B-1B production in a "performance readiness review." In November, the first wing carry-through structure was shipped, again ahead of schedule, and in February the third subassembly, the engine nacelles, was placed aboard railroad cars for shipment to Palmdale, California.

Flight testing on two of the four prototypes continued during the summer of 1984. Airplane number 2 (the second

WING CARRY-THROUGH STRUCTURE

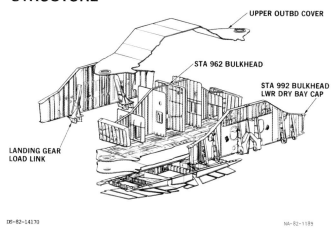

UPPER OUTBD COVER

STA 962 BULKHEAD

STA 992 BULKHEAD
LWR DRY BAY CAP

LANDING GEAR
LOAD LINK

DS-82-14170

NA-82-1189

The primary strength of an airplane is located where the fuselage and wing spars intersect. A large airplane with wings that swing presented a unique engineering challenge. Rockwell devised a section of fuselage called the "pass-through" with hinge holes on each side. This critical fuselage section utilized titanium and was fabricated at Columbus.

B-1A, tail number 74-0159) crashed near Edward AFB on August 29, 1984. The escape capsule (unique only to the first three B-1As) was activated, but a parachute malfunctioned. Two Air Force crew members survived, but Rockwell test pilot Doug Benefield perished.

Assembly complete, the rollout ceremony for the first B-1B was held at Palmdale, California, on September 4, 1984, and the maiden flight occurred on October 18. The new bomber met all its test objectives in a three-hour, ten-minute flight. Less than a year later, on June 27, 1985, the first B-1B was delivered to Strategic Air Command (SAC) at Dyess AFB. By October 1986, Columbus had reached a production rate of four ship sets of B-1B assemblies per month. The FIF for aircraft no. 100 was shipped on September 18, three days ahead of schedule; the wing carry-through structure was shipped on October 23; and the nacelles followed in December.

This marked the end of B-1B production at Columbus. The cycle of boom to bust was complete; however, this time there was nothing following. The Soviet empire had crumbled. The administration of Bill Clinton was eager to cash in on the "peace dividend." The United States was then the sole surviving superpower, and all parts of the military were being trimmed. The boneyard at Davis-Monthan was awash in early-model B-52s culled from the fleet and parked for the last time. With engines gone cold, massive shears arrived to chop airframes into scrap metal.

The B-1B Lancer was flown hard in the skies over Iraq and Afghanistan. The precision dropping of conventional bombs was their forte. Sometimes, to rattle an unsophisticated enemy with rural agrarian upbringing, the American ground troops would invite a Lancer to descent from high altitude and make a low-level pass over the battlefield in full afterburner. Massive noise and concussion rendered enemy ground troops flustered and shaken.

B-1B Lancers were designed for eight to ten thousand flight hours. Average actual hours are now over twelve thousand, and airframes are beyond their anticipated thirty-year service life. Loitering in the skies over Afghanistan and Iraq with heavy bombloads and wings extended has been problematic. Stress cracks have appeared in the wings' leading and trailing tabs, upper-wing splice bolts, and drain holes, as well as on the dorsal and shoulder longerons and ribs.[3] As this is written, news reports indicate the following:

With Pentagon officials expecting budgets to remain flat or decline over the next several years, one of the Air Force's biggest challenges will be finding ways to reduce costs in other programs to accommodate the B-21 as production ramps up.

The ability to fly in proximity and even within defended airspace, a stealth bomber offers an ideal combination of survivability, range, and weapons capacity. The aircraft's stealthiness adds substantially to the production cost, but the tradeoff is an aircraft that can carry less expensive, short-range weapons such as glide bombs.

None of the great powers, however, is willing to part completely with an existing bomber fleet, despite aircraft designs that date back to the late 1940s. Leveraging heavy investments in new propulsion, sensors and weapons, the US, China, and Russia will breathe new life into their aging Cold War–era platforms. . . .

Draft appropriation bills for fiscal 2021 in Congress include the Air Force's request to retire 17 B-1s and funnel the operating-cost savings to modernize what would be the remaining 45 aircraft in the fleet. The bomber renaissance also is seeing transformation of the Cold War–era fleets of the Chinese and Russian Air Forces.[4]

Current plans are to retire both B-1 and B-2 bombers when a new bomber from Northrop Grumman, the B-21 Raider, enters service. The B-21 will join the last remnants of the Stratofortress production run—the B-52H dating from 1961–1962. The B-52H has low airframe hours. Why? Older B-52s were sent to the Vietnam War and flown hard. They are now retired and mostly scrapped. Only flown to maintain aircrew proficiency, the B-52H defended the homeland while parked on alert status. Why are the newer bombers being retired first? The answer is called mission-capable rate. Airliners are measured by "dispatch reliability," which airlines expect to be nearly 100 percent. The Boeing B-52 Stratofortress enjoys a higher mission-capable rate than either of its two compatriots.

The B-1B Lancer is a warplane with a checkered history. Caught in shifting political winds, it was started, canceled, and then restarted. Its service history was equally turbulent. Grounded with engine and other technical problems, it sat out the first Gulf War. Yet, like a phoenix, it returned as a fearsome and unstoppable weapon over the insurgent desert battlefields of the Middle East. USAF photo

Early in the Rockwell B-1 era, a news reporter arrived at a base to craft a story about the awesome new bomber. She interviewed the enlisted troops and then stopped to confirm her facts. "Again, what is the name of this big airplane?" The answer was B-1, but by the time it got into print it was morphed into "BONE." Everybody had a good laugh, and Bone became a popular term of endearment. The B-1B Lancer is the last active warplane bearing the DNA of North American Aviation, Inc.

A B-1B Lancer bearing tail number 86-0124 takes to the air on September 17, 2007. It proudly proclaims the identity of Dyess AFB and the inscription of the commander, 28th Bombardment Squadron. Such markings inspire esprit de corps among unit members.

Epilogue

Termination of the XFV-12A program in 1981 presented an existential threat to the Columbus Division. Production orders for the RA-5C Vigilante, T-2 Buckeye, and OV-10 Bronco were complete, and there were no new programs on the horizon. Since 1979, Columbus had been surviving on small subcontracts: an engine pod–tooling contract for Boeing 767-200s, a modification contract for the Marine Corps' OV-10D Bronco, and a development contract from the Naval Air Development Center for a lightweight, high-pressure hydraulic system, plus preliminary study contracts for the VTXTS (a future trainer) and VFMX (a future fighter). Evidence of Columbus's precarious future was everywhere—even the plant name was changed with ominous frequency.

Rockwell established a new headquarters in a nine-story high-rise at Seal Beach (a suburb south of Los Angeles). In April 1979, the Rockwell International Board combined Inglewood and Columbus into a single entity called the "Military Aircraft Division." Then in July, the board resurrected the North American name, calling it "North American Aircraft Operations—Columbus Facility." Sign painters changed the famous North American Aviation name on the plant at least twice.

The final shipment of B-1B nacelles in December 1987 marked the end of Rockwell's aircraft work at Columbus. Rockwell abandoned the plant in December 1988. Structural work for the X-31A prototypes remained at Palmdale under Cecil Cline. X-31 engineering was moved away from Columbus.

Why was the MDC C-17 Globemaster III needed? The Lockheed C-141 Starlifter was the Air Force's primary airlifter starting in 1965. The fleet of 285 served the US well; however, they were flown hard, starting with the Vietnam War, during peace, and in the other conflicts that followed. War weary after three decades of hard service, the McDonnell Douglas C-17 Globemaster II was deemed a worthy replacement, and contracts were awarded. Factory space at Columbus was initially considered necessary to meet the demand. Including exports, 279 were built between 1991 and 2015, primarily to rejuvenate Air Mobility Command's fleet of primary airlifters. Just as North American Aviation assumed the Columbus lease from Curtiss-Wright in 1950, McDonnell Douglas assumed the lease from Rockwell in 1988.[1]

The Air Force transferred possession to MDC for C-17 Globemaster III, MD-80, and DC-11 production. An employment level of two thousand was projected, but it

Sections of the space shuttle fabricated in Columbus included fuselage fore and aft of the cargo bay, plus a flap located on the rear bulkhead beneath the powerful Rocketdyne-built trio of main engines.

An aerial photograph of the Columbus plant shows the original construction in the upper center. Nearly fifty years of usage resulted in many changes and additions. Nolan Leatherman collection

Plant Area and Utilization

Rockwell International

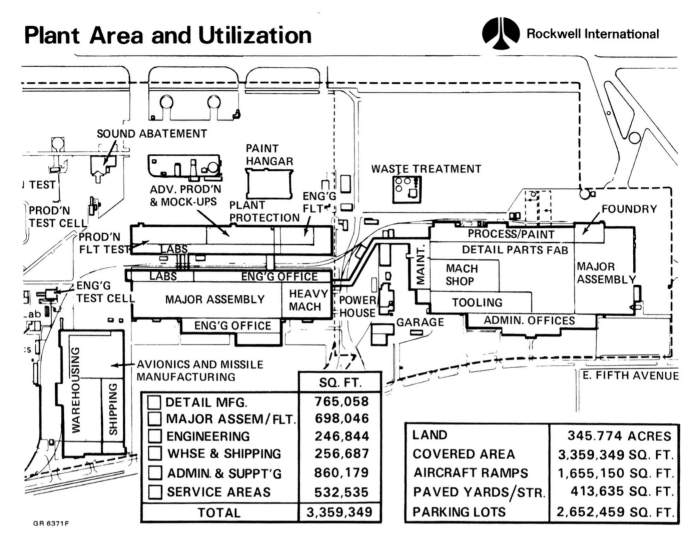

	SQ. FT.
☐ DETAIL MFG.	765,058
☐ MAJOR ASSEM/FLT.	698,046
☐ ENGINEERING	246,844
☐ WHSE & SHIPPING	256,687
☐ ADMIN. & SUPPT'G	860,179
☐ SERVICE AREAS	532,535
TOTAL	3,359,349

LAND	345.774 ACRES
COVERED AREA	3,359,349 SQ. FT.
AIRCRAFT RAMPS	1,655,150 SQ. FT.
PAVED YARDS/STR.	413,635 SQ. FT.
PARKING LOTS	2,652,459 SQ. FT.

GR 6371F

The layout of the Columbus plant during the waning days of Rockwell occupied nearly 300 acres. In an industry where building size is expressed as acreage, the main factory structure consumed 77 acres of roofing material. Nolan Leatherman collection

never exceeded 1,200. Three and a half years later, in August 1992, MDC announced plans to relocate more work to Long Beach, California, leaving the Columbus plant vacant. For the first time since the plant was built in 1941, no defense contractor occupied the facility. Without the familiar rat-a-tat-tat of rivets being bucked, the vast plant sat in eerie empty silence. The Air Force invoked its industrial-plant divestiture authority by offering the property for sale. It was acquired by the Schottenstein Stores Corporation, a Columbus-based holding company of numerous retail and manufacturing ventures.

Accountants generally ascribe a forty-year life to factories and other buildings for purposes of calculating depreciation. Sure enough, many of the wartime airplane factories were showing their age by the mid-1980s. Like every other abandoned airplane factory, site environmental remediation is needed because of fuel and various other spilled chemicals too often leave behind contaminated groundwater.

Obsolete electrical and other internal systems, insufficient ceiling heights for modern aircraft, and leaky roofs invite dismantling by the wrecking ball. The Kansas City B-25 factory, and the NAA main plant at LAX were torn down in 1986, so the valuable land beneath could be repurposed. The end for the Columbus plant came in December 1988. Some other plants, including Boeing Plant II in Seattle, the Consolidated factory at San Diego, the former Vultee complex of Downey, and the sprawling Ford Willow Run B-24 factory lingered a bit longer.

Rockwell International did a poor job of protecting the heritage of North American Aviation. For some executives, semi truckloads of records, photographs, and artifacts constitute an avoidable expense. The photographic collection of the Dallas plant was lost. Wind tunnel and other models disappeared. Original ink drawings on vellum from several locations were shipped to the Columbus plant, stored away from view, but then dragged onto the factory floor after a water pipe burst. There dates ranged from the 1930s and into the 1960s. The drawings ranged a broad spectrum from mundane small parts to very large exploded-views and training manual illustrations created by gifted artists. Many got wet. Some suffered damage; however, vellum is a sturdy medium and not easily destroyed. Estimates of the archival drawing count range from 40,000 to 60,000.

A concerned employee, Ken Jungeberg, stepped forward to intervene. Jungeberg obtained permission to preserve the collection. With the help of friends and a rented truck, most ended up stored at his personal airplane hangar near Lebanon, Ohio, for the next thirty-two years until they found a more enduring home.

The Troublesome China Connection

Most of the equipment and tools left by McDonnell Douglas Corporation (MDC) were sold at auction in May 1994, but some items, such as the Cincinnati Milacron five-axis profilers installed for B-1B production, were far too specialized and sophisticated for any local machine shop. At that time, MDC was in negotiations to build forty civilian airliners in China, and the machinery would be invaluable for that joint venture. A team of Chinese aviation officials were invited to Columbus to inspect the machinery, and a sale was negotiated. An export license was obtained from the US Department of Commerce, with the strict condition that the computer-driven machines could be used only to manufacture commercial aircraft parts. The Chinese buyers

Airplane factories have large metal-working machinery mostly hidden away from public view. Highly skilled operators establish computer programs that grind away mountains of aluminum shavings with great precision. All scrap will be sold and recycled. John Andrew collection

agreed to the restriction, but a 1995 Commerce Department investigative report revealed that six of the machines were sent to a military plant in Nanchang that produces Silkworm cruise missiles and A-5 attack aircraft.

The Commerce Department report concluded that the Chinese purchaser, China National Aero-Technology Import and Export Corp. (CATIC), "illegally, knowingly and willfully diverted" the equipment. A federal grand jury investigation into the transaction resulted in an indictment[2] of CATIC and McDonnell Douglas Corporation. According to Bonni Tischler, assistant commissioner for investigations for the United States Customs Service, this was the "first time a Chinese Government entity has been indicted for violations of US export laws."[3] The case was resolved on May 11, 2001, when CATIC entered a plea of nolo contendere (a plea of "no contest" that neither admits nor denies guilt). The Chinese corporation was sentenced to pay a fine of $1 million and suffer a revocation of its export privileges for five years. MDC agreed to an administrative penalty of $1.32 million and denial of its export privileges for ten years. Both parties had their export denials suspended in exchange for an agreement to comply with all Export Administration Regulations and cooperate in any administrative enforcement proceeding against other parties.

Missiles of Columbus

Research turned up a listing of missiles produced at the Columbus plant. Like a military airplane, missiles are often given a designation and name. Categories include air-to-surface missile (designated ASM), air-intercept missile (AIM), and surface-to-air missile (SAM). "Modular Guided Weapon" is a euphemism for a guidance mechanism wrapped around a conventional steel bomb.

> Hornet Anti-Tank ASM
> Terminal Homing Flight Test Vehicle
> Redhead and Roadrunner Target Missile
> Low-Altitude Short-Range Missile
> Condor Standoff Tactical ASM
> Mk. 84 Explosive—Ordnance Modular Guided Weapon (2,000 lbs.)
> M-117 Explosive—Ordnance Modular Guided Weapon (750 lbs.)
> Mk. 84 Explosive—Infrared Modular Guided Weapon (2,000 lbs.)

The Demise of North American Aviation

Like the slow passing of a large, old oak tree, the demise of NAA played out over years. During his prime and facing adversity, Dutch Kindelberger anticipated the customer needs, fabricated the perfect aircraft to meet them, and then (as the chief salesman) twisted the arm of officials to get them sold. As the 1960s arrived, Dutch and his inner circle were slowing down. Corporate history is littered with the corpses of companies (both large and small) that expire at (or near) the forty-year mark because their aging founders lacked a succession plan. As Kindelberger's health declined, so did his connections with governmental decision makers. Friendships with the "old timers" were long gone by 1961. F-111 and other defense contracts were landing in Texas, the home state of Lyndon Johnson. Lacking an infusion of fresh blood, NAA's direction began to drift.

Despite the cautionary note, the prosperity continued. Sales first hit $1 billion in 1957 and doubled by 1964 as NAA climbed the list of largest US companies from number 28 to number 19. While seemingly losing momentum, NAA was still holding a portfolio of projects of national importance. Apollo, with engineering and manufacturing based at Downey, was a massive project driven by incredible time constraints. To date, it is the only project to successfully land and retrieve a human from the moon. The Saturn second stage, also built by NAA, was an essential part of Apollo. Rocketdyne type J-2 engines were engineering marvels that melded thrust, reliability, great strength, and light weight.

Everybody was confident that follow-on space projects would continue. First stops at the moon certainly would be quickly followed by Mars and other galactic destinations. After Apollo, Space Shuttle would be a useful interim project to keep the Downey facility occupied and workers gainfully employed. The section of the space vehicle housing astronauts was called "orbiter" by Rockwell and NASA workers. Guidance systems from Anaheim were still needed. Separately, global positioning system (GPS) satellites were entering gestation at Seal Beach.

The Palmdale and Columbus plants shouldered most of what remained of aircraft contracts. The relationship was collaborative. The XB-70 utilized a unique proprietary skin fabricated of honeycomb steel to cope with heat generated at Mach 3. Some of those parts were fabricated at the Columbus plant.

The Air Force chief of staff was then a crusty World War II–era bomber general named Curtis LeMay (1906–1990). The election of John Kennedy swept a youthful, number-crunching math whiz named Robert McNamara into the Pentagon's top job. The cocky McNamara and resolute LeMay were at loggerheads. The new arrival was a proponent of missiles, and with the Vietnam War heating up, the whiz kid outmaneuvered the old cigar-chomping general. Many of McNamara's decisions were misguided at best—especially his handling of the Vietnam War. The value of a weapon system such as the B-70 was to force the Soviets to spend disproportionately on defense. Defensive radars, interceptors, and surface-to-air missiles do not threaten the United States. Despite incredible technological advancements, Curtis LeMay's B-70 program died at the hands of McNamara. The combined loss of the B-70 bomber, F-107, and F-108 fighter was a painful blow to NAA.

Atwood, ever stoic on the outside, was no doubt reeling on the inside. He knew that Boeing, Lockheed, and Douglas had airliner sales to bridge the gaps in government business. After having suffered repeated rejection at the hands of fickle military procurement officials, Atwood longed to bring stability to a business lacking a mitigating private-sector presence. Survival at the mercy of congressional appropriations was proving untenable.

The aerospace business has always been a rollercoaster, where winning a primary contract results in hiring booms,

Whether in combat or politics, the word "defeat" was not in Curtis LeMay's vocabulary—until he tangled in 1961 with Robert McNamara regarding replacing the Boeing B-52 Stratofortress with a fleet of North American B-70 Valkyries.

Cocky, brash, and outspoken, Robert McNamara ruffled feathers with most everybody, including military brass, defense contractors, and the grunts counting dead bodies in the tropical heat of Vietnam. Yet, he retained the full confidence of two presidents, Kennedy and Johnson.

Progressive heart failure was taking its toll even as the "old man" remained chairman of the board. On July 27, 1962, Dutch Kindelberger, the founder, the perennial optimist, and driving force behind NAA, passed away at age sixty-seven. The grief and disbelief permeated NAA everywhere, from the factory floor to the executive suites.

Other companies strictly enforced mandatory retirement at age sixty-five. There were very few exceptions. Other companies also practiced succession planning. Executives were rotated, and those who floundered were weeded out. Kindelberger ran NAA as a family business, even after his only son (Howard, known to the family as "Bud") died in an equestrian accident at age eighteen in 1940. Dutch provided lifetime loyalty to his trusted associates, and it was most often reciprocated. Lee Atwood was a close family friend—almost a surrogate son. Other family-run large businesses have faced serious management challenges—including Douglas Aircraft, McDonnell Aircraft, Ford Motor Company, and Anheuser-Busch brewing.

By 1962, nothing in the United States seemed more important than military defense and going to the moon. A major slice of federal budgetary pie (both NASA and Pentagon) was earmarked for NAA. Programs that were ending (e.g., F-100 Super Sabre and Hound Dog) had performed well, and new projects were off to a great start.

and contract cancellations (or completions) can be followed by wholesale layoffs. Seniority offers some protection. Managers do their best to preserve core competencies by holding on to those with critical skills; however, a certain level of business is needed to generate the cash to pay for all the overhead expenses (e.g., security, fire protection, public relations, legal, the wind tunnel, and an office in Washington, DC).

Kindelberger's forte was aircraft design, followed by high-rate airframe production. Space and its related products were outside his comfort zone. A younger executive, Harrison "Stormy" Storms (1915–1992), emerged as the feisty leader at Downey who pushed his Missile & Information Systems team forward and into peaceful space projects. By late 1960, Kindelberger's health further declined, and Lee Atwood replaced him as president. Lee was reserved, scholarly, and collaborative rather than confrontational. As the antithesis of earthy Dutch Kindelberger, with his salty (but straightforward style), Atwood was a gentlemanly and quiet intellectual who read and could quote Shakespeare. The more introverted lifelong understudy was now fully in charge, and his dysfunctional side was starting to show.

Lee Atwood and Al Rockwell (right) sit together for a portrait ca. 1967. Akin to a wreck on the freeway, this merger was a marriage made in hell that destroyed America's most accomplished aerospace company.

Harrison "Stormy" Storms was a 150-pound (dripping wet) human dynamo who joined NAA during World War II and clawed his way to the top of the Apollo program. His career abruptly ended because three Apollo astronauts were the tragic victims of a fatal launchpad fire in January 1967.

Lee Atwood clutches a cigarette in a chilly scene with NASA's powerful and charismatic chief rocket scientist, Wernher von Braun. Von Braun's résumé included wartime service as a Nazi major in the SS. Like a fledgling bird in an undersized nest, Lee Atwood pushed aside two better-qualified peers (Chuck Gallant and Harrison Storms) to retain the presidency of NAA, a job for which he was not well suited.

The internal optimism at NAA, as America's premier aerospace company, was never higher. The new projects (nuclear, rockets, space, and guidance) had come to overshadow the traditional business of building airplanes.

The bond between Dutch and Lee Atwood was a close partnership and personal friendship forged over three decades. Lee Atwood found himself alone at the storm-

tossed helm. Kindelberger was always in "go" mode and needed somebody nearby and trusted to act as a brake on his propensity to overcommit. Atwood was that person. Asking pointed questions and double-checking the data was an attribute when working with Dutch; however, without Dutch, constantly demanding more data became an impediment to making decisions and moving the business forward.[4]

In a tale that mixes rumor with facts, multiple NAA "old-timers" have volunteered to the authors that Kindelberger knew of Atwood's limitation and was contemplating a solution. Furthermore, it was Kindelberger's plan that Charles "Chuck" J. Gallant would succeed him; however, Dutch dithered and then passed away before any action was taken.

Gallant, born in 1911, was sixteen years junior to Dutch. Gallant was another defector from Douglas Aircraft who joined NAA in 1935. Chuck earned the respect of Dutch by adroitly handling the construction of the wartime plants at Kansas City and Dallas, where his initial role was factory systems, including electricity, water, and air-conditioning. Later, he helped perfect the automobile-style assembly lines. From 1950 to 1959, he was the overall plant manager at Columbus. In 1959, Gallant was returned to Los Angles and joined the elite top tier of executives reporting directly to Kindelberger. Then, in 1962 (at the age of fifty-one) Chuck Gallant suddenly departed the NAA payroll to "spend more time with family." Our sources assert that Atwood got wind of the plan, and a Machiavellian plot emerged. Gallant was sacked when the opportunity arose. Lee Atwood was more vicious and conniving than he outwardly appeared. Gallant was covertly sacrificed by Atwood so Atwood could save his own skin.

The mounting daily loss of combat pilots over Vietnam plus the death of test pilots at home had unfortunately become routine. But it was the untimely demise of the three astronauts in the launchpad inferno at Cape Kennedy, fueled by pure oxygen, on January 27, 1967, that was far more devastating to the national psyche. The blame for the fatal Apollo 1 fire fell upon NAA. It would redefine the remainder of Lee Atwood's life. Four years had elapsed since the passing of Dutch Kindelberger. Atwood, outwardly a shy but trusting person, found himself alone at the storm-tossed helm.

Some observers assert that NASA leadership (Wernher von Braun et al.) expected either Harrison Storms or Lee Atwood to be sacked. Harrison Storms, a plucky senior executive at Downey with many of Kindelberger's traits, was scapegoated and pushed aside. Like Chuck Gallant before him, Harrison Storms was another capable insider who was more openly sacrificed by Lee Atwood so he could again save himself. But plenty of blame asserting faulty electrical and other shoddy work within the Apollo capsules remained on Atwood's shoulders. Harrison Storms remained on the payroll in a minor headquarters assignment. The balance of his life was spent searching diligently for his next big break. Sadly, it never came. Congressional investigations and bloviating politicians kept the fatal Apollo 1 fire at the top of the news. Atwood's testimony before the Senate investigative committee remains public record.

Like Kindelberger, Al Rockwell was an engineer (MIT graduate) and entrepreneur with an intense interest in aviation. The family-run conglomerate Rockwell Standard was based on manufacturing truck parts. In 1958, an Oklahoma-based fabricator of executive airplanes was acquired and renamed Aero Commander. Atwood's relationship with Dutch was long standing, rewarding, and mutually beneficial. Like a mate who has lost a spouse, and after pushing two peer "siblings" out of the nest, Lee Atwood, himself the son of a preacher, was lonely and searching for another workplace "father" figure with whom to bond.

Atwood took an international trip in 1966 and found himself seated on an airliner adjacent to Willard F. "Al" Rockwell (1914–1992), another personable industrial magnate. The two travelers struck up a conversation and immediately hit it off. Both men spoke of their business goals. It turned out that the Rockwell family, already holding Aero Commander, harbored even-bigger aviation aspirations. Atwood remained shaken in the wake of the fatal Apollo fire. Al Rockwell, a savvy negotiator experienced in mergers, invited Atwood to join forces with him at the industrial altar.

To Atwood, Mr. Rockwell may have seemed like an ideal business partner to replace Kindelberger, Aviation was cyclical. "Maybe," Atwood likely thought, "truck parts will bring stability and dampen the boom-and-bust cycle inherent within aerospace." Fatherly Al Rockwell could really turn on the charm—when it served his purpose. Atwood accepted the proposition from Mr. Rockwell despite sharp protests from other NAA executives. NAA was then worth over $2 billion. Rockwell Standard was valued at $600 million, with debt nearly equal to equity. Merger with the much-smaller truck parts conglomerate yielded North American Rockwell (NAR), one of the nation's largest companies. The minnow (the little Rockwell company) devoured the whale (the aerospace giant known as North American Aviation, Inc.). The knot was tied in September 1967, but the honeymoon was brief.

The newly merged company was initially named North American Rockwell, with Lee Atwood as the president. It may have appeared to Atwood that Al Rockwell would fill Kindelberger's benevolent shoes as chairman. A whiz at math but a klutz at reading nuanced interpersonal relationships, Atwood had seriously miscalculated. The merger soon digressed into a marriage forged in hell. Lacking an annulment clause, the workplace climate quickly turned toxic, to the detriment of thousands of shocked NAA career employees.

Their work lives too frequently became hellish as their aerospace roots were trampled.

The board of directors at each premerger company numbered twelve. The new enterprise not coming together. Feuding, cultural clash, and disharmony are common in the postmerger workplace. Atwood despised confrontation. Lacking the personality traits to diffuse it, he first cowered and then retreated from strife. Meanwhile, the merger-savvy Al Rockwell and his like-minded progeny seized the opportunity and approached Lee with a solution: "Two dozen board members is an unwieldy number. Let's retire everybody who is age seventy or older." Atwood consented, not realizing that it was his advocates who were betrayed. The Rockwell clan and their minions were now in full control. A fatal stake had been driven into the heart of NAA. The merger was a disaster. NAA was now on a trajectory to oblivion.

Each corporate name change made the name "Rockwell" more prominent as "North American" faded. Changes to signage were frequent. A glance at the 1972 Rockwell corporate telephone directory finds Mr. Willard F. "Al" Rockwell Jr. as chief executive officer and chairman of the board. It seems that Ralph H. Ruud was the only recognized Rockwell corporate officer with an NAA pedigree. The brand was sullied by a protracted series of headline-grabbing national tragedies:

Date	Event
6/8/66	XB-70 midair collision; 2 pilots die.
1/27/67	Apollo 1 launchpad fire; 3 astronauts are fatalities.
8/29/84	B-1A crash kills Rockwell test pilot Doug Benefield.
1/28/86	Space shuttle *Challenger* launch explosion; 7 dead
2/1/03	Space shuttle *Columbia* reentry fire; 7 astronauts perish.

With the Vietnam War winding down, the Air Force was in search of a new air superiority fighter, to be designated F-15. Leveraging the success of the versatile F-4 Phantom II, the McDonnell Aircraft Corporation of St. Louis won the contract. Meanwhile, the blame for the loss at NAR landed upon Lee Atwood, and it was the excuse that Al Rockwell needed to fire him. Atwood later recalled, "I spent over $35 million dollars bidding on the F-15 and the B-1, and I was really savagely criticized for it because we had just merged with Rockwell, and most of those people couldn't understand it. In fact, I got a letter

A portfolio that included intercontinental supersonic bombers, truck parts, the Aero Commander line, and a celebrity spokesman named R. A. "Bob" Hoover was a facade. The family dream of a prospering giant aerospace company named Rockwell crumbled.

(via telegram) from Al Rockwell, which in most-bitter terms gave me six hours to tender my resignation. I still have a copy of it." Atwood held out until the next board of directors meeting to resign. It was 1969, and Lee was at the traditional retirement age of sixty-five when he joined Storms and Gallant on the list of banished executives.

Married, but without children, Lee Atwood stood as the de facto leader for the loyal workers who retained strong affinity to NAA. He remained respected and dignified despite the morass of his own creation. The charming Lee Atwood could strum a guitar and sing at social gatherings. He attended alumni events and accepted speaking invitations.

The postmerger Rockwell view of NAA was condescending but understandable. In some ways, the situation had reverted to the circumstances at Dundalk in 1934. The enterprise had run out of gas and stopped moving forward. The transmission was in park, the emergency brake was set, and the driver's seat was vacant. A visionary spark plug with aerospace credentials (like Kindelberger, Chuck Gallant, or Harrison Storms) was needed. Such people are rare. No such savior emerged from a culture steeped in truck parts.

Even when wounded, big corporations die slowly. The 1984 head count stood at 106,000: 44,730 were hourly (touch labor) workers, 17,000 were professional engineers or scientists, and 44,270 performed other salaried duties. A quarter of the workforce (or 26,000 employees) worked on the B-1 bomber project. There was an alarming dearth of new projects in the backlog after NavStar, Space Shuttle, and B-1B were completed. Rockwell International was clearly failing to win new aerospace business.

Each business unit was scrutinized on the basis of quarterly financial results. Each reacted by building a fence around themselves. Balkanization with interdivisional bickering emerged. There was insufficient collaboration to cycle talent between them. Older employees retired as projects were completed, while younger employees got laid off. All focus was on the quarterly financial reports. Decisions were risk adverse. Critical defense and space

workers departed the company and were not replaced. North American's management, many veterans of the aircraft trade, were quietly retiring. The Rockwell aerospace workforce fell from 106,000 employees in 1984 to 22,000 at the end of 1996.

If a tree is ailing, then none of its branches can long survive. The Columbus plant was performing well at a time when other parts of NAR were becoming underutilized. Yet, the Ohio operations were vacated well before the Rockwell divestiture. The scattered remaining pieces of NAR were swept into Boeing, effective December 6, 1996. Most were subsequently sold off or shut down. The Missile Division at Duluth, Georgia, was first to go, in January 1997. Later, Downey was torn down, Anaheim vacated, and Rocketdyne divested to Pratt & Whitney. Boeing shareholders were poorly served by the Rockwell aerospace acquisition because of the environmental liability for cleanup projects at Crenshaw, the Santa Susana test site, and elsewhere.

Lee Atwood was active in speaking and writing during his long retirement. Two topics were favorites: the P-51 Mustang cooling system and the tragic Apollo 1 test pad fire. Atwood was among the nearly one hundred people on hand on June 10, 1992, when the California Museum of Science and Industry bestowed its lifetime achievement award upon Harrison Storms. Atwood used his speech to assert that neither North American Aviation nor Harrison Storms was responsible for the Apollo 1 fire: "He was innocent of the deaths of those people, completely innocent." Despite an assertion delayed by twenty-five years, Atwood's outspoken and public defense gave comfort to Stormy. Harrison Storms's passing came a mere month later, on July 11, 1992.

Atwood remained a gentleman to the end, by never expressing anger or frustration regarding events (many of his own instigation) that destroyed the great company that Dutch Kindelberger had entrusted solely to him, starting in 1960. John Leland "Lee" Atwood quietly passed away at age ninety-four on March 5, 1999.

What Happened at Curtiss?

The first chapter depicts the XP-87 in an unfavorable light. Research turned up a letter from Richard A. Morely dated September 27, 1998. The open letter states in part, "You may want to include this as part of the Curtiss archives." More important are insights into the postwar business climate within Curtiss-Wright (C-W) Corporation. Despite Morely's assertions, the XP-87 was rightfully rejected because it was overweight, underpowered, too slow, and otherwise unfit for military service in the jet age:

The beginning of the end of Curtiss-Wright's Airplane Division came when their XP-87 Blackhawk was canceled in its entirety on October 15, 1945. The findings of the review board clearly favored the competitor, Northrop's XF-89 Scorpion, for several reasons. The report led to the termination of the program.

The Secretary of the Air Force, A. S. Barrows, had the final approval of either airplane. Harry Truman, now president, remembered his difficulties with Curtiss-Wright when he was senator back during World War II. Further, he must have wondered why with all the cash C-W had in the bank ($135 million) that they would not spend one cent for research and development. Plus, he probably could not understand the Wall Street champions, the financial wizards who now controlled the company, playing musical chairs with all the C-W general managers. Truman, known to have a "get even" attitude, sure had influenced Barrows' final decision which led to the procurement of Northrop's Scorpion in quantity.

The Findings Report was not complete as a number of XP-87 advantages were omitted[;] therefore the Review Board did not have a complete picture of the flight test activity. The procurement recommendation was made on this basis.

The wing on the XP-87 was altitude limited. The Air Force made the decision that the airplane should operate higher—up to 70,000 feet. C-W priced another wing which was cost excessive. The regular engineering personnel normally associated with design review, pricing[,] and cost negotiations were not involved with the contract amendment. This was handled by upper-level management[,] presumably to ensure reduction of other program losses. The original wing design, limited to approximately 45,000 feet, was in conformance with the altitude requirements established by the Air Force! Further, the findings report revealed the Northrop XP-89 was favored by the project pilots, specifically Maj. Richard Johnson. It was simply a better airplane in part due to the wing on the XP-87. It was unfortunate indeed, however, there was no doubt that Curtiss-Wright was "screwed." It remains to be seen whether it was done by themselves, or by the Air Force, or by Harry Truman.

Earlier, Guy Vaughan, C-W's president, had a meeting with Barrows which turned ugly, many harsh words were exchanged, and Vaughan was thrown out of Barrows' office. Vaughan retired from Curtiss soon thereafter.

All this led to a big giant step downward in the demise of the Airplane Division.

Prior to the entry of the United States into World War II (about the same time that Germany invaded Poland in 1939), Curtiss-Wright was expanding in every area. Robert Earle, who was in charge of propellor [sic] operations at Buffalo, was made Curtiss-Wright vice-president in charge of the Propellor [sic] Division and the Airplane Division. Earle was a Navy man, pilot, spent a couple of years in the Washington office[,] as was assistant to the General Manager before becoming involved with propellors [sic]. Bob Earle was probably the last hope for the Airplane Division at Columbus.

Earle had received an RFP from BuAer for an anti-submarine warfare (ASW) shipboard airplane. Knowing that Columbus was desperately in need of a product, he contacted Walter Tydon, then former chief engineer at Buffalo and XP-87 project[,] and told him to do anything possible to get aboard the program. Tydon was transferred to the New York office[,] where he immediately began to organize the proposal. He went on an ASW exercise with the Navy to obtain firsthand the information required for the RFP submittal.

Tydon made several attempts to attract the Navy to accept the Curtiss-Wright proposal even though there were no requirements for the additional effort:

A full-scale plywood mockup impressed the BuAer personnel.

Wind tunnel model tests were conducted at Cornell's aeronautical lab[,] which was donated to the University by Curtiss-Wright at the closing of Buffalo operations (Tydon had to wait in line with other contractors to use the facility because his ex-employees did not show him any preference).

The last bonus was an appendix showing other applications that [aircraft] carriers lacked—cargo airplane (COD—carrier on-board delivery), litter, and personnel transport.

The replacement for Guy Vaughan was an ex-machine shop foreman who worked his way up to director of manufacturing engineering at the Ford Motor Company, Roy Hurley. He was a dynamic person; however, he had no formal education, was not aero-oriented, and knew nothing of aircraft R&D. He would not listen to how the aeronautical community operates.

In September 1949, BuAer notified Curtiss-Wright and Grumman that they would be awarded study contracts. In addition, Hurley said he would be in the New York office the following day. Instead of helping to celebrate the contract, Hurley announced to the stunned C-W personnel that he was going to visit Admiral Pride at BuAer the following day and tell him that Curtiss-Wright would not accept an experimental order. He would only accept a production contract. The rest is history. Grumman got the contract and Curtiss-Wright was out of the military airplane business. It was not the demise any-more, it was the burial.

In November 1950, Curtiss-Wright was removed from the Columbus facility, and North American Aviation became the new tenant at 4300 East Fifth Avenue.

Signed, Richard A. Morely

Glossary

This matrix is followed by a list of common acronyms and abbreviations. It is provided to assist readers.

Pay grade	Navy and Coast Guard	Army, USAF, and Marines	Insignia
O-1	Ensign	Second lieutenant	Gold Bar
O-2	Lieutenant (junior grade)	First lieutenant	Silver Bar
O-3	Lieutenant	Captain	Dual Silver Bars
O-4	Lt. Commander	Major	Gold Leaf
O-5	Commander	Lt. colonel	Silver Leaf
O-6	Captain	Colonel	Eagle
Above O-6	Admiral	General	Stars

Common Acronyms, Initialisms, and Abbreviations	
Admiral, Adm.	Air Force base, AFB
General, Gen.	Chief of naval operations, CNO
Colonel, Col.	Curtiss-Wright Aeronautical company, C-W
Captain, Capt.	Joint Chiefs of Staff, JCS

Comment: Impact of Warplanes on Automobile Design

The Vigilante debuted in 1958, at the same time the newest automobiles were sprouting fins and other aviation-themed adornments—as depicted by the pink 1959 Cadillac. Considered big, fast, and beautiful in the eyes of many Americans, the Detroit automobile became a metaphor for the Pentagon's newest warplanes. Designers emulated the long, crisp, and clean lines as personal expressions of jet-age power and speed. Every suburban garage could hangar the family's personal example. Settling into the driver's seat of a 1962 Buick is reminiscent of a cockpit

rife with gauges, switches, and knobs adorned with dollops of chrome. Like vestigial vertical stabilizers, fins first appeared on Chevrolets with the iconic 1957 model. Versions of the overendowed Oldsmobile Rocket 88 arrived at dealers with semitruck-sized 455-cubic-inch V-8 engines. No catapult was required to feel the acceleration. As measured by fin size, 1959 was the apex year. The Cadillac also sported cone-shaped, red-glowing taillights, symbolic of the flame-belching afterburners found on fighter planes.

A pink 1959 Cadillac emulates the sleek fighter jet that first flew in 1958, with fins and cone-shaped taillights that are a metaphor for the flame-belching afterburners on the hottest warplanes, such as Vigilante. Alamy CTTCRF

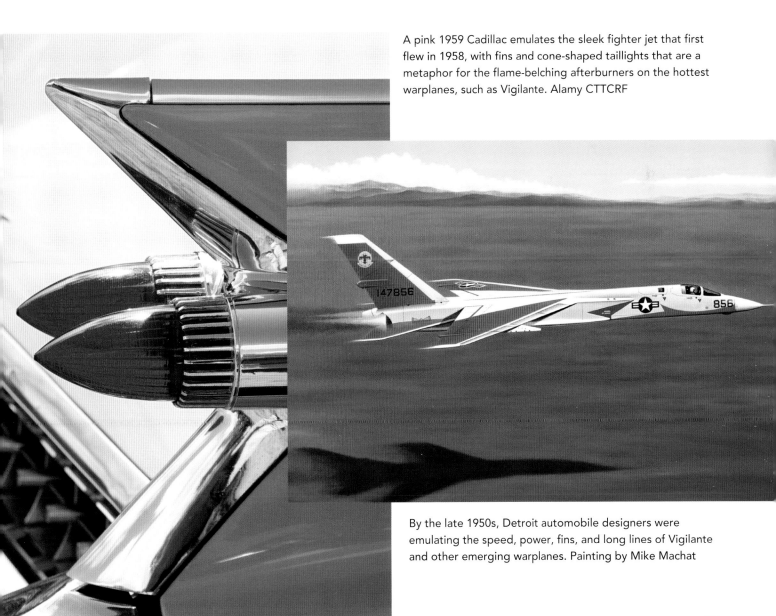

By the late 1950s, Detroit automobile designers were emulating the speed, power, fins, and long lines of Vigilante and other emerging warplanes. Painting by Mike Machat

Endnotes

Chapter 1

1. "Accept Your Heritage," undated NAR Columbus Division employee magazine article.

2. Louis R. Eltscher and Edward M. Young, *Curtiss-Wright, Greatness and Decline* (Woodbridge, CT: Twayne, 1998), 86–89.

3. Bill Norton, *American Aircraft Development of World War II* (Stroud, UK: Fonthill Media, 2019), 27.

4. Bert Kinzey, "SB2C Helldiver," *Detail & Scale* 52 (1997): 6.

5. Norton, *American Aircraft Development of World War II*, 30–33.

6. Peter Bowers, *Curtiss Aircraft, 1907–1948* (Annapolis, MD: Naval Institute Press, 1987), 417.

7. Douglas Knerr, "Lustron: How an Ohio Company Almost Changed American Housing," *Timeline* 22 (April–May 2005): 18–33), accessed January 23, 2021.

8. "Case History of the XF-87 All-Weather Fighter," *AAHS Journal* 38, no. 1 (Spring 1993): 20–31.

9. Marty J. Isham and David R. McLaren, *Northrop F-89 Scorpion History* (Atglen, PA: Schiffer, 2004).

Chapter 2

1. Seahorse aboard *Shangri-La* came from three sources: Philadelphia Field Service Representatives report (in NAA files); Ed Rusinek, "The Sea Trials of the P-51 Mustang 'Seahorse,'" *NAAR Bulletin*, Summer 2002, 5–6; and ship's log from Ghost Gray website, accessed January 16, 2021.

2. Kindelberger's view of the air war in Korea was found in an NAA history brochure prepared by the Columbus Division, circa 1960.

3. *Aviation Week*, November 13, 1950, 57.

4. Paul McCormick, "Dutch Kindelberger's Columbus Gamble," *NAA Retiree's Bulletin*, Fall 2008, 10.

5. Ibid., 11.

6. Warranty deed filed with Franklin County, dated April 3, 1989.

7. Richard A. Morley, "Ed Gillespie: The World's Oldest Test Pilot?," *AAHS Journal* 46, no. 3 (Fall 2001): 173.

Chapter 3

1. William E. Scarborough, "The North American AJ Savage, Part One: Establishing the Heavy Attack Mission," *The Hook*, Tailhook Association, Fall 1989, 31.

2. From 1798 until 1949, the secretary of the Navy was a member of the president's cabinet. Assignment to the Department of Defense was seen by many admirals as a downgrade and therefore a threat that contributed to the dysfunctional behavior exhibited during the revolt of the admirals.

3. Jeffrey G. Barlow, *Revolt of the Admirals* (Washington, DC: Naval Historical Center, 1994), 123.

4. David McCullough, *Truman* (New York: Simon & Schuster, 1992), 738–40.

5. Barlow, *Revolt of the Admirals*, 247.

6. Ibid., 250.

7. Ibid., 260–62.

8. Ibid., 289.

9. Hill Goodspeed, "Record Setters Soar in Hangar Bay One," *Foundation* 38, no. 2 (Fall 2017): 32–36.

10. www.tailsthroughtime.com/2015/08/the-atomic-neptunes-navys-interim.htm.

11. Scarborough, "The North American AJ Savage," 31.

12. Ibid., 33.

13. Ibid., 34–35.

14. Jim Pearce, *A 20th Century Guy: An Autobiography* (Goodyear, AZ: Sonya Steiner, 2008), 245.

15. Tommy H. Thomason, *Strike from the Sea: U.S. Navy Attack Aircraft from Skyraider to Super Hornet, 1948–Present* (Forest Lake, MN: Specialty Press, 2009), 50–54.

16. Kevin Thompson, *North American Aircraft, 1934–1999*, vol. 2 (Santa Ana, CA: Narkiewicz/Thompson, 1999), 35–36.

17. Steve Ginter, *North American AJ-1 Savage* (Simi Valley, CA: S. Ginter, 1992), 12.

18. Richard A. Leyes and William A. Fleming, *The History of North American Small Gas Turbine Engines* (Washington, DC: National Air & Space Museum, Smithsonian Institution, 1999), 530–31.

Chapter 4

1. Frank Compton, "November Seven Nine Zulu," *Sport Aviation*, June 1983, 37.

2. Morley, "Ed Gillespie," 175.

3. Compton, "November Seven Nine Zulu," 38.

4. Ibid., 39.

5. Avco Lycoming Corporation press release, undated draft.

6. *Aviation Week & Space Technology*, April 1, 1963, 31.

7. Gary Wheatley, "Trojan Horse," *Warbirds International?*, 22.

Chapter 5

1. Leyes and Fleming, *The History of North American Small Gas Turbine Engines*, 35–40.

2. NAA Preliminary Flight Test Report NA-46-1013, Model No. XFJ-1, BuNo 39053, 4.

3. Gordon Swanborough and Peter M. Bowers, *United States Naval Aircraft since 1911* (New York: Funk & Wagnalls, 1968), 325.

4. Scholer Bangs, *Aviation Week*, March 22, 1948, 13.

5. Steve Ginter and Ron Picciani, *North American FJ-1 Fury*, Naval Fighters 7 (Simi Valley, CA: S. Ginter, 1983), 15.

6. A. Kevin Grantham, "The 1946–1949 Bendix Trophy Races," *Warbirds International*, July 2006, 30–37.

7. Tommy H. Thomason, *US Naval Air Superiority* (Forest Lake, MN: Specialty Press, 2008), 42.

8. NATC Report, *Carrier Suitability XFJ-2*, 2–4.

9. Steve Ginter, *North American FJ-2 Fury* (Simi Valley, CA: S. Ginter, 1984), 2; and Duncan Curtis, *North American F-86 Sabre* (Marlborough, UK: Crowood, 2000), 118–21.

10. Bob Hoover, *Forever Flying* (New York: Atria Books [Simon & Schuster], 1997), 172.

11. NATC Report, *Carrier Suitability Tests XFJ-2*, 12.

12. *Board of Inspection and Survey (BIS) Report*, August 3, 1955, 2.

13. Steve Ginter, *North American FJ-3/3M Fury*, Profile Publication 88 (Simi Valley, CA: S. Ginter, 2010), 44.

14. Ray Wagner, *The North American Sabre* (New York: Doubleday, 1963), 99–101; and Curtis, *North American F-86 Sabre*, 122–24.

15. Tommy H. Thomason, "Non-aerodynamic Wing Fences," www.tailspintopics.com, accessed July 2, 2016.

16. Francis K. Mason, *North American FJ Fury*, Profile Publication 42 (Leatherhead, UK: Profile Publications, 1965), 10.

17. Email from Duncan Curtis to author, June 28, 2018.

18. David K. Stumpf, *Regulus: America's First Nuclear Submarine Missile* (Nashville: Turner, 1997), 73–74.

19. Ibid., 182.

20. Curtis, *North American F-86 Sabre*, 126.

21. *Approach*, February 1957, reprinted in Steve Ginter, *FJ-4/4B Fury*, 5–7.

22. BuNos 139287, Carrier Suitability; 139289, Flight Test—Stability and Control; 139290, Flight Test—Engine Performance; 139291, Electrical; 139292, Service Test; 139293, Armament; and 139294, Carrier Suitability and Service Test.

23. Thomason, *Strike from the Sea*, 97.

24. See Thomason, *Strike from the Sea*, 89–90, for a complete discussion of LABS.

25. Curtis, *North American F-86 Sabre*, 132.

26. Earl Berlin, *North American F-86H Sabre "Hog,"* Air Force Legends (Simi Valley, CA: S. Ginter, 1999), 2–6.

27. Ibid., 76–77.

28. Ibid., 77.

Chapter 6

1. Erwin J. Bulban, "T2J Designed," *Aviation Week*, May 13, 1957, 52–59.

2. Press release, "Westinghouse Jet Engine Logs Two-Millionth Hour of In-Flight Operation."

3. Bulban, "T2J Designed," 52–59.

4. Cmdr. John Moore (retired), *The Wrong Stuff: Flying on the Edge of Disaster* (Forest Lake, MN: Specialty Press, 1997), 185.

5. Correspondence from commander, NATC, to chief, bureau of aeronautics, July 27, 1959. An aerodynamic stall is the sudden reduction in the lift generated by an airfoil. Stall strips are small triangular shaped objects attached to the leading edge of a wing to enhance stability prior to the onset of a stall.

6. Mark Frankel and Tommy H. Thomason, *Training the Right Stuff* (Atglen, PA: Schiffer, 2016), 151–52.

7. Correspondence from chief of naval air training to CNO, August 29, 1968.

8. Ed Gillespie, "View from the Cockpit," *Air Enthusiast*, October 1973, 169–71.

9. *T-2B Variable Stability Advanced Trainer*, North American Brochure NA 64H-313, April 1, 1964, 4.

10. *T-2D [sic] Trainer Technical Summary*, North American Aviation / Columbus North American Rockwell, NR69M-80, March 10, 1969.

11. Frankel and Thomason, *Training the Right Stuff*, 238–48.

Chapter 7

1. NAGPAW—For a brief postwar period, it was fashionable at North American for product names starting with "NA." The list included Native, Navajo, Navion, and others.

2. George Gehrkens, *The A-5 Vigilante*, Sea Wings documentary movie.

3. Robert I. Stanfield, *Aviation Week*, May 26, 1958, 30.

4. Nolan Leatherman, interview with author.

5. Early Vigilantes assigned to Pax River: BuNo 146694 through 146702 and 147850 through 147854.

6. Capt. George Klett, USN (Ret.), "The Half-Life of an Aircraft," *Foundation*, Spring 2002, 50.

7. Cmdr. John Moore, USN (Ret.), "To Mach 2 or Not to Mach 2," *NAA Retirees Bulletin*, Fall 2001, 5.

4. Nolan Leatherman, interview with author.

5. Early Vigilantes assigned to Pax River: BuNo 146694 through 146702 and 147850 through 147854.

6. Capt. George Klett, USN (Ret.), "The Half-Life of an Aircraft," *Foundation*, Spring 2002, 50.

7. Cmdr. John Moore, USN (Ret.), "To Mach 2 or Not to Mach 2," *NAA Retirees Bulletin*, Fall 2001, 5.

8. Capt. R. A. "Bob" Elder, USN (Ret.), "Vigi Vignettes," *The Hook*, Tailhook Association, Winter 1980, 26.

9. Report of Service Acceptance Trials, vol. 1:4.

10. Hill Goodspeed, "North American Rockwell A3J (A-5) Vigilante," *Wings of Fame* 19 (2000): 51.

11. Klett, "The Half-Life of an Aircraft," 48–52.

12. Goodspeed, "North American Rockwell A3J (A-5) Vigilante," 63–65.

13. Ibid., 65.

14. Ed Gillespie, "Vigilante Recollections," *American Aviation Historical Society Journal* 46, no. 2 (Summer 2001): 178–79.

15. For detailed histories of Vigilante in Vietnam War combat, see Charles Stafrace, *North American RA-5C Vigilante*, Warpaint 97 (Bletchley, UK: Warpaint Books, 2014), 27–51.

16. Hill Goodspeed, "North American Rockwell A3J (A-5) Vigilante," 81.

17. Letter from George Klett to Boom Powell, February 25, 2004.

18. Roger L. Wood, *The A-5 Vigilante, an Enduring Chapter of America's National Defense History*, 10.

Chapter 8

1. W. H. Beckett and K. P. Rice, "The OV-10 Story: Innovation vs. 'the System,'" OV-10 Association website, Fort Worth Aviation Museum, accessed March 27, 2021.

2. Steven Ginter, Howie Auten, Jim Fink, and Johnny Knebel, *Convair Model 48 Charger*, Naval Fighters 39 (Simi Valley, CA: S. Ginter, 1997), 48.

3. Ibid., 6.

4. *North American Take-Off* (plant newspaper), July 12, 1965, 1–3.

5. Donald E. Fink, "North American Accelerates COIN Work," *Aviation Week & Space Technology*, February 8, 1965, 20.

6. C. E. Cook, A. G. Lane, and T. T. Smiley, "Rough Terrain Demonstration of the OV-10A," AIAA Paper 69-316, 13.

7. Memo from G. R. Gehrkens to R. F. Walker, president, NAR Aerospace and Systems Group, September 19, 1969.

8. Interview with Archie Lane by the author on October 8, 2019.

9. "Remembering Desert Storm: 10 Years Later," OV-10 Bronco Association, accessed January 25, 2021.

10. William E. Burrows, *Air & Space Smithsonian*, March 2010, 67.

11. Interview with Archie Lane.

Chapter 9

1. Clarence A. Robinson, "XFV-12 May Spur Navy VTOL Family," *Aviation Week & Space Technology*, April 16, 1973.

2. Mr. Ron Murphy and Cmdr. Ernest L. Lewis, Naval Air System Command, "XFV-12A Thrust Augmented Wing Prototype Aircraft," undated paper, 474.

3. Ibid., 475.

4. Tommy H. Thomason, unpublished manuscript, preliminary draft, September 10, 2000.

5. H. Andrews, R. Murphy, and I. Wilken, "The XFV-12A- Reflections and Some Lessons," AIAA-90-3240, paper presented at the AIAA/AHS/ASEE Aircraft Design, Systems, and Operations Conference, held in Dayton, Ohio, September 17–19, 1990, 1–19.

6. Ibid., 15–18.

7. "V/STOL Technology Advances Expected," *Aviation Week & Space Technology*, January 31, 1977, 70.

8. Charles E. Schneider, "Rockwell Proposes VTOL C-130 Version," *Aviation Week & Space Technology*, October 6, 1975.

9. Excerpted from the Boeing Company X-31A web page, accessed January 5, 2021; and "X-31A Fact Sheet," NASA Dryden Flight Center, accessed February 24, 2021.

Chapter 10

1. Dennis R. Jenkins, *B-1 Lancer: The Most Complicated Warplane Ever Developed* (New York: McGraw-Hill, 1999), 46.

2. Frank Greve, "Rockwell and the B-1," *Capitol Magazine* insert, *Columbus Dispatch*, April 8, 1984, 19.

3. John Tirpak, "Restoring Broken Bones," *Air Force* (magazine), January–February 2021, 32–33.

4. Steve Trimble, *Aviation Week & Space Technology*, January 10, 2021, 59.

Chapter 11

1. Excerpted from *Footprints*, Rockwell International, 1988, and oral interview with Nolan Leatherman, July 27 and August 2, 2018.

2. *US News & World Report*, February 5, 1996, 41.

3. "US Indicts McDonnell-Douglas and Chinese in Equipment Deal," *New York Times*, October 20, 1999.

4. The demise of NAA was adapted by John Fredrickson from his book *NAA in the Jet Age* (Atglen, PA: Schiffer, 2019), chap. 16.

Bibliography

Adcock, Al. *T-28 Trojan in Action.* Carrolton, TX: Squadron/ Signal Publications, 1989.

Avery, Norm. *North American Aircraft, 1934–1998.* Vol 1. Santa Ana, CA: Jonathan Thomas, 1998.

Blackburn, Al. *Aces Wild: The Race for Mach 1.* Wilmington, DE: Scholarly Resources, 1999.

Bowers, Peter M. *Curtiss Aircraft 1907–1947.* Annapolis, MD: Naval Institute Press, 1979.

Casey, John W., with Jon Boyd. *North American Aviation: The Rise and Fall of an Aerospace Giant.* 2nd ed. Tucson, AZ: Amethyst Moon, 2011.

Curtis, Duncan. *North American F-86 Sabre.* Marlborough, UK: Crownwood, 2000.

Frankel, Mark A., and Tommy H. Thomason. *Training the Right Stuff.* Atglen, PA: Schiffer Military History, 2016.

Ginter, Steve, *North American AJ Savage.* Simi Valley, CA: Steve Ginter, 2010.

Ginter, Steve. *North American FJ-3/3M Fury.* Simi Valley, CA: Steve Ginter, 2010.

Ginter, Steve. *North American Rockwell T-2 Buckeye.* Simi Valley, CA: Steve Ginter, 1986.

Ginter, Steve. *North American T-28 Trojan.* Simi Valley, CA: Steve Ginter, 1981.

Gray, Mike. *Angle of Attack: Harrison Storms and the Race to the Moon.* New York and London: W. W. Norton, 1992.

Hoover, Robert A., and Mark Shaw. *Forever Flying.* New York: Atria Paperback, a division of Simon & Schuster, 1996.

Katz, Kenneth P. *The Supersonic Bone: A Development & Operational History of the B-1 Bomber.* Havertown, PA: Pen & Sword Books, 2022.

Lloyd, Alwyn T. *A Cold War Legacy: A Tribute to Strategic Air Command,1946–1992.* Missoula, MT: Pictorial Publishing, 2000.

McMaster, H. R. *Dereliction of Duty: Lyndon Johnson, Robert McNamara, the Joint Chiefs of Staff, and the Lies That Led to Vietnam.* New York: HarperCollins, 1997.

Moore, John. *Wrong Stuff: Flying on the Edge of Disaster.* Lake Forest, MN: Specialty Press, 1996.

Murray, Russ. *Lee Atwood: Dean of Aerospace.* Pittsburgh, PA: Rockwell International, 1980.

Powell, Robert B. *Vigilante: 1200 Hours Flying the Ultimate US Navy Reconnaissance Aircraft.* North Branch, MN: Specialty Press, 2019.

Simone, William J. *North American F-107A.* Simi Valley, CA: Steve Gintner, 2002.

Thomason, Tommy H. *US Naval Air Superiority Development of Shipborne Jet Fighters, 1943–1962.* North Branch, MN: Specialty Press, 2007.

Thompson, Kevin. *North American Aircraft, 1934–1999, Vol. 2.* Santa Ana, CA: Jonathan Thompson, 1999.

Tuttle, Jim. *Eject! The Complete History of US Aircraft Escape Systems.* Minneapolis: MBI, 2002.

Wilson, Stewart. *Sabre, MiG-15, and Hunter.* Western Creek, Australia: Aerospace Publications, 1995.

Index